Backpacking Tennessee

ALSO BY JOHNNY MOLLOY

Day Hiking the Daniel Boone National Forest

Trial by Trail:
Backpacking in the Smoky Mountains, new updated edition

Mount Rogers National Recreation Area Guidebook:
A Complete Resource for Outdoor Enthusiasts, 3rd edition

Johnny Molloy

BACKPACKING TENNESSEE

Overnight Trail Adventures from the Mississippi River
to the Appalachian Mountains

THE UNIVERSITY OF TENNESSEE PRESS
Knoxville

LIBRARY OF CONGRESS CATALOGING-IN-PUBLICATION DATA
Names: Molloy, Johnny, 1961- author.
Title: Backpacking Tennessee : overnight trail adventures from the
Mississippi River to the Appalachian Mountains / Johnny Molloy.
Description: First edition. | Knoxville : The University of Tennessee Press, [2022] |
Summary: "The latest hiking guide from veteran trail documentarian Johnny Molloy
is made up of forty overnight backpacking trips that range from the well-known trails
of the Smoky Mountains and Cumberland Plateau to lesser-known areas
in smaller state parks and national forests. Molloy includes an introduction, trail details,
maps, and safety tips for long hikes in the backcountry"—Provided by publisher.
Identifiers: LCCN 2021053313 (print) | LCCN 2021053314 (ebook) |
ISBN 9781621907381 (paperback) | ISBN 9781621907398 (pdf)
Subjects: LCSH: Backpacking—Tennessee—Guidebooks. | Hiking—Tennessee—Guidebooks. |
Trails—Tennessee Guidebooks. | Tennessee—Guidebooks.
Classification: LCC GV199.42.T2 M64 2022 (print) | LCC GV199.42.T2 (ebook) |
DDC 796.5109768—dc23/eng/20211207
LC record available at https://lccn.loc.gov/2021053313
LC ebook record available at https://lccn.loc.gov/2021053314

Contents

EAST TENNESSEE
AND THE APPALACHIAN MOUNTAINS

Acknowledgments

Thanks to all the trail blazers, trail maintainers, backpacking clubs and all the folks who keep the pathways coursing through the Volunteer State, so backpackers like us can enjoy them. Thanks also to all who have joined me on the trail, backpacking in Tennessee, especially my wife, Keri Anne.

Introduction

Looking for great places to go backpacking? The state of Tennessee is blessed with plentiful tracts of wild lands, places where new and experienced backpackers can find large parcels of terrain laced with trails and places to trek and camp for days—or a day. These backpacking destinations present crashing waterfalls, dramatic overlooks and historic highlights—and alluring campsites to pitch your tent in the backcountry, where you can relax before a calming campfire and escape from electronic chains that bind us to the daily grind.

A Tennessee backpacking adventure can lead to destinations high and low, from the bluffs along the Mississippi River at Fort Pillow State Park to the highlands of Smoky Mountains National Park, and a wealth of land between. Tennessee's unforgettable backpacking destinations lead through federally designated wildernesses and scenic areas such as Virgin Falls State Natural Area amid the geologically fascinating Cumberland Plateau.

The Volunteer State is a backpacker's paradise, as evidenced by 94 miles of the Appalachian Trail running exclusively through it, along with another 160 trail miles more shared with North Carolina. Great Smoky Mountains National Park, Big South Fork National River & Recreation Area, Land Between the Lakes National Recreation Area plus the Cherokee National Forest preserve well over a million acres containing thousands of miles of trails, presenting a multitude of overnighting opportunities. Additionally, Tennessee state parks offer numerous backpacking destinations within their collection of special preserves.

So where to start backpacking in Tennessee? That is where this book comes into play. It contains 40 specific backpacking adventures covering over 650 miles of trails, every mile of which I hiked for this guide (whether I'd hiked them before or not and nearly all of them I had). My resume also includes having backpacked over 2,500 nights in 40 states throughout the United States, with more than 600 nights backpacked in my home state of Tennessee alone. That experience, combined with writing over 80 outdoor related guidebooks on backpacking, hiking, camping, paddling and bicycling should give you confidence in this book, a guide to help you make the most of your time backpacking in Tennessee.

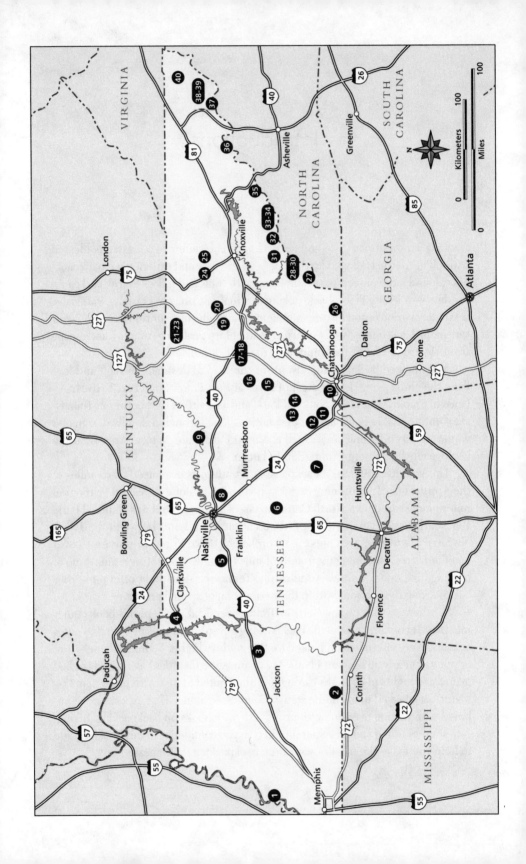

It all started with a backpacking trip at Great Smoky Mountains National Park, an adventure that ultimately launched me into a career as an outdoor writer. As the backpacking trips continued, life lessons learned while in the backcountry, such as persistence in the face of obstacles, patience when you have miles and miles to go, and acceptance of your circumstances when they are less than ideal I would apply to life in general. So can it be with you, whether you are new to backpacking or a rising veteran of the great outdoors.

To see vistas, waters and wildlife—to backpack Tennessee—and be able share them with you has brought me to the realization that purchasers of *Backpacking Tennessee* are banking their money and their free time that Johnny Molloy knows what he is talking about. This is serious business and I take it seriously!

One of the joys of my occupation is sharing my love of the outdoors with you. And as a native Tennessean, my love of our state's natural splendor raises the stakes even higher. I want y'all to see, smell, hear and feel what lies out there, in the back of beyond, while backpacking Tennessee. As electronics further infiltrate every aspect of our lives, we are losing our connection with nature. Backpacking provides a means to get outside, to explore, to stimulate our mental, physical and spiritual selves in the great outdoors.

You can hit the trail with friends and family, together discovering and sharing the God-given beauty of the Volunteer State. While backpacking Tennessee you can soak-in horizon-to-horizon vistas from rock outcrops atop the Cumberland Plateau, wander among massive old growth trees in the Smokies, ramble alongside lakes in Middle Tennessee, traipse through wildflower-filled lowlands in the Mississippi River delta, trek amid regal pine woods or wander along brawling rivers.

This book includes different types of backpacks in varied settings with varying layers of difficulty. Most backpacking adventures detailed are two-night trips typical for the weekend backpacker, yet additional backpacks range from 2-mile, one-night family treks to multi-day, 50-plus mile adventures.

The backpacks not only feature fine trails and campsites but also scenic sights—cataracts such as Savage Falls, overlooks like Blackstack Cliffs and waters like Cordell Hull Lake. Well-known "must do" destinations such as the Appalachian Trail, the Cumberland Trail and the Smokies high country are included, but undiscovered gems like the upper Bald River Wilderness, Big Hill Pond State Park and Henry Horton State Park increase your Tennessee backpacking possibilities.

This book also delivers "must know" information for you, so you can more adeptly execute successful backpacking adventures: how to get to the trailhead, how far the backpack is, hike difficulty, when to go, where the campsite are, what you are going to see along the way and where you are within reason at any given moment of the hike. Each hike includes all the above, along with an easy-to-scan map, trail mileage chart and photo to help you build a mental picture of the area. Additionally, scattered within this "where-to" guide are "how-to" backpacking tips and tricks guaranteed to make your outdoor adventures run more smoothly. These helpful tidbits will boost your quest for becoming the best backpacker you can be.

I hope this guide will inspire you to create your own adventures and make memories that will leave you and your loved ones wanting more, and to want to share the great outdoors with still others. The reason I travel and explore the outdoors is simple: The world is a beautiful place! Life is for living. Do everything now. Don't wait. Go now. Backpacking in Tennessee can be so exciting—you never know what is going to happen next, what is around the bend in the river, what is over the next ridge or what the weather will bring. But I can guarantee you that using *Backpacking Tennessee* will bring a wealth of adventures and memories to last a lifetime.

Backpacking in Tennessee

Look at a map of Tennessee. Several things will strike aspiring Volunteer State backpackers. First, the state extends from the highlands of the Appalachians westerly over the rampart that is the Cumberland Plateau, through the valleys of the Tennessee and Cumberland Rivers and onward to the Mississippi River coastal plain to the Big Muddy itself, hundreds of miles. This varied terrain ranges from 6,643 feet, westerly all the way down to 338 feet where the Mississippi River flows past Memphis. Backpacking Tennessee includes backpacking trips traveling amidst the highest and lowest points in the state. Thus, backpackers can adventure through the elevation extremes in the Volunteer State. These varied heights harbor wide-ranging ecosystems containing diverse flora and fauna, augmenting your outdoor experience.

Tennessee is blessed with a wealth of public lands where you can enjoy backpacking—national parks, national forests and national recreation areas as well as state parks, forests and wildlife management areas. Tennessee features America's most famous and most visited preserve– the one and only Great Smoky Mountains National Park—that offers first rate backpacking. However, additional federal lands offer more backpacking possibilities—starting with the 640,000 acre Cherokee National Forest. Within it lie 11 federally designated wildernesses through which backpacks in this guide course. Additionally, more backpacking trails wind through 125,000 acre Big South Fork National River & Recreation Area and 170,000 acre Land Between the Lakes National Recreation Area. Tennessee state parks manage an additional 200,000 acres of trail laden territory. Finally, Tennessee's state-held public lands also harbor trails for backpackers. This adds up to a lot of land to explore by foot, enhancing the experience via overnight backpacking.

The diversity of terrain, habitat and trails is reflected in the backpacking adventures that you can undertake here in Tennessee. Starting from west to east you can walk the Chickasaw Bluff Trail at Fort Pillow and march through history atop bluffs above the Mississippi River. Next, you find the 30-plus mile trail system at Big Hill Pond State Park weaving past waters and hills near the Mississippi state line. Natchez Trace State Park & Forest presents surprisingly undulating terrain and seclusion.

Middle Tennessee has its own destinations, including Land Between the Lakes. The backcountry hike at Henry Horton State Park rises above the alluring Duck River. The Bearwaller Gap Trail twists along the steep shores of Cordell Hull Lake while another shoreline backpack uses the Volunteer Trail at Percy Priest Lake.

Moving east you come to Tennessee's magnificent Cumberland Plateau. Trek along cliff edges and admire wild waterfalls at Savage Gulf State Natural Area. Meld gorgeous rivers, mining history, and superlative camping at Obed Wild & Scenic River, using Tennessee's special path—the Cumberland Trail. Trek across swinging bridges and through vast woodlands at Fall Creek Falls. Enjoy wildflowers galore at Frozen Head State Park. Find arches, rockhouses and other geological wonders at the Big South Fork National River & Recreation Area.

Farther east you cross the Tennessee River valley where family backpacks at Norris Dam State Park and Big Ridge State Park await. Still farther east you reach the Appalachian highlands. Here, backpackers have ample opportunities to hike the Appalachian Trail. Backpacks that include the world's most famous footpath stretch from Great Smoky Mountains National Park north to Iron Mountain near the Virginia state line, including the segment where the AT wanders through the world famous balds of Roan Mountain.

Other Appalachian Trail backpacks are parts of loops, such as the Silers Bald Backpack where you can see mountain streams, meadows and the rare spruce-fir forest that cloaks only the highest mantles of the Smokies. And don't forget rustic backcountry destinations in the Cherokee National Forest such as Citico Wilderness, with its clear-as-air streams, or the untamed montane terrain of Joyce Kilmer-Slickrock Wilderness, and lesser visited Big Frog Wilderness. Yet other Tennessee icons are included among the backpacks here—among them the Bald Mountains and Watauga Lake. Along Brookshire Creek you can camp in solitude and fish for native brook trout.

Yet there are places to backpack beyond the mountains. Destinations such as Tims Ford State Park, Long Hunter State Park and Montgomery Bell State Park provide shorter but accessible backcountry experiences for residents of Middle Tennessee. And finally you have two backpacking adventures in Tennessee state forests and wildlife management areas—the vast wilds of Scotts Gulf and Prentice Cooper State Forest, overlooking the Grand Canyon of the Tennessee River down Chattanooga way—top off the mosaic of backpacking opportunities in the Volunteer State.

WEATHER

Tennessee experiences all four seasons in their entirety, and given the state's elevations—from over 6,600 feet to under 400 feet—the Volunteer State might be experiencing them all simultaneously! Summer can be warm, with occasional downright hot spells in the western lowlands and sometimes Middle Tennessee. The mountains in the east will be cooler. Morning backpackers can avoid heat and the common afternoon thunderstorms. A smart phone equipped with internet access allows hikers to monitor storms as they arise, but don't count on service in mountain hollows and remote national forest areas.

Backpackers are drawn outdoors in increasing numbers when the first northerly fronts of fall sweep cool clear air across Tennessee. Crisp mornings, great for vigorous backpacks, give way to warm afternoons, more conducive to relaxing around the campsite. Fall is drier than summer. Winter will bring frigid subfreezing days, chilling rains and snows, especially in the mountains. There are also fewer hours of daylight. However, a brisk hiking pace and smart time management will keep you warm and walking while the sun is still above the horizon. Each cold month has a few days of mild weather. Make the most of them.

Spring will be more variable. A warm day can be followed by a cold one. Extensive spring rains bring re-growth, but also keep backpackers indoors. But any avid trail trekker will find more good backpacking days than they will have time to hike in spring and every other season. A good starting point to plan your backpack is to check monthly averages of high and low temperatures and average rainfall for each month in Murfreesboro, roughly in the center of the state. Elevation and specific location will lead to different exact temperatures. Below is a table showing each month's averages for Murfreesboro. This will give you an estimate of what to expect each month.

Month	Average High	Average Low	Precipitation
January	47 degrees	26 degrees	4.5 inches
February	51	28	4.4
March	61	36	5.4
April	71	45	4.5
May	78	54	5.1
June	86	63	4.7
July	89	67	5.0
August	89	66	3.7
September	83	58	4.4
October	72	45	3.5
November	61	37	4.5
December	51	30	5.4

HOW TO USE THIS GUIDEBOOK

This guidebook covers backpacking adventures throughout Tennessee. The backpacks are divided into four primary regions—West Tennessee, Middle Tennessee, Cumberland Plateau, then East Tennessee and the Appalachian Mountains. The following is a sample of what you find in the information box at the beginning of each Tennessee backpack:

Abrams Creek Backpack

THE BACKPACK

The description begins with a short overview of the backpack, to give you a flavor of the adventure. It is followed by an information box:

Distance & Configuration: 19.7-mile loop
Difficulty: Moderate
Outstanding Features: Streams, remoteness, Smokies history
Elevation: 1,099 feet low point, 2,038 feet high point
Scenery: 4
Solitude: 3
Family Friendly: 4
Canine Friendly: 0 (Dogs not allowed)
Fees/permits: Fee-based permit required
Best season: Year-round, late spring and early fall best
Maps: National Geographic #229 Great Smoky Mountains National Park
For more info: Great Smoky Mountains National Park, 107 Park Headquarters Road, Gatlinburg, TN 37738; (865) 436-1200; nps.gov/grsm

From the information box, we can see that the trip is a 19.7-mile loop trek, and it is moderate, mainly due to minimal elevation change, especially for being inside Great Smoky Mountains National Park. Along the way you will enjoy multiple mountain streams, seclusion, and view Smokies history. Elevations along the trek will range from 1,099 feet to 2,038 feet, giving you an idea of elevation changes as well as climatological considerations due to elevation, which in this case are minimal.

The scenery is a 4 on a scale of 1 to 5, with 5 being the best. So expect a scenic trip. Solitude is a 3, so you should expect company along the hike. The family friendly scale is a 4 meaning it can be a favorable family backpacking destination. The canine friendly rating is a 0 since pets are not allowed in the Smokies backcountry. The lower the number the less friendly the backpack is for your dog. A fee based backcountry permit is required to undertake this hike. Best season tells you the prime times to enjoy the backpack. In this instance, the best time is spring and fall.

Maps tells you the best maps to use for the hike. A high quality map is included with each hike description in this guide and should suffice. However, use the recommended map to augment the book map. This is followed by trailhead directions along with trailhead coordinates you can plug into your device to help you get there. For More Info tells you the governing body of the area backpacked, as well as pertinent phone numbers and websites should you want to endeavor further research on your own.

Following that is a rendition of the backpack, including must know tips for the trek, as well as not to be missed highlights and what to expect while out there, the feeling, the vibe of the adventure. Each hike description ends with "Mileages," a quick reference table of mileages and milestones along the way.

Some backpacks include an informational sidebar. The sidebars, usually accompanied with a lesson learned on the trail, offer tips and advice to help you become a better and more complete backpacker. These sidebars are paired with particular backpacks because those backpacking trips likely have a scenario where the sidebar applies.

BACKPACKER CHECKLIST

There is a reason why "hike your own hike" is a popular phrase in backpacking circles. Items needed for a backpacking trip that are dear to me may not seem so essential to you. A way to determine what you (and your group) need is to go down this list, assemble the items then get out there and hit the trail. After each trip, assess your gear. Did you bring everything you needed? Did you need everything you brought? Next, adjust your gear list for the next trip, continuing to refine your list.

In order to execute the best trip possible go through the following sequence of questions and considerations:

- Physical ability, trip desires and expectations—what are the physical abilities of you and your party? What length and duration of trip do you desire? What are the group expectations? Are y'all each carrying your own food/gear or sharing gear? What is the weather forecast?

- Now, go from your feet to your head to determine what clothing you will need. Next check the needs of your shelter, bedroom, bathroom, bedroom, and kitchen. Other miscellaneous gear possibilities follow. The key is to take everything you need and no more.
- Shoes: hiking shoes/boots and camp shoes/sandals.
- Clothes: socks, long pants, short pants, t-shirt, long sleeve button up shirt with collar, vest, jacket/poncho, bandanna, hat/toboggan, gloves, extra clothes as needed or desired.
- Backpack.
- Shelter: tent, tarp, or under the stars.
- Bedroom: closed cell sleeping pad, ultra-light air mattress, sleeping bag, pillow.
- Bathroom: toothbrush/paste/floss, toilet paper, lotion, biodegradable soap, pack towel.
- Kitchen: food, spices, water purification (filter, tablets, boil), cookware (cup, spoon, knife, pot, potholder, frying pan, spatula), cooking sources (stove or fire/grill).
- Hiking implements: trekking poles, ultralight camp chair, maps, compass, lighter, fire starter, medical kit, cord (enough to hang food from bears), headlamp, lantern, solar powered light.
- Other Items to consider: phone/cord/solar charger, spare batteries, bug dope, trash bag, GPS, weather radio, aspirin, book, radio, camera, cards, vitamins, watch, sunscreen, lip balm, extra batteries, sunglasses, small towel, binoculars, wildlife identification books/apps.

Just remember, backpacking Tennessee is about the experience, not the stuff you carry. Be prepared, but prepare to enjoy your time interacting with nature. My personal rule of thumb is to carry no more than 15% of my body weight, and closer to 10% if I can get away with it. Use this rule of thumb for yourself, no matter your weight. It will work for you and kids, too.

Most importantly, carve out some free time, get out there then make some memories backpacking Tennessee.

BACKPACKING SUMMARY CHART

	Distance (miles)	Difficulty	Highlights
West Tennessee			
1 Fort Pillow Backpack	1.4	Easy	Short hike, good campsite, views
2 Big Hill Pond Loop	12.6	Moderate	Trail shelters, views, swamp boardwalk
3 Natchez Trace Backpack	25.4	Moderate-difficult	Lakeside camping, wildflowers, primitive trail
Middle Tennessee			
4 Land Between The Lakes Backpack	18.3	Moderate	Historic Civil War routes, old homesites
5 Montgomery Bell Loop Backpack	10.5	Easy-moderate to Difficult	Trail shelters, streams
6 Henry Horton Backpack	3.8	Easy	Cedar glades, bluff campsite
7 Tims Ford Backpack	12.7	Moderate	Lake views, suspension bridges, lake access
8 Long Hunter Backpack	11.0	Moderate	Percy Priest Lake, views, good campsites
9 Bearwaller Gap Trail	6.2	Moderate	Bluffs above Cordell Hull Lake, views
Cumberland Plateau			
10 Pot Point Backpack	12.1	Moderate	Views, arch, good campsites
11 Foster Falls Backpack	4.6	Easy	Foster Falls, gulf views, good campsites
12 Grundy Forest Backpack	3.5	Easy	Old trees, geology, waterfalls, historic CCC camp
13 Great Stone Door Backpack	18.9	Difficult	Great Stone Door, waterfalls aplenty
14 Savage Gulf Loop	20.0	Moderate-difficult	Views aplenty, Hobbs Cabin, Savage Falls
15 Fall Creek Falls Backpack	12.1	Moderate	Waterfalls galore, swinging bridges
16 Scotts Gulf Backpack	14.6	Moderate	Overlooks, waterfalls, solitude
17 Virgin Falls Backpack	10.6	Moderate	Virgin Falls, other waterfalls, Martha's Pretty Point
18 Cumberland Mountain Backpack	8.1	Easy-moderate	Attractive streams, family backpack
19 Obed River Backpack	4.8	Easy-moderate	Bluffs, great campsite, rivers

20 Frozen Head Backpack	18.2	Moderate-difficult	Frozen Head tower, wildflowers in season, campsites
21 Honey Creek Backpack	28.0	Difficult	Geology, waterfalls, views, campsites, streams
22 Big South Fork Loop	55.3	Difficult	Multi-day trip, views, waterfalls, geology, challenge
23 Twin Arches Backpack	21.7	Moderate-difficult	Twin Arches, Needle Arch, Slave Falls, Laurel Fork Creek
East Tennessee & Appalachians			
24 Norris Dam Backpack	4.4	Easy	Historic trails, easy trek, good family trip
25 Big Ridge Backpack	9.3	Easy-moderate	Lake views, lakeside camping
26 Big Frog Wilderness	17.9	Moderate-difficult	Big Frog Mountain, views, cascades
27 Upper Bald River Wilderness	17.4	Moderate	Upper Bald River Falls, newer wilderness area
28 Citico Creek Wilderness	17.7	Difficult	Gorgeous streams, waterfalls, views from Bobs Bald
29 Rocky Flats Backpack	11.7	Moderate-difficult	Rocky Flats homesite, Citico Creek gorge, views
30 Joyce Kilmer Slickrock Wilderness	11.8	Moderate	Views, swimming, fishing, Wildcat Falls
31 Abrams Creek Backpack	19.7	Moderate	Streams, remoteness, Smokies history
32 Bote Mountain Backpack	21.4	Difficult	Appalachian Trail, Smokies history
33 Silers Bald Backpack	25.6	Difficult	Views from high country, cascades along Fish Camp Prong
34 Old Settlers Backpack	44.4	Difficult	Best historic backpack in the Appalachians
35 Snake Den Backpack	18.2	Difficult	Old growth forests, views, waterfall, homesites
36 Bald Mountains Backpack	17.0	Difficult	Blackstack Cliffs, Big Firescald Ridge, waterfalls, remoteness
37 Roan Highlands	30.0	Difficult	Grassy balds, spruce-fir highlands, views extraordinaire
38 Laurel Fork Backpack	18.5	Difficult	Mountain stream, waterfalls, views
39 Big Laurel Branch Wilderness	20.7	Moderate-difficult	Views, wilderness, Watauga Lake
40 Shady Valley Backpack	41.9	Difficult	Long loop, views, resupply opportunity

BEST TENNESSEE BACKPACKING TRIPS BY CATEGORY

Best Backpacks for Beginners

Best Backpacks for Families

Best Backpacks for Water Lovers/Anglers

Best Backpacks for Waterfall Lovers

Best Backpacks for Views

Best Backpacks for Geology

Best Backpacks for Solitude

Best Winter Backpacks

Best Long Backpacks

Backpacking Tennessee

West Tennessee

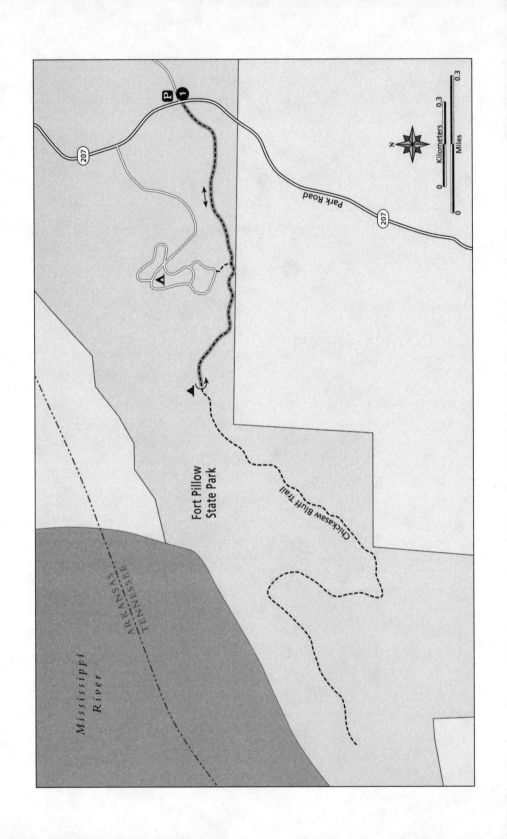

Mississippi River

ARKANSAS
TENNESSEE

Fort Pillow
State Park

Chickasaw Bluff Trail

Park Road

207

207

P 1

N

Kilometers   0.3
0

Miles   0.3
0

1

Fort Pillow Backpack

THE BACKPACK

This is the most westerly backpack in the Volunteer State. Although short, the trek takes you to a campsite on a high bluff overlooking the Mississippi River, and makes for a great family destination. In addition, you can follow the Chickasaw Bluff Trail beyond the campsite to enhance the trip.

Distance and Configuration: 1.4-mile figure there-and-back
Difficulty: Easy
Outstanding Features: Camping atop Mississippi River bluffs
Elevation: 413 feet high point, 316 feet low point
Scenery: 4
Solitude: 5
Family Friendly: 5
Canine Friendly: 5
Fees/permits: Contact park office
Best season: October through April
Maps: Fort Pillow State Park
For more info: Fort Pillow State Park, 3122 Park Road, Henning, TN 38041, 731-738-5581, www.tnstateparks.com
Finding the Trailhead: From the junction of TN 54 and US 51 in Covington, head 8.5 miles north on US 51 to TN 87. Turn left onto TN 87 and follow it 17 miles to TN 123, Old Fulton Road. Turn right onto TN 123 and follow it 1 mile to the state park. The Chickasaw Bluff Trail starts on the left shortly after entering the park. Parking is on the right at the Butterfly Garden area just after passing the Chickasaw Bluff Trail. GPS trailhead coordinates: 35.626870, -89.853603

This campsite sits on the edge of Chickasaw Bluff overlooking the Mississippi River.

This fine Tennessee state park was preserved due to its place in Civil War history. The setting is North Chickasaw Bluff, overlooking the mighty Mississippi River and the state of Arkansas. Back when the War Between the States was fought, the Mississippi River flowed directly below North Chickasaw Bluff, making the hilltop an ideal place to locate a bastion to control boat traffic on the Mississippi River (The river has since changed, oxbowing away from the bluff). So, back in 1861, the Confederate Army constructed battlements here to defend the river. The next year what became Fort Pillow was engaged in battle. Eventually the Union bombarded Fort Pillow into submission, and it was abandoned by the Confederates then taken by Union forces.

However, the action wasn't over at Fort Pillow. In 1864, legendary fighter Nathan Bedford Forrest won Fort Pillow back for the South. The war then passed Fort Pillow by. In 1971, the 1,642-acre state park was established, and these majestic bluffs overlooking the Mississippi River—ostensibly preserved for their historical importance—also protected this special natural resource of Tennessee.

Therefore, today we can hike some 20 miles of park pathways, including the Chickasaw Bluff Trail that leads out to a backcountry campsite. The hike is short but more challenging than you might expect, yet its mere 0.7 mile distance makes it doable by even toddling backpackers. And the level large campsite is a worthy destination, on a bluff edge overlooking the river. Don't worry by the way; a cable barrier stretches along the edge of the bluff at the campsite, keeping things safe. The site also includes a fire ring with surrounding benches, a picnic table and privy. Grassy flats at the campsite form ideal tent sites. Make sure and contact the park office for the latest information for obtaining an overnight camping permit at the primitive backcountry campsite.

The signed Chickasaw Bluff starts near the park entrance, a little ways back toward the park entrance from the Butterfly Garden parking area. Pick up the track as it heads west along the edge of field and forest under sweetgum, sassafras and tulip trees, as well as oaks. Quickly enter full blown forest. Note the abundance of vines draped among the forest giants, lending a junglesque aspect. You will also notice the sharp drop-offs that fall away from the hillside on which you walk. The gullied woodland is created by rain runoff cutting its way toward the Mississippi River.

The trail drops sharply to a bottom to reach the base of a gully at 0.3 mile, then ascends just as sharply. Roller coaster into another gully, then pass a spur trail leading right to park's auto accessible campground at 0.4 mile. Look for big beech trees. Ahead, the singletrack trail picks up an old roadbed. The hiking eases as you level off on the bluff and before you know it at 0.7 mile you are at the backcountry primitive campsite. The partly grassed and partly wooded site lends a pleasant aspect, with plenty of room for a family campout. I have stayed here several occasions. Leafless winter allows for better views of the river 180 feet below. Spring and fall are ideal, but stay away in the hot and buggy summertime. Woe to the soldiers who manned Fort Pillow during that season.

Our stay should be much more pleasant. After setting up camp, consider taking the Chickasaw Bluffs Trail an additional 1.3 miles to its end, enjoying more river views during the leafless time of year, then back to your bluff top camp at this historic Tennessee preserve.

Mileages

0.0	Chickasaw Bluff trailhead
0.4	Spur to auto campground
0.7	Primitive backcountry campsite
1.4	Chickasaw Bluff trailhead

OUTFITTING YOUR BACKPACKER KITCHEN

Backcountry cooks, since they are transporting their food and cooking implements on their back, must judiciously factor weight and space. My backpack always contains a small grill, an aluminum pot that I do not mind putting over the fire, a pot grabber, a small knife and a spoon. Sometimes I tote an aluminum frying pan when cooking pancakes or fish. Don't forget the spatula!

If two or more of you are backpacking together then y'all can split the cooking items: one takes the grill and the other takes the frying pan, and one person carries the pot. Aluminum pie tins make for great lightweight and reusable plates.

Don't be afraid to tweak your cook kit for different seasons and circumstances. For example, if you are going on a long distance Appalachian Trail backpack, you might want to pare down your cook kit, whereas a relaxing, shorter distance summer trip you can bring the extras and engage in some serious campfire cookery.

Consider the following items for your backpacking adventure:

Camp stove: Backpacking camp stoves range from white gas models with tanks to those with canisters and a whole cook kit built around the stove. All backcountry models should be single burner. Stoves using canisters can be problematic, unless you are using a brand new canister you never know exactly how much fuel is in the canister. Therefore, I recommend stoves using white gas. Alcohol stoves are very lightweight and use less fuel but backpackers are limited by the energy output of the alcohol stove. They can boil water for coffee or reconstituting a freeze-dried meal but forget any actual cooking over them.

Cook Kit: Cook kits come in a wide variety of sizes and weights, from nearly weightless titanium sets to sets so big and bulky they belong on a wagon train. Just make sure you have enough pots, plates and cups for everyone on the trip. Also, if you are handling hot stuff have a plan, whether it is bringing a pot grabber, using bandannas or a chef mitt.

Grill: Have a grill big enough to cook your meats and other goodies for everyone in the party. Visualize how you will be using a grill. Will you be setting it up on rocks? Does it have legs? I use a very small, titanium grill when going solo, but a bigger one when in a group.

Frying pan: Frying pans can be used for more than just fish. They can be used to sauté vegetables, stir fry rice, make quesadillas and of course make breakfast. Backpacking-size aluminum frying pans with a folding handle make toting and stowing them practical.

Cup: Plastic cups are preferred. Make sure they are durable enough, can be used for hot or cold drinks and can hold adequate amounts. Insulated cups are good for winter, but in milder weather end up keeping your coffee too hot for too long. No glass in the backcountry.

Utensils: The spoon is the most versatile utensil in the backcountry. It can do almost anything that a fork can, yet a fork cannot quite do with a spoon can. That must be why they invented what is known as a "spork," which looks like a spoon except it has tines on the front. Plastic ones are lightest.

I bring an ultralight one-blade knife when by myself, but a more elaborate one if in a group. Make sure your knife includes a can opener if you are toting canned goods.

Cooking in the backcountry can be challenging. However, with the right utensils and frame of mind, it can not only be fun but also enhance your backpacking experience.

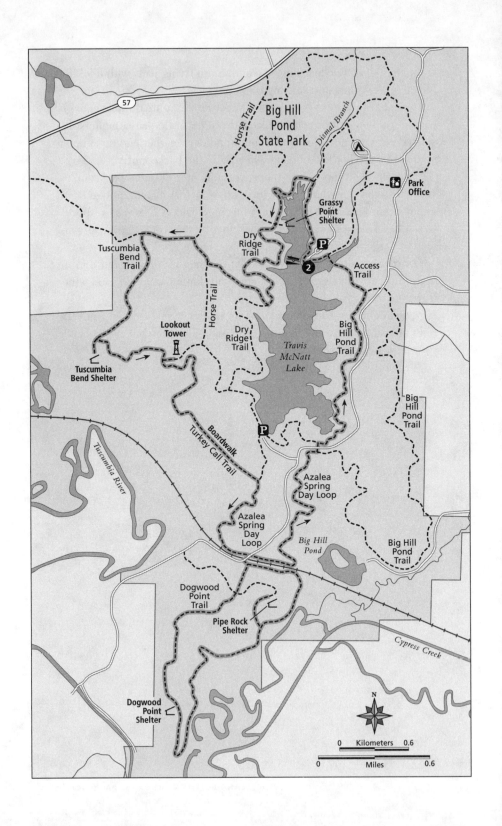

Big Hill
Pond
State Park

57

Horse Trail

Dismal Branch

Park
Office

Grassy
Point
Shelter

Dry
Ridge
Trail

Tuscumbia
Bend
Trail

P

Access
Trail

2

Horse Trail

Dry
Ridge
Trail

Lookout
Tower

Big
Hill
Pond
Trail

Tuscumbia
Bend Shelter

Travis
McNatt
Lake

Big
Hill
Pond
Trail

Tuscumbia River

Boardwalk
Turkey Call Trail

P

Azalea
Spring
Day Loop

Azalea
Spring
Day
Loop

Big Hill
Pond

Big Hill
Pond
Trail

Dogwood
Point
Trail

Pipe Rock
Shelter

Cypress Creek

Dogwood
Point
Shelter

N

0   Kilometers   0.6

0   Miles   0.6

2

Big Hill Pond Loop

THE BACKPACK

This scenic backpack will make you rethink West Tennessee. Here, make a loop around and beyond Travis McNatt Lake over hills cut by clear spring-fed creeks and across Dismal Swamp. Gaze upon the landscape from a hilltop observation tower. Four trail shelters at four designated campsites enhance the experience and add variety to the adventure.

Distance and Configuration: 12.6-mile figure eight loop
Difficulty: Moderate
Outstanding Features: Dismal Swamp boardwalk, trail shelters, lookout tower
Elevation: 594 feet high point, 374 feet low point
Scenery: 4
Solitude: 4 (Lookout Tower and Dismal Swamp areas can be busy)
Family Friendly: 3
Canine Friendly: 3
Fees/permits: Contact park office
Best season: October through April
Maps: Big Hill Pond State Park
For more info: Big Hill Pond State Park, 1435 John Howell Road, Pocahontas, TN 38061, 731-645-7967, www.tnstateparks.com
Finding the Trailhead: From Selmer, head 7 miles south on US 45 to TN 57. Turn right and head 10 miles west on TN 57 to the Big Hill Pond entrance, which will be on your left. Follow the main park road a half mile then veer right toward the boat ramp. Parking is in the lot above the boat ramp. GPS trailhead coordinates: 35.058371, -88.727397

Big Hill Pond State Park is set in hills rising above the Tuscumbia River, just north of the Mississippi state line. The combination of river, swamp, hills, streams and

Trekking across the Dismal Swamp boardwalk.

a lake create a scenic wooded haven through which travel 30 miles of trails. The entire pathway system has been designated a National Recreation Trail. You can execute a 12 mile loop that visits all four backcountry trail shelters/campsites as well as the major highlights of this preserve. Winter trips here are recommended, with relatively mild weather and shelters in which to sleep. Summer is untenable, with heat and bugs in abundance. Trips of 1-2 nights are recommended, especially with a short first day at Grassy Point Shelter.

Make sure and stop by the park office for the latest permitting information before you set out. The backpack leaves the boat launch area on the Dry Ridge Trail, northbound along handsome 165-acre Travis McNatt Lake, fed by Dismal Branch and small spring creeks trickling down the hollows. The singletrack trail winds along the lakeshore, shaded by pines, dogwood, ironwood and beech.

This bridge leads you across Travis McNatt Lake.

Boardwalks cross tinkling spring branches. By 0.5 mile you are at the head of Travis McNatt Lake. Here, a trail goes right toward the park auto accessible campground, while our route heads left, crossing marshes of Dismal Branch and Dismal Branch itself via intermittent bridges bordered by alder thickets. Rise steeply away in hardwoods, turning south on a richly-wooded hillside. At 1.0 mile, a spur leads left to the Grassy Point Shelter. Typical of the shelters here, it is a wooden cabin with a door, screened windows, and bunks inside. All have a fire ring outside and some shelters also offer a picnic table. This campsite overlooks Travis McNatt Lake.

The hike continues south along the west side of the impoundment, winding in and out of hollows rich in ferns. You are across the boat launch at 1.5 miles. Circle around another hollow and reach an easy-to-miss intersection atop a ridge at 2.1 miles. Here, cut acutely right, northwest, to reach the Horse Trail at 2.5 miles. Hike north on the wider track in pine-oak woods then head left on the signed Tuscumbia Bend Trail at 2.6 miles. This hiker-only old road runs atop a ridge dotted with outcrops under forest. At 3.2 miles, the track splits with a faint but

Dogwood Point trail shelter awaits your arrival.

marked path dropping left off the ridge. Most hikers miss this and stay with the old roadbed. The two alternate routes merge at 3.6 miles, and a spur leads a short ways to the Tuscumbia Bend Shelter, set on a little rise above Dismal Swamp. A nearby stream provides water. This shelter can be heavy with mosquitoes during the warm season.

The backpack continues as the Tuscumbia Bend Trail cruises the margin between Dismal Swamp and rising hills, only to climb away from the swamp and reach the spur to the park lookout tower at 4.3 miles. Head left here 0.1 mile to find the 70-foot observation turret, allowing nearby looks at Travis McNatt Lake as well as forests and hills to the distant horizon. Join the Turkey Call Trail as it winds down a rocky hillside to reach Dismal Swamp and the famed swamp boardwalk at 5.2 miles. Here you cross a seasonally inundated cypress swamp on an elevated wood platform. This is a true highlight of the backpack and a must for every park visitor. After a half-mile of thrills, meet the Azalea Spring Day Loop. Turn right, still bordering Dismal Swamp. Come along the Southern Railway and cross the tracks at a park road at 6.4 miles. You will return here later. For now, join the southbound Dogwood Point Trail. There are two legs of the path—make sure to leave from the southbound leg, not the leg going along the railroad tracks.

The Dogwood Point Trail rises into hickory-oak hills, reaching the Dogwood Point Shelter at 7.5 miles, attractively set in hardwoods on a bluff above Cypress Creek and its attendant swamps. The swamp below is your water source for this shelter, 0.3 mile distant. From the shelter, the Dogwood Point Trail dips to bottomlands then turns north on a steep slope betwixt the Cypress Creek swamps and adjacent hills, a juxtaposition of environments that makes Big Hill Pond State Park special. At 8.9 miles, curve into a hollow to meet an old grassy road heading left. This track leads 0.2 mile up the hollow and to the Pipe Rock Shelter. Water can be had from a seasonal creek near the intersection of the old road and the Dogwood Point Trail. Otherwise you can get it from the nearby swamps.

The Dogwood Point Trail continues the margin between swamp and hill, coming next to the Southern Railway at 9.3 miles. Climb along the rail line then make the rail crossing at the road where you were earlier. After crossing the tracks at 9.7 miles, rejoin the Azalea Spring Day Loop, paralleling the tracks before climbing north into hardwood hills, rising above the actual Big Hill Pond. At 11.0 miles, come near a park road, cross it and head right on the Big Hill Pond Trail, hiking north on the east side of Travis McNatt Lake. A nest of user created trails and blazes can make this area confusing. Roll in scenic wooded hillside in and out of hollows, enjoying lake views through the trees. At 12.2 miles, the Big Hill Pond Trail heads right while we stay left with the Big Hill Pond Access Trail, descending to the lake. Reach the shoreline at 12.5 miles, then cross a super scenic hiker bridge across a lake embayment. Once across the water, head left along the shoreline, returning to the boat launch, concluding the backpack at 12.6 miles.

Mileages

0.0	Boat launch
1.1	Grassy Point Shelter
2.6	Tuscumbia Bend Trail
3.6	Tuscumbia Bend Shelter
4.4	Lookout tower
5.2	Dismal Swamp Boardwalk
6.4	Cross railroad tracks
7.5	Dogwood Point Shelter
8.9	Spur left to Pipe Rock Shelter
9.7	Cross railroad tracks a second time
11.0	Cross park road
12.6	Boat launch

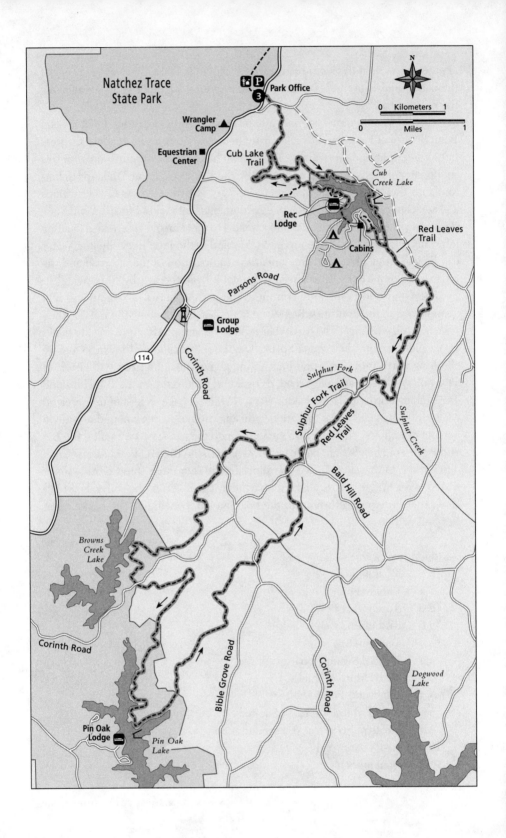

3

Natchez Trace Backpack

THE BACKPACK

This surprisingly demanding adventure traces the Red Leaves Trail alongside three lakes, with two shelters available for overnighting. Most of the hike is on navigationally challenging primitive track that will test your route finding skills. After starting you will come to developed Cub Creek Lake area, with a camping shelter and day use amenities before striking south in remote Sulphur Fork drainage, heading along hardwood ridges and wildflower rich bottoms. Loop down past Browns Creek Lake then along Pin Oak Lake to find a second trail shelter. After backtracking a bit, your return route skirts the south side of Cub Creek Lake.

Distance and Configuration: 25.4-mile figure eight loop
Difficulty: Moderate-difficult due to distance and hills
Outstanding Features: Lakeside camping, wildflowers, primitive trail
Elevation: 650 feet high point, 463 feet low point
Scenery: 4
Solitude: 4 (Cub Lake area can be busy)
Family Friendly: 1
Canine Friendly: 2
Fees/permits: Fee-based reservable campsite permit required
Best season: Mid-fall through mid-spring
Maps: Natchez Trace State Park, Red Leaves Trail
For more info: Natchez Trace State Park, 24845 Natchez Trace Rd., Wildersville, TN 38388, 731-968-3742, www.tnstateparks.com
Finding the Trailhead: From exit 116 on I-40 east of Wildersville, take TN 114 south for 1.7 miles to the park visitor center on your right. GPS trailhead coordinates: 35.796250, -88.264417

It is hard to believe, but this West Tennessee backpack sports around 2,500 feet of ups and downs if hiked in its entirety. That's a lot of rolling into and out of

Overlooking Pin Oak Lake.

hollows at the historic Civilian Conservation Corps developed state park and forest comprising 48,000 acres. Two backcountry shelters are available for camping, as well as the park campground, since the route loops directly by it. I recommend a two night adventure using the shelters. A shorter, 7 mile one-night trip could be done by circling Cub Creek Lake.

Go only during the recommended window. Summer is too hot, buggy and overgrown. Be apprised the Red Leaves Trail becomes very primitive beyond Cub Creek Lake, with a faint trailbed and lesser markings, adding a navigational component to the challenge. You will get turned around. Just keep the last blaze in sight and look for the next blaze ahead. The route does cross roads, availing bailout options. You will work around blowdowns. The creek bottoms are scenic, and often have bridges and boardwalks over wide shallow seeps as well as deep gullies. Autumn will present the driest trail conditions and colorful leaves. Winter

This bridge takes you across Cub Creek Lake.

avails solitude. Spring can be somewhat mucky but the lively creeks, wildflowers and budding trees add value.

Each trail shelter is a three sided open fronted wood refuge with four bunks, a table and overhanging porch. A fire ring is nearby. Water can be had from the nearby lakes. Each shelter does have tent sites. The following is a detailed mile-by-mile route description for you to use.

Mileages

0.0 Join the Red Leaves Trail as it leaves the east side of TN 114, not the Red Leaves Trail segment leaving directly from the visitor center parking lot

0.1 Cross Creek Lake Trail, a dirt road, head left, then split right on singletrack in oaks

0.5	Bridge streams in bottomland of sweetgum, beech and ferns
0.7	Reach an intersection. Here, stay left with the Red Leaves Trail, as the Cub Creek Trail (hiking trail) leaves right
1.3	Bridge streams in bottomland near marshes of Cub Creek Lake
1.6	Come along the shore of Cub Creek Lake
2.1	Right on Cub Creek Lake Trail, a gravel road, and follow it over the dam of Cub Creek Lake
2.2	Leave road right, back on singletrack Red Leaves Trail
2.4	Reach Cub Creek Lake shelter via a short spur, continue along lakeshore
3.3	Intersection; here stay straight with now-faint Red Leaves Trail, as the Cub Creek Trail (hiking trail) leaves right. Ascend a hollow
3.8	Cross paved Parsons Road; drop south into Sulphur Fork watershed, bridging tributaries of Sulphur Fork, occasionally working along the side slopes of hollows, full of mayapples, trillium, trout lilies and rue anemone in spring
5.5	Red Leaves Trail climbs abruptly right up a hill, heading northwest
6.0	Cross Sulphur Fork Trail, a gravel road, enter pines back on foot trail
6.1	Turn right onto Sulphur Fork Trail (road), southbound
6.2	Bridge Sulphur Fork via culvert; curve right with road then split left onto Red Leaves Trail. Head up a hollow, then climb out of bottoms
7.1	Cross Sulphur Fork Trail (road); continue on foot trail crossing lesser gravel road then curve left, paralleling gravel Bald Hill Road
7.4	Intersection. Begin lower loop of Red Leaves Trail by splitting right on blazed doubletrack. Cross gas line clearing, then drop to cross creek
8.3	Cross paved Corinth Road. Enter pines, traverse hills and hollows, undulate
10.2	Come along Browns Creek Lake, leave the shore after 0.4 mile, climb
11.0	Cross paved Browns Creek Lake Road, enter forest with many dogwoods
11.9	Pop out onto doubletrack dirt road, curve right, head southwest on easy track

12.3	Spur left onto singletrack, descend, cross tributary
13.0	Cruise along shore of cedar-heavy Pin Oak Lake
14.0	Reach Pin Oak trail shelter on point. Excellent lake views. Beyond here continue up embayment, heading northeast
14.4	Leave the lake, climb away from bottom
15.2	Right on primitive doubletrack Boyd Woods Road
15.6	Leave left from the road. Stay with blazes
16.6	Cross paved Corinth Road. Dive into Sulphur Fork watershed
17.0	Bridge Milton Branch in narrow scenic bottoms, climb
17.9	Cross gravel Bald Hill Road. Stay with singletrack trail heading right
18.0	Complete lower loop of Red Leaves Trail. Backtrack northeast
19.2	Bridge Sulphur Fork via culvert, ascend
21.6	Cross paved Parsons Road
22.1	End backtrack. Head left on Cub Lake Trail (hiking trail). Bridge a stream in bottoms, then turn north
22.5	Emerge onto paved Cabin Road. Head toward the lake then follow Cabin Road left, passing Cabin 11. Dip to low spot then climb to head right on step near Cabin 12. Cross arm of Cub Creek Lake on a pedestrian bridge then come near the state park campground (potential camping). Cross a second bridge over another arm of Cub Creek Lake.
22.8	Right along north bank of Cub Creek Lake. Pass through picnic area, then turn left up to the Recreation Lodge. Once at the lodge, head left in parking lot then cut right back onto foot trail.
23.1	Pass first of two intersections with Fern Nature Trail. Work up tributary
24.0	Pass spur leading left to Taylor Trail, a dirt road
24.3	Bridge uppermost gully of Cub Creek tributary
24.7	Reach intersection with Red Leaves Trail. Backtrack
25.4	Return to the visitor center, completing the backpack

CHOOSE THE RIGHT BACKPACK
FOR YOUR HIKE

Backpacks have come a long way the past fifty years. I'm talking about backpacks used for overnight excursions as opposed to daypacks used for school, work and day hiking. In the bad old days, backpacks were a simple aluminum frame holding a nylon pack with a few pockets. Unpadded straps went over your shoulders and around your waist. Known as external packs (due to the external aluminum frame), these became more deluxe, with padded shoulder straps, waist belt and a dizzying array of pockets for stowing your gear.

External packs served well in their day. My longest non-resupplied backpack ever—15 nights in Great Smoky Mountains National Park—was done with an external pack. As time rolled on, the internal backpack came into vogue. As its name implies, the frame is built into the pack.

Today, internal frame packs have supplanted external frame packs in popularity. Sure, there are still plenty of external frame backpacks out there, but internal frames rule the roost. I use only internal packs these days.

Internal packs fit closer to your body and are more compact, whereas external frame packs are generally bigger and bulkier, but have more pockets, which help organization and loading. Internal pack users have to take more of a "duffel bag" approach to their loading, though assorted pockets and pouches are now incorporated into most internal packs. Most importantly, internal packs are significantly lighter, the lightest being a mere 1.5 pounds, more often around 3 pounds, versus 5 pounds for your average external pack.

For the backpacker, which pack you choose is a matter of personal taste. For example, when going off trail or on shorter trips I prefer a sturdy internal pack. Internal packs are narrower and can squeeze through brush and between boulders without catching. The sturdier internals are more durable.

The ultralight internal packs are designed for longer treks, typically Appalachian Trail thru-hikers going ultralight head-to-toe. The ultralight internals are designed to be carried on cleared, maintained trails and are less sturdy or durable. Consider a more durable internal pack when backpacking through Tennessee's Cherokee National Forest, where lesser-maintained trails can be rough on a pack.

Your starting point for choosing a backpack is fit. Head to your nearest outdoor store and try on various packs, or borrow a friend's pack. Switch packs with someone while on a trip. The more types of packs you try, the more likely you are to find one suiting your needs. Specialty outdoor retailers often rent packs.

Ask yourself the following questions? How much money do you want to spend? How often do you plan to backpack? How long is your typical trip? Name brand packs offer quality and durability. Consider how much gear you like to carry. Do you like to bring everything but the kitchen sink? Or do you carry only the barest of necessities?

If you want to pare down your gear, buy a smaller pack. Far too often, I see backpackers with huge packs designed for a 2-week trip when their average trip is two days. No matter how long you go, be discerning when choosing the right pack for your backpacking adventures.

Middle Tennessee

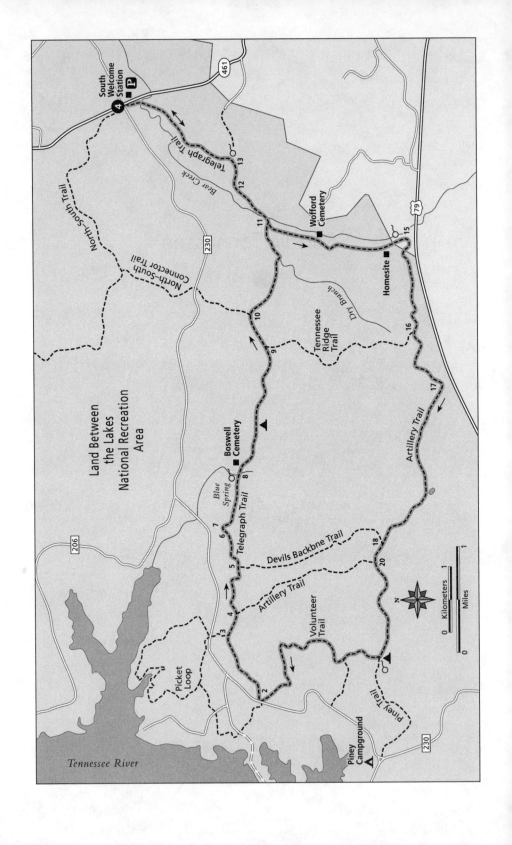

Land Between
the Lakes
National Recreation
Area

Tennessee River

North-South Trail

North-South Connector Trail

South Welcome Station

Telegraph Trail

Bear Creek

Wofford Cemetery

Homesite

Dry Branch

Tennessee Ridge Trail

Boswell Cemetery

Blue Spring

Telegraph Trail

Devils Backbone Trail

Artillery Trail

Volunteer Trail

Artillery Trail

Picket Loop

Piney Trail

Piney Campground

N

Kilometers

Miles

4

Land Between the Lakes Backpack

THE BACKPACK

This overnight adventure explores the Fort Henry Trails area of Land Between The Lakes National Recreation Area. Here, you will traverse the hills and hollows of this peninsula dividing between the Tennessee and Cumberland Rivers. Start on the Telegraph Trail then loop your way west across Tennessee Ridge to Fort Henry Branch. Your return trip takes you across more valleys and low ridges. The elevation changes are moderate and good campsites can be found throughout the trek. Cross trails make shorter loops possible.

Distance and Configuration: 18.3-mile balloon loop
Difficulty: Moderate
Outstanding Features: Historic Civil War routes, old homesites
Elevation: 682 feet high point, 371 feet low point
Scenery: 3
Solitude: 4
Family Friendly: 4
Canine Friendly: 4
Fees/permits: None required
Best season: September through mid-May
Maps: Fort Henry Trails
For more info: Land Between The Lakes National Recreation Area, Golden Pond, KY, 42211, https://www.landbetweenthelakes.us.
Finding the Trailhead: From Dover, TN, head south on US 79 for 5 miles to access The Trace. Turn right on The Trace and drive north for 3.4 miles to reach the welcome station on your right. GPS trailhead coordinates: 36.520638, -87.917671

Shared with the state of Kentucky and managed by the US Forest Service, Land Between The Lakes National Recreation Area (LBL) truly lives up to its name,

Trails at LBL often skirt fields where wildlife can be seen.

offering a multiplicity of land and water based outdoor activities, including swimming, fishing, boating, camping, mountain biking—and backpacking.

The Fort Henry Trails of LBL, 30 collective miles collectively designated as a National Recreation Trail, run among the hills and hollows of the recreation area's south end, allowing hikers to retrace the footsteps of Civil War soldiers who fought here. The Fort Henry Trail System is concentrated in the southwest end of LBL. There are no designated backcountry campsites, though backpackers often overnight near springs and on streamside flats. Creeks hereabouts are usually flowing but don't count on stream water in autumn or during dry years, though winter and spring will find the creeks flowing well. Avoid backpacking at LBL in summer.

To keep hikers oriented in the Fort Henry trail system, numbered trail signs are located at trail junctions. These numbers are referred to as "points." Start this backpack on the Telegraph Trail. It leaves south as a mown path from FR 230 (The long-distance North-South Trail leaves north from here, Kentucky bound) and at 0.2 mile crosses Bear Creek in a flat. This could be a ford and will give you an idea of water levels for the hike ahead. From there, climb sharply up the nose of a hickory-oak ridge dividing Bear Creek from Bee Branch, leveling off at 0.8 mile. Dip to reach Point 13 at 1.4 miles. Descend an old road then come to Kirkmans Camp Spring and an old homesite at 1.6. Campsites can be found

Trailside view of Bear Creek.

hereabouts and in flats a bit downtrail. Thomas Kirkman received a land grant from the state of Tennessee in 1845. He built an iron furnace on this land not far from this spring. It is hard to imagine the community that sprang up around the iron furnace among today's woods and fields. The community was short-lived however, as the Civil War interrupted production at the furnace.

Soon pass Point 12 and continue along flats beside Bear Creek, crossing the stream again to reach Point 11 at 2.1 miles. Begin the loop portion of the back-pack, heading left on the Peytona Trail, named after Kirkman's Peytona Furnace. Peytona was a famous racehorse back in 1845.

Leave the Telegraph Trail at Point 11. Immediately cross the Dry Branch streambed and enter a field. Circle around the right hand side of the field before reentering woods, coming alongside Bear Creek, then find the small Wofford Cemetery. Climb a hill, then return to the main trailbed. Pass a homesite on your right with concrete steps and wire-encircled water well. Reach Point 15 at 3.7 miles, near US 79. Notice the blue and black slag rocks, byproducts of 1800s iron industry. Turn right here, away from nearby US 79 and wind uphill toward Tennessee Ridge, passing more homesite relics. An old road enters as the trail reaches Point 16 and the Tennessee Ridge Trail at 4.8 miles.

Stay left with the Peytona Trail on a dry ridge replete with chestnut oak while the Tennessee Ridge Trail forms the divide separating the Tennessee River watershed from the Cumberland River watershed. Descend to cross a streambed in Lick Hollow. Wildflowers abound in this north-facing cove in spring. Climb to reach Point 17 at 5.5 miles. A roadbed leads acutely left 0.1 mile to US 79. We leave right on the Artillery Trail, named after US Grant's use of the track to haul men and supplies from Fort Henry to Fort Donelson during the Civil War. Today you follow an old wide track that makes easy hiking amidst pines, oaks and hickories.

At 6.7 miles, the path veers right at an old homesite with a pond to your left. Stay on the old track to reach Point 18 at 7.3 miles. Here, the interesting Devils Backbone Trail leaves right. Keep straight with the Artillery Trail then reach Point 20 at 7.5 miles. Here, the Artillery Trail splits right while we head left, now on the Piney Trail. A mixture of shortleaf pines and oaks cloak a steep sided ridge. The walking is easy and the Piney Trail descends to South Piney Creek and a campsite at Point 21 at 8.7 miles.

The loop leaves right here on the Volunteer Trail, as the track rolls through low hills divided by wide creek bottoms, reaching and crossing intermittent North Piney Creek at 9.9 miles. Climb into oak hills then drop to reach Point 2 at 10.7 miles. Forest Road 230 is just to your left. Head right here, joining the Telegraph Trail, which you will follow all the way back to the trailhead.

The Telegraph Trail traverses a wide bottom where Fort Henry Branch splits into numerous ribbons, some flowing, some not, under maple, ash, and sweetgum. Reach Point 3 at 11.5 miles. Here, a field is in view, and the Telegraph-Picket Trail leaves left 0.3 mile toward FR 230. The Telegraph Trail keeps east in hickory-oak forest with fields still in view to your left, north. Make Point 4 and meet the Artillery Trail at 11.7 miles.

The Telegraph Trail continues working east, to reach Point 5 and the Devils Backbone Trail at 12.4 miles. Here, you will find a campsite, spring in a creekbed and the Devils Backbone Trail. Our route, the Telegraph Trail, bridges a stream, then skirts the edge of the field to reenter woods, now climbing and reach Point 6. Continue easterly in hardwoods to meet gravel Forest Road 400 and Point 7 at 12.9 miles. Turn right here and trace FR 400 as it undulates then ends at an earthen barrier near Panther Creek, at Point 8 at 13.5 miles. Cross Panther Creek on a wood hiker bridge.

Soon pass the Boswell Cemetery #1 on your left. It has only one known grave. A campsite is in the vicinity. From this bluff, observe beaver dams and ponds below. Ascend from the watershed on an old eroded wagon track shaded by chestnut oaks. Pass a dry campsite at 13.9 miles and continue ridge running to reach Point 9 and the Tennessee Ridge Trail at 14.9 miles. The Telegraph Trail continues straight, passing a successional field on the right. Make an easy track over a rolling ridge to meet the Fort Henry North/South Trail Connector and Point 10 at 15.2 miles. Stay right with the Telegraph Trail along a rib ridge between two feeder streams of Dry Branch. Descend among cedars to reach a field and bottomland, curving along the field to come alongside Dry Branch. The lush streamside woods and bluffs of Dry Branch are an appealing contrast to the hilltop oak-hickory forest. At 16.2 miles, reach Point 11. You have completed the loop portion of the backpack. From here, it is a 2.1 mile backtrack to the trailhead, concluding the trek.

Mileages

0.0	FR 230 near South Welcome Station
1.6	Kirkmans Camp Spring
2.1	Join Peytona Trail
3.7	Point 15
5.5	Point 17
8.7	South Piney Creek and a campsite at Point 21
11.5	Point 3
12.4	Point 5, campsite, spring
13.5	Point 8, campsite ahead
13.9	Dry campsite
15.2	Point 10
16.2	Point 11
18.3	FR 230 near South Welcome Station

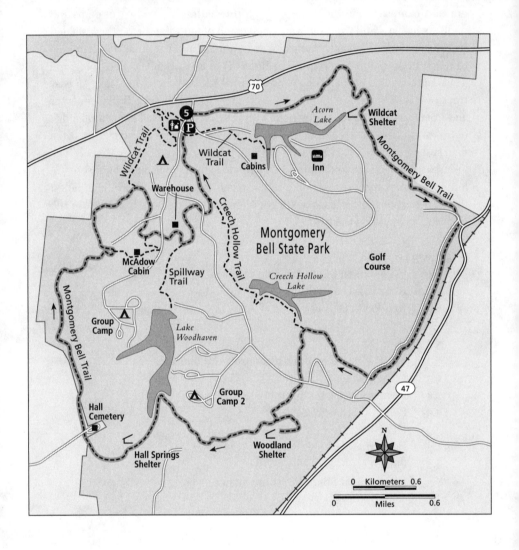

70

5

Wildcat Trail

Wildcat Trail

Warehouse

McAdow Cabin

Spillway Trail

Montgomery Bell Trail

Group Camp

Lake Woodhaven

Group Camp 2

Hall Cemetery

Hall Springs Shelter

Woodland Shelter

Cabins

Inn

Acorn Lake

Wildcat Shelter

Montgomery Bell Trail

Montgomery Bell State Park

Creech Hollow Trail

Creech Hollow Lake

Golf Course

47

N

Kilometers   0.6

Miles   0.6

5

Montgomery Bell Loop

THE BACKPACK

This backpack, great for novices or families, loops around active Montgomery Bell State Park, making a scenic circuit while accessing three backcountry trail shelters where you can overnight. The historic state park features clear streams, lakes and wooded hills through which to hike. First, surmount an oak ridge to reach Wildcat Shelter and a pair of creeks. Then climb into uplands, circling past the park golf course to reach the Woodland Shelter. Come near Lake Woodhaven before passing Hall Springs Shelter. The final part of the loop leads among historic ore mines and park facilities.

Distance and Configuration: 10.5-mile loop
Difficulty: Easy-moderate
Outstanding Features: Trail shelters, streams
Elevation: 836 feet high point, 599 feet low point
Scenery: 3
Solitude: 2
Family Friendly: 4
Canine Friendly: 4
Fees/permits: Camping fee and permit required
Best season: Mid-September through May
Maps: Montgomery Bell State Park
For more info: Montgomery Bell State Park, 1020 Jackson Hill Road, Burns, TN 37029, 615-797-9052, www.tnstateparks.com
Finding the Trailhead: From Exit 182 on I-40 west of Nashville, head west on TN 96 11 miles to US 70 near Dickson. Turn right on US 70, then head 4 miles east to the state-park entrance, which will be on the right. Enter and park at the office on your right. The loop begins on the main park road near the old park headquarters. GPS trailhead coordinates: 36.101322, -87.284941

Evening falls on the Wildcat Shelter.

Taking a break from the rain at the Woodland Shelter.

This loop backpack makes for a fine starter hike. The Montgomery Bell Trail (MBT) loop can be easily shortened using a shortcut trail, but you could also make a really easy 2 night trip using the entire MBT. The full 10.5 mile circuit is a winner any way you slice it. The three trail shelters are all recommended sites and reservations are required. There is a maximum one night stay per shelter. The trails are well marked and maintained as they roll between hill and hollow, allowing for a bit of challenge but overall pretty easy.

This state park and this backpacking trail were named for Tennessee's principle iron industrialist of the early 1800s, Montgomery Bell. Start the MBT from the park office. Walk back toward the park entrance on the main park road, crossing Wildcat Creek on the road bridge. Shortly reach the historic stone park headquarters building on your right. Pick up the MBT just beyond the building. Climb an old woods road onto a hickory-oak-cedar ridge. The hollow dropping steeply to your right stores Lake Acorn, one of three park impoundments. Drop off the ridge toward Wildcat Hollow at 1.0 mile. Step over a small branch, then reach Wildcat Creek. Descend along Wildcat Creek to cross a large feeder stream at 1.5 miles. Above you stands Wildcat Shelter, overlooking the streams. The wooden refuge, like the other two shelters, is three sided, open in the front and offers sleeping spots for 6 or so backpackers. A fire ring stands out front.

From the shelter, the MBT heads up the hollow of the large feeder branch, replete with small bluffs and dancing shoals, crossing it twice. The creek breaks into small feeder branches as you head upstream. At 2.1 miles, the MBT climbs from the hollow along concrete park-boundary markers, placed there at the park's 1930s inception.

Come to a gravel park-service road at 2.5 miles. Turn left and follow the road toward TN 47, then turn right off the road onto a wide, easy doubletrack running under tall oaks and pines, along with cedars. The park golf course can be seen through the trees. At 3.6 miles the MBT leaves abruptly right into upper Creech Hollow. Descend along gathering streams that empty into Creech Hollow Lake. At 4.2 miles, make a trail intersection within sight of the impoundment. Here, the Creech Hollow Trail heads right along its namesake lake then on toward the park office. The MBT leaves left, climbing to cross a paved park road at 4.5 miles. Keep southwesterly, dipping to yet another hollow then meet the spur trail to the Woodland Shelter. The spur circles around the upper hollow 0.3 mile to reach the wooden refuge, set on a hillside overlooking a stream blow. The camp also offers a privy.

Back on the main MBT continue your tour of the fine state park, replete with attractive forests that are a joy through which to walk. Come to an overlook of Lake Woodhaven at 5.9 miles. Soak in a view then hike along an arm of the lake in sycamore and beech. Leave the tarn, coming to the rebuilt Hall Springs

Shelter at 6.4 miles (The old shelter was crushed by a tree in 2019). Hall Spring lies below.

The MBT circles a hollow then emerges at the Hall Cemetery on the edge of the park at 6.7 miles. Continue north along the park boundary, passing near houses. The trail becomes hillier as you dip to bridge a stream at 7.1 miles then climb again. At 7.7 miles, turn east into Jackson Hollow, paralleling the cascading stream to pass an intersection with the Ore Pit Loop then reach a clearing and a replica of the Sam McAdow cabin, build where the original stood, at 8.1 miles. Back in 1810, a Christian revival swept rural areas of our country. Doctrinal differences led McAdow and others to form their own denomination—the Cumberland Presbyterian Church—during this time of spiritual enrichment.

Climb away from the cabin, passing a spur trail to the lonesome grave of Dorothy Lowe. She lived just two years in the early 1900s. Climb into the old ore pits. These holes, now rounded with time and grown over with trees, are the remains of pits dug to extract the area's iron ore. A forest rich with regal white oaks, shows the enduring healing powers of nature. The ore was fed into Laurel Furnace, located inside what are now the state park bounds, and the molten mass flowed into iron molds then shipped off to build a growing country.

At 8.7 miles, the Wildcat Trail leaves left toward the park office. The MBT descends to cross the paved park road leading to the McAdow Cabin at 9.1 miles. Climb to pass the other end of the Ore Pits Loop. Cross another park road at 9.3 miles, then dip to circle around the park warehouse. Bridge the outflow of Lake Woodhaven at 9.5 miles. Here, the Spillway Trail leaves right but we stay left to climb very sharply to cross yet another park road then meet the other end of the Creech Hollow Trail at 10.0 miles. You're almost back. Stay left with the MBT and descend to come within sight of the park office, concluding the fine state park backpack at 10.5 miles.

Mileages

0.0	Park office
1.5	Wildcat Shelter
4.2	Come near Creech Hollow Lake
4.8	Spur to Woodland Shelter
6.4	Hall Springs Shelter
8.7	Intersection with Wildcat Trail
10.5	Park office

PRACTICE TRAIL ETIQUETTE

We associate backpacking with wild places. But even when you are in the back of beyond, there is a certain amount of decorum that accompanies backpackers. After all, we don't want to act like a bunch of heathens just because we are beyond the glare of an electric light. Keep the following considerations in mind concerning proper trail behavior.

Whether you're on a county, state, or national park trail, always remember that great care and resources (from God's handiwork as well as from your tax dollars) have gone into creating these trails. Don't deface trail signs or trees. It takes a long time for trees to grow big enough to be carved into. There's no need to let passersby that you were here.

Hike on open trails only. Respect trail and road closures. Ask if you are not sure. There's usually a valid reason if a trail is closed—storm damage, mudslides, wildlife breeding area, etc. Avoid possible trespassing on private land. Imagine if that private land were yours. Obtain all permits and authorization as required. For example, Great Smoky Mountains National Park requires a backcountry permit for overnight backpacking.

Leave only footprints. Be sensitive to the ground beneath you. This also means staying on the existing trail and not blazing any new trails. Mudholes can get wider and wider if walked around by everyone.

Have you ever reached an overlook only to find trash accompanying your view? Pack out what you pack in—and more. No one likes to see the trash someone else has left behind.

Never spook wildlife. An unannounced approach, a sudden movement, or a loud noise startles most animals. A surprised animal can be dangerous to you, to others, and to themselves. Give them plenty of space. After all, the wilderness is the only home they have.

Honor leash laws. Most trails require keeping Fido on a 6-foot leash. Some pet owners think their dog is special and leash laws don't apply. I can't tell you how many times I've been jumped on by a dog with muddy feet while their owners are simultaneously yelling at the barking canine, creating a chaotic and unpleasant scene for everyone. Think of your fellow backpackers before setting your dog free. Unleashed dogs will also chase wildlife and perhaps become lost.

Plan ahead. Know your equipment, your ability, and the area where you are hiking—then prepare accordingly. Be self-sufficient at all times; carry necessary supplies for changes in weather or other conditions. Most backpacking accidents/rescues start with ill-prepared walkers overestimating their abilities. They become tired or worried, then make poor decisions, turning a bad situation worse. In contrast, a well-executed trip is a satisfaction to you and to others. It builds your confidence and makes you desirous to return again.

Finally, be courteous to other hikers, bikers, equestrians you encounter on the trails. Bikers should yield to hikers and equestrians. Hikers should yield to equestrians. If encountering a horse, get well off the trail, be still and talk in smooth tones. Horses can sometimes be scared of hikers with packs on, so if wearing a pack, step to the downhill side of the trail to make yourself seem smaller.

A little etiquette goes a long way in smoothing things out while roughing it on the trail.

6

Henry Horton Backpack

THE BACKPACK

This fun little overnighter at Henry Horton State Park leads you through Middle Tennessee's unique hickory-cedar forests and cedar glades to an overnighter camp on a bluff above the Duck River. Start at the park's camp store, then visit sinkholes, springs, homesites and rock outcrops en route to your wooded camp above the longest river entirely within the boundaries of the Volunteer State. Next, day, make an easy riverside jaunt back to the trailhead.

Distance and Configuration: 3.8-mile loop
Difficulty: Easy
Outstanding Features: Cedar glades, bluff campsite
Elevation: 709 feet high point, 635 feet low point
Scenery: 3
Solitude: 3
Family Friendly: 5
Canine Friendly: 4
Fees/permits: Camping fee required
Best season: Mid-September through mid-May
Maps: Henry Horton State Park
For more info: Henry Horton State Park, 4209 Nashville Highway, Chapel Hill, TN 37034, 931-364-2222, www.tnstateparks.com
Finding the Trailhead: From Exit 46 on I-65 south of Nashville, head east on TN 99 13 miles to US 31A. Turn right on 31A and follow it south a short piece to the Henry Horton State Park. Take the right turn toward the state-park campground on River Road and follow it 0.3 mile to turn left toward the campground and camp store. The Hickory Ridge Trail starts to the right of the camp store as you face it. GPS trailhead coordinates: 35.591153, -86.702327

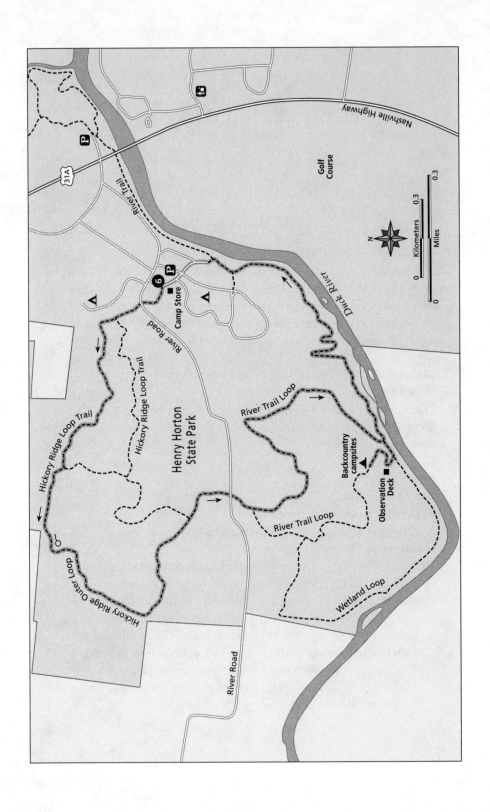

The backpack takes you along the banks of the Duck River.

I've been visiting Henry Horton State Park for decades and was very pleased when they expanded the trail system and added a backcountry campsite, ideally situated on a bluff above the Duck River, making a good thing better. If you've never been here, backpacking is a fine way to experience the woods and waters named for a Tennessee governor. There are two reservable sites, each with a fire ring and benches. Water can be had from the nearby Duck River but since the hike is short, consider bringing all your own aqua, using river water to put out your campfire or to make coffee. Campsite reservations are required. Permits are available online or at the camp store.

The Hickory Ridge Trail is your conduit to the backpacker campsite. Leave the camp store, crossing River Road entering the hickory-cedar woods found in this part of the Volunteer State. You will also find sinkholes and cedar glades, one of the state's rarest habitats. These openings in cedar forests appear barren but are habitat to very rare plants. The limestone cedar glades and hickory-cedar forests are usually accompanied by sinks, caves, and water seeps, revealing the

Duck River bottomland.

area's karst topography, a fancy word for holey eroded ground where water and rock interplay beneath the surface, resulting in both springs and sinks. At first glance, cedar glades resemble a flat rock parking lot grown over with weeds. But these weed-looking plants are actually some of the life that is so rare in this rare habitat, such as Tennessee coneflower and Pyne's ground plum.

At 0.2 mile, the loop part of the Hickory Ridge Loop Trail leaves left. Stay right, passing by a linear primitive auto-accessible campground. Ahead, wind among sinkholes, as well as old rock piles and fence lines. It is hard to believe this thin-soiled land was used for agriculture, but about the whole park was at one time. At 0.6 mile, reach a trail junction and stay right with the Hickory Ridge Outer Loop. The trail remains mostly level, traversing woods. Come to a rock walled spring at 0.8 mile. Beyond here, the loop curves south, still in hickory-oak-cedar woods.

At 1.1 miles, walk through a cedar glade. Middle Tennessee is the planetary epicenter for these peculiar habitats. Return to cedar woods and reach an intersection at 1.5 miles. Here, turn right, southbound, to cross River Road and meet the River Trail, full name Adeline Wilhoite River Trail Loop. Stay left, winding in and out of cedar glades and former fields mixed with woods, with numerous old fence lines—both stone and wire—bordered with Osage orange trees. Look around for relics from the farming days, as the forest rises among the fields. This is a good area to spot deer. At 2.1 miles, the River Trail Loop curves south. Descend the bluff above the Duck River then reach an intersection at 2.5 miles. The Duck River is just a few feet away. Head right, downstream, and walk a short distance to climb to a 35-acre former field, now restored to native grasses using prescribed fire. Here you will find an observation deck rising over the meadows, as well as the mown portion of the Wetland Trail. Climb the tower then climb the hill to reach the backcountry campsite at 2.7 miles. The recommended two campsites are in level woods, with a fair distance between them. Each site has a table and fire ring. Bring your water or treat it from the Duck River.

Next day, backtrack to the Duck River, then follow the River Trail upstream, sometimes winding through bottoms and sometimes along the river bank where you get good looks at the waterway. Notice the occasional islands in the stream. At 3.7 miles, head left on a short spur trail leading into the park campground. From there, walk through the campground back to the camp store, completing the rewarding Middle Tennessee backpack.

Mileages

0.0	Camp store
1.7	Left on River Trail Loop
2.7	Backcountry campsites
3.8	Camp store

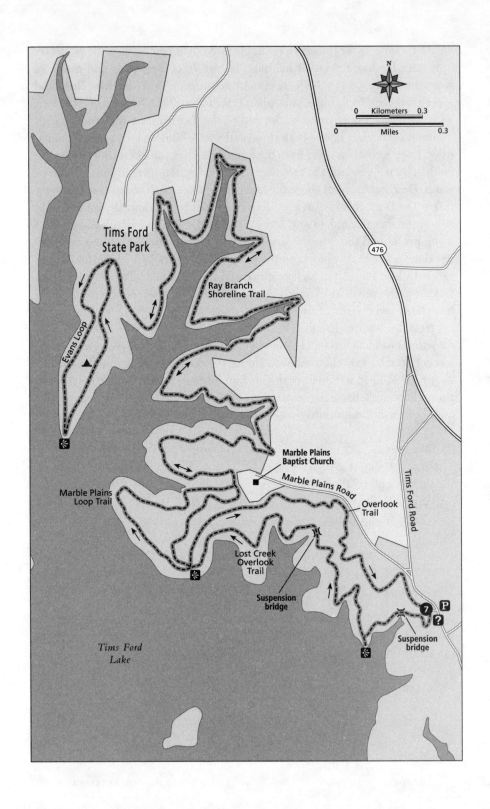

Tims Ford State Park

Ray Branch
Shoreline Trail

Evans Loop

476

Marble Plains
Baptist Church

Marble Plains Road

Marble Plains
Loop Trail

Overlook
Trail

Tims Ford Road

Lost Creek
Overlook
Trail

Suspension
bridge

Tims Ford
Lake

Suspension
bridge

7
P
?

N

0   Kilometers   0.3

0   Miles   0.3

7

Tims Ford State Park Backpack

THE BACKPACK

This attractive lakeside overnight trek leads atop over suspension bridges and past views to a lesser visited peninsula of Tims Ford State Park, with waterside access before rising to reach a backcountry campsite, once site of a farmstead. Your return route involves both backtracking and new trail.

Distance and Configuration: 12.7-mile figure-eight loop
Difficulty: Moderate
Outstanding Features: Lake views, suspension bridges, lake access
Elevation: 997 feet high point, 890 feet low point
Scenery: 4
Solitude: 3
Family Friendly: 3
Canine Friendly: 2
Fees/permits: Fee-based reservable campsite permit required
Best season: Fall through spring
Maps: Tims Ford State Park
For more info: Tims Ford State Park, 570 Tims Ford Drive, Winchester, TN 37398, 931-968-3536, www.tnstateparks.com
Finding the Trailhead: From exit 111 on I-24 near Manchester, take TN 55 west for 12.4 miles to Tullahoma, then keep straight on Carroll Street and straight on Clement Street to quickly meet and turn left on TN 130 south, Westside Street. Follow TN 130 south for 3.6 miles then veer right on TN 476 and stay with it for 7.1 miles to turn right onto Tims Ford Road and follow it for 0.5 mile to turn right into the state park visitor center parking lot. GPS trailhead coordinates: 35.220306, -86.255167

Tims Ford State Park came to be when the Elk River was dammed back by Tennessee Valley Authority in 1970, creating Tims Ford Lake. The park consists of

View of Tims Ford Lake from a designated overlook.

2,200 acres of mostly shoreline where steep-sided hollows drop into fingerlike coves and embayments. It is along the shoreline this backpacking adventure travels, allowing nearly continuous watery vistas when the leaves are off the trees. The destination is a formerly settled peninsula along Ray Branch embayment. Tree-lined fence rows delineate former pastureland from forest.

The first part of the trip is on scenic and popular day hiking trails. As you face the visitor center, join the Lost Creek Overlook Trail to your right, west. The natural surface singletrack path descends into a sloping hollow of beech and cedar. Meet the first hiker suspension bridge at 0.1 mile. This long wooden span stretches across a hollow below. At 0.3 mile, a spur goes left to a point and vista on Tims Ford Lake. From there, work around more steep-sided hollows to find another very long hiker suspension bridge at 0.8 mile. This one is over 120 feet long! Continue hiking westerly to reach a designated overlook at 1.3 miles. Here, a platform opens south into Tims Ford Lake, revealing the islands and waters of the now submerged Elk River, with the Cumberland Plateau rising as a formidable rampart in the background. From here join the Marble Plains Loop Trail, still heading west, now on less sloped land. The trail turns you into the Ray Branch embayment, with which you will become very familiar. Dip to an old roadbed then climb east to a trail intersection near Marble Plains Baptist Church at 2.2 miles. Here, head left on the Ray Branch Shoreline Trail, leaving any crowds behind. This path continues the pattern of tracing the shoreline into and out of finger embayments of the greater Ray Branch embayment. The singletrack, well maintained trail often comes near private property while wandering through dogwoods, sweetgum and tulip trees. The path is more level than not, even as it works along sloped hollows. Under normal conditions the streams flowing into the hollows will be dry.

At 4.9 miles, circle around the head of Ray Branch embayment. Now turn south down the west side of Ray Branch embayment. Cruise around one finger embayment then resume south, very close to the shore, winding through cedar thickets before turning northwest, away from the water. At 6.1 miles, reach a trail intersection. Here, the Evans Loop begins. Stay right, curving to the west side of the peninsula. The land drops off sharply, but here atop the peninsula you will see signs of habitation—wire fencing, metal artifacts and old fence rows lined with big trees.

Descend to reach the point of the peninsula—now at water level—at 6.7 miles. Here lies a small, slightly sloped unofficial campsite with stellar views to the south. This camp is used by boaters and backpackers who don't realize the official campsite is actually uptrail a bit. At 6.9 miles—after climbing from the water—a short spur leads left to a level tree-shaded signed camp with a metal fire ring. The closest water is back at the shoreline campsite at 6.7 miles.

From the official campsite follow an old roadbed north, then complete the Evan Loop at 7.3 miles. Begin backtracking 3.9 miles on the Ray Branch Shoreline Trail, to rejoin the Marble Plains Loop Trail near Marble Plains Baptist Church at 11.2 miles. Keep south here, returning to the lake overlook at 11.6 miles. Enjoy another elevated vista of Tims Ford Lake, then join the paved (and easy) Overlook Trail. It leads you back to the visitor center and trailhead, completing the backpack at 12.7 miles.

Mileages

0.0	Visitor Center
0.8	Second suspension bridge
1.3	Official overlook
2.2	Join Ray Branch Shoreline Trail
6.1	Right on Evans Loop Trail
6.7	Reach lakeshore, unofficial campsite
6.9	Evans Loop campsite

In spring, the backpack will take you by shooting star wildflowers.

CHOOSE YOUR BACKPACKING FOOTWEAR WISELY

My friend Bryan and I were backpacking the Bald Mountains of Greene County in the Cherokee National Forest. A slow moving tropical storm dumped inches of rain on us and raised area streams to scary heights. We waited a whole day and night for the waterways to drop, stranded between potential trail exits.

The next day we came to Jennings Creek, a brown flowing fury. My impatience clouded my sanity and we hiked forward, trying to ford the swollen stream. I pushed through and made it. Bryan did too, minus a shoe, torn off his feet. Once across, we inventoried our situation and bee lined to the nearest road, Bryan hiking with two pairs of socks in lieu of his lost shoe. Wrong shoes, wrong place.

Another time I was embarking on a backpack in the Big Frog Wilderness. The early fall skies promised a good trip. Hiking pal John Bland and I took the Big Creek Trail, aiming for the Big Frog Mountain. I hadn't made a quarter mile in my brand new boots when my heels started heating up. Uh, oh.

A mile further, I was limping and asking for Band-Aids from John. We cut the day short, camping on small creek. By the time we reached Big Frog Mountain the next day my heels resembled hamburger meat. I was relegated to barefoot camp tender while John did the camp chores. Next day, I hobbled to the nearest trailhead while John got the car and picked me up. Right shoes, bad fit.

When dropping a significant amount of hard-earned dough on a boot, consider having them fitted by professionals at outdoor stores. Fit is more important than brand name or shoe type or numerical shoe size.

When choosing backpacking footwear, consider the typical terrain through which you hike. Are the trails rough and rocky? Are they steep or are they smooth and widely graded? Many backpackers can get away with low top hiking shoes if the trails are moderate and their pack is light. However, if you don't have strong ankles as I do, go with shoes that give ankle support. If the trail is rough consider additional support, using boots with a metal shank in them and a more rugged sole. Heavier boots are preferable in winter, for warmth and snow protection.

Backpackers have a dilemma when considering footwear. They desire shoes that will support a fully loaded backpack while hiking, and also are comfortable in camp. Having two pairs of shoes on your person during a backpacking trip adds weight, though camp shoes, such as flip flops, get lighter all the time. If you are going to do a lot of hiking, or going on a very long trip I strongly recommend having quality trail shoes with quality sole. And if you find a brand that works for you, stick with that brand.

When backpacking you literally carry your own weight so you live with your decisions, for better or worse. Remember, a successful backpacking adventure starts from the ground up —with your shoes.

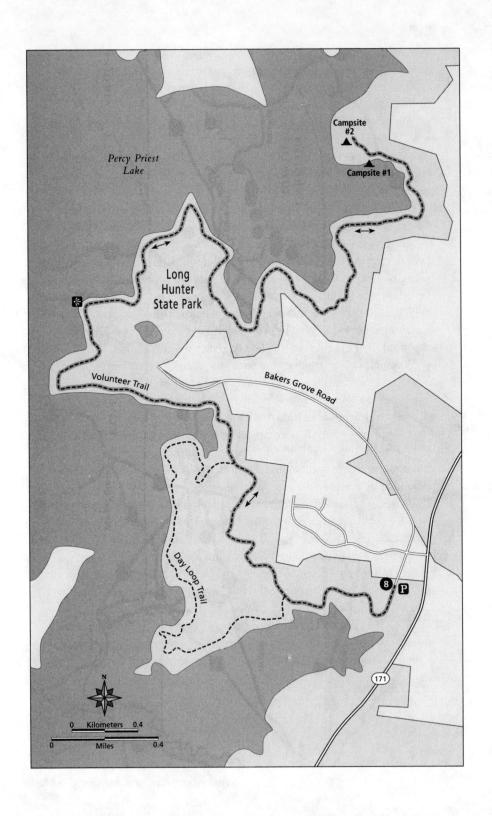

Percy Priest
Lake

Campsite
#2

Campsite #1

Long
Hunter
State Park

Volunteer Trail

Bakers Grove Road

Day Loop Trail

8

P

171

N

0   Kilometers   0.4
0   Miles   0.4

8

Long Hunter Backpack

THE BACKPACK

This overnight adventure at Long Hunter State Park takes place on the shores of Percy Priest Lake. Start at Bakers Grove on the Volunteer Trail, glimpsing the lake while trekking amid cedar and rock before climbing through oaks. Come back along the shore to travel along the water to a fine pair of campsites on the Suggs Creek arm of the scenic impoundment.

Distance and Configuration: 11.0-mile there-and-back
Difficulty: Moderate
Outstanding Features: Percy Priest Lake, views, good campsites
Elevation: 611 feet high point, 492 feet low point
Scenery: 3
Solitude: 2
Family Friendly: 3
Canine Friendly: 4
Fees/permits: Camping fee required
Best season: October through April
Maps: Long Hunter State Park
For more info: Long Hunter State Park, 2910 Hobson Pike, Hermitage, TN 37076, 615-885-2422, www.tnstateparks.com
Finding the Trailhead: From Exit 226 on I-40 east of downtown Nashville, take South Mount Juliet Road, TN 171, south 4.2 miles. Veer right at the split as TN 171 becomes Hobson Pike. Keep forward 1.8 miles farther, turning right on Bakers Grove Lane. Drive just a short distance, then turn left on Bakers Grove Road and follow it a short distance to the parking area at the dead end. GPS trailhead coordinates: 36.101771, -86.553654

Back in 1960, what became Long Hunter State Park was a sleepy rural area east of Nashville. In 1968 the Stones River was dammed and Percy Priest Lake came

Soak in views of Percy Priest Lake on this backpack.

to be. The state of Tennessee negotiated a 99 year lease with the US Army Corps of Engineers to create a state park that included 33 shoreline miles of Percy Priest Lake. More than a half-century has passed and Nashville has grown exponentially. The current land value of Long Hunter State Park would boggle the mind.

The park features over 30 miles of trails in four areas, including the Volunteer Trail that leads to a backcountry campsite, availing a shoreline backpacking opportunity in the shadow of Nashville. And what a pretty hike it is, running along the shore, through cedar woods and oak stands, betwixt limestone outcrops, into creek vales and along peninsulas jutting into the lake. Remember, fee based camping reservations must be made in advance, either online or in person at the state park office. There are two backcountry campsites that can be reserved. Campsite 1 is more popular as it is closer to the lake, while Campsite 2 offers isolation atop a wooded hill about 100 yards distant. You must bring or treat your water. No other amenities are on site. Access to the sites is by foot only. As far as when to go, the cooler the weather the better, for Percy Priest Lake can get clogged with noisy motor boats during the warm season.

The hike is not difficult and has only a few hills. The ground can be stony in places but overall the route is well marked, maintained and in good shape. Leave the Bakers Grove parking area on the Volunteer Trail, with which runs in conjunction with the Day Loop Trail. Trundle down an old gravel road flanked with tightly grown cedars, along with hickory and oaks. Reach a boardwalk spanning a wet-weather drainage area that forms the cove of Percy Priest Lake to your left. You will pass along many such coves along with peninsular points before reaching the backcountry campsite.

Long Hunter State Park got its name through a man named Uriah Stone. The Stones River was named for him. Back in the 1700s, this part of the world was a howling wilderness when the inexorable tide of colonists filtered over the Appalachians. Uriah Stone was among the men reaching this far flung area in search of animal hides before returning east to sell them. The hunts would sometimes last a year or more, and men like Uriah Stone became known as long hunters.

It was somewhere in this vicinity, on this tributary of the Cumberland River that Uriah Stone was double-crossed by a French long hunter with whom Stone had partnered. The Frenchman made off with the hides they had gotten thus far. The tale of Stone's ill luck passed on among other long hunters, and the name of this river became Stones River.

The Stones River valley, aka Percy Priest Lake, leaves your view. Wander through boulder gardens then come to an intersection at 0.5 mile. Here, the Day Loop Trail leaves left to make a circuit on a peninsula. We stay right, gently climbing over a rocky hill upon which grows red bud, shagbark hickory and oak. At 0.9 mile, pass a sinkhole to your left and the remains of an old farm pond on your right, slowly filling in with forest debris, almost an ephemeral wetland. Cut through an old stone fence before reaching another intersection at 1.2 miles. Here, stay right with the now lesser used singletrack Volunteer Trail, rolling amidst rocky woods. Note cacti rising forth from the thin soils. The path now stays close to the lake, falling into a pattern of mimicking the shoreline, remaining more level than not.

Lake views open up and user created trails lead to clear spots where you can gander out on the impoundment. The warmer the weather the more boats you will see. At 2.5 miles, reach a point opening due west where an old road heads directly into the lake. This was an early incarnation of Old Hickory Boulevard, rerouted when the lake came in the 1960s. The view open west down the Stones River Valley. At 3.2 miles, turn into the Suggs Creek embayment. Traverse among taller oaks. Cross a pair of streams at 3.9 and 4.4 miles, continuing to skirt the shore. At 5.5 miles, come to Campsite 1, set in a flat not far from the shore and an outcrop where you can access the lake. Campsite 2 is up a hill to your right. After overnighting you can add new mileage to the adventure by taking the Day Loop Trail back.

Visualize yourself overnighting at this campsite.

Mileages

0.0	Bakers Grove trailhead
0.5	Right with Volunteer Trail
1.2	Right with Volunteer Trail
2.5	View
5.5	Campsites
11.0	Bakers Grove trailhead

LIGHT OPTIONS FOR THE LONG NIGHTS OF WINTER

A friend and I were backpacking Long Hunter State Park. At noon, a December sun stretched low overhead, then fell to the west, elongating the shadows of leafless, skeletal trees. A creeping chill pushed into our campsite with the darkening dusk.

It wasn't even 5 o'clock. But it was time to light our campsite.

For this backpacker, camping goes on, despite the short days and long nights, when fall's golden light turns to winter's pale weak rays and don't even stick around that long. In Murfreesboro, the geographic center of Tennessee, the hours of daylight reach a low of 9 hours 43 minutes of sunshine per day. That leaves 12 plus hours of darkness. And for the backpacker that can be a long time.

However, backpackers have an array of light options, from old-fashioned candles to ultralight headlamps. Depending on the situation I use them all to illuminate the night, to not only help stay awake, but also to gather wood, cook dinner, slip into the sleeping bag and keep from stumbling around the campsite.

Candles still have their place. They give a soft light, perfect for general illumination. A little foil will enhance candle brightness and also block a breeze that makes them burn fast or blow out. An upside: Candle wax dripped onto kindling makes for a good emergency fire starter. A downside: their subjectivity to wind—also you simply can't carry them around. Small, battery operated lanterns are yet another option. They use 2-3 small batteries and provide decent illumination.

Headlamps are the best all-around backpacking light. Here, a battery operated light is connected to a strap fitting around your head. The headlamp is hands free and the beam shines wherever the user is looking. These generally operate on AAA batteries, leaving them lightweight. Variations of this include small lights, operated by nickel-sized watch batteries that clip onto the bill of a ball cap. Headlamps are best for backpackers because they weigh so little. Check your batteries before embarking on your backpack!

Lightweight, plastic solar charged lights, such as those by Luci, are inexpensive, weigh mere ounces, yet can spread a soft light onto a campsite when hung from a nearby tee or line, for stumble-free camping. These are slow recharging in winter, so have it fully charged before departing, and don't expect much recharging during a winter trip.

What about a hand-held flashlight? They are still used by a few backpackers, and still have their place, mostly as a backup for the other light options during the long nights of winter.

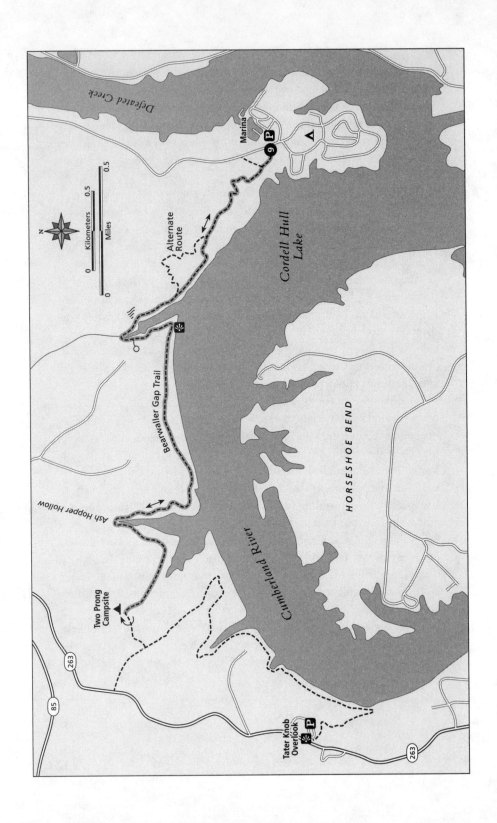

9

Bearwaller Gap Trail

THE BACKPACK

This official National Recreation Trail will challenge you as it traverses the steep and attractive hills rising from Cordell Hull Lake to reach a backcountry campsite set in the head of a hollow. Leave Defeated Creek Recreation Area to climb high bluffs with lake views before dropping to a stream hollow only to climb yet again to a stellar vista. From here turn into a pair of hollows, the second of which harbors your destination, Two Prong backcountry campsite, a fine place to overnight.

Distance and Configuration: 6.2-mile there-and-back
Difficulty: Moderate, does have steep segments
Outstanding Features: Bluffs above Cordell Hull Lake, views
Elevation: 822 feet high point, 504 feet low point
Scenery: 4
Solitude: 3
Family Friendly: 2
Canine Friendly: 3
Fees/permits: None required
Best season: October through April
Maps: Bearwaller Gap Hiking Trail
For more info: Defeated Creek Recreation Area, US Army Corps of
    Engineers, 140 Marina Lane, Carthage, TN 37030, 615-735-1034,
    www.lrn.usace.army.mil
Finding the Trailhead: From Exit 258 on Interstate 40 east of Lebanon,
    take TN 53 north 4 miles, and continue straight as the road changes
    into TN 25 west. Keep forward 6 more miles to reach TN 80. Turn
    right on TN 80 north and follow it 2.5 miles to TN 85. Turn right on
    TN 85 east, and follow it 3.6 miles to Defeated Creek Recreation
    Area. Turn right and follow the recreation area road 1.4 miles to
    a parking area on the right near the picnic shelter just before the
    campground. GPS trailhead coordinates: 36.302955, -85.909967

Passing a quaint cove of Cordell Hull Lake.

The Bearwaller Gap Trail is both challenging and beautiful and a welcome addition to Middle Tennessee backpacking possibilities. Though it is but 3.2 miles to Two Prong backcountry campsite, the Bearwaller Gap Trail does extend for 2.6 miles farther to an alternate trailhead at Tater Knob Overlook on TN 263. If upon arriving at the campsite and you desire a little more trail treading you can add the distance to the overlook and back to your trek. Or you can make it a one-way adventure using two vehicles (The Tater Knob Overlook trailhead is gated in winter). The scenery en route to Two Prong campsite offers a lot—wet weather waterfalls, tall bluffs, lake views, wildflowers and signs of human habitation, namely old rock walls.

Therefore, the Bearwaller Gap Trail is deserving of its status as a federally designated National Recreation Trail. Though bears are largely absent from Middle Tennessee these days you will likely see deer along the way. Begin the backpack, heading uphill from the signed trailhead at Defeated Creek Recreation Area on a fence lined trail. Soon cross an old road then climb into a rock garden shaded by hackberry, hickory and chestnut oak trees. Stinging nettle could be troublesome here in summer.

The blazed path switchbacks upwards to level out at 0.5 mile. Congratulations, you just climbed 300 feet. Cruise along the wooded bench then reach a trail split. The main route goes left while the "easier" route goes right. Go left, descending a very stony, very steep slope with Cordell Hull Lake making its curve at Horseshoe Bend, visible through the trees. Watch your footing on this steep slope. Trekking poles come in handy here. By 0.9 mile the extremely narrow trail arrives at a saner slope, and the alternate route sneaks in on your right. Cross a dry streambed, then turn into a cove of the lake. At 1.1 miles cross the naked rock of a stream, with small waterfalls both above and below the trail. Curve around the cove stepping over a pair of streambeds over which water may or may not be flowing. After curving around the cove, pass a spring on your right in the brush at 1.2 miles. Look for the concrete block catch basin with the rocked-in springhead just above that. The developed spring is a sign that a home was once nearby.

The Bearwaller Gap Hiking Trail reaches a point and rock outcrop overlooking the lake at 1.4 miles. Soak in views to the south, down the impoundment, created by the damming of the Cumberland River, framed by hills beyond. From the overlook, the path ascends a slender but steep wooded ridge, topping out 320 feet above the lake. Descend from the knob as quickly as you climbed. Cross an intermittent streambed at 2.1 miles.

From here turn into the Two Prong embayment, skirting the shoreline into Ash Hopper Hollow. Beard cane borders the track. Step over the streambed of Ash Hopper Hollow then come alongside a stone fence paralleling the trail at 2.8 miles. Look also for another stone fence heading straight up the hillside. Curve into the second hollow, climbing to make Two Prong backcountry campsite at 3.1 miles. This locale is hard against a steep hill but has flat tent sites, a covered spring, three fire pits, a small covered shelter, picnic table, and an outhouse. This is your well-earned overnight destination.

If you want to continue the Bearwaller Gap Trail, ascend the wide roadbed ahead, topping out on a level ridgeline, only to descend to a rocky streambed. Circle a steep hollow beside stone walls, coming to the lake and an old homesite. Keep along a bluff above the shore with views of the Cordell Hull Dam to your south, then make a final climb for Tater Knob, where you can enjoy a wide view of the hills and waters of this land, 2.4 miles from the Two Prong campsite.

Mileages

0.0	Defeated Creek Picnic Area
0.5	Trail splits
0.9	Trail comes together
1.4	View
3.1	Two Prong campsite
6.2	Defeated Creek Picnic Area

Soak in this fine view en route to the campsite.

ABOUT WATER IN THE BACKCOUNTRY

I drink untreated water. No I'm not talking about down Mexico way (I did that and got sick). I'm talking about drinking water in the backcountry in the United States. I've drank from swamps down in Florida and wilderness rivers in New Mexico. I've drank from alpine lakes high in the California Sierras and iron-rich lakes in Minnesota. Locally, I mean springs, swamps, rivers, lakes and creeks here in Tennessee.

Face it, while backpacking, we cannot bring all the water we will need to drink. That means we will have to obtain water from local sources. Backpackers are faced with the dilemma while in the back of beyond: do I drink the water?

I am in the minority, but I drink the water directly from the source and don't treat it. To the chagrin of my backpacking compadres I haven't gotten sick. However, consider the following do-as-I-say-not-as-I-do advice: Treat your water.

So what can drinking bad water do? Microbes such as giardia and cryptosporidium get in your intestines and disrupt your life with excessive gas, diarrhea and other unpleasantries. Giardiasis—the illness caused by giardia—won't ruin your average backpacking trip, as it takes 1 to 2 weeks for symptoms to appear. But once symptoms crop up expect to be ill for 2 to 6 weeks. Weight loss and dehydration follow. A doctor's a gut-relieving prescription and plenty of fluids may help with the symptoms, which will eventually run their course, resulting in one painful weight loss program.

Treating your water has become a lot easier these days, but let's harken back for a moment. The old method was to boil your water for at least a minute—there's nothing like hot water to sate a big thirst! It is not convenient either, you have to wait until after your water is boiled, which means you have to have made a fire or broken out a camp stove. Then came the pump filters—you literally pump your water through a device that filters out the demon microorganisms. Pump filters were once bulky but are now smaller and commonly used.

Many people use chemical water treatments. Iodine was the choice of days gone by, but it has an awful taste and gives you iodine breath, which ain't good. Nowadays we have products like Aqua Mira, where you mix two drops of chemicals, making chlorine dioxide, and wait 30 minutes, then your water is fine. Again, the wait is a problem but it is the lightest option. Buying a water bottle with a built-in filter is an easier choice. Simply fill your water bottle then suck through a straw, which forces the water through a built-in small filter, which needs to be replaced often. UV filters are another option—using ultraviolet rays to kill the bad things in the aqua. These products, such as Steripen, use batteries, which can die.

Simple filters such as the gravity fed Sawyer are lightweight, cheap and last for years. They use special microbe blocking membranes and operate using gravity—or squeeze pressure if in a hurry. The filters are used in undeveloped countries throughout the world.

No matter your method, treating your water is smart. Otherwise, you may spend your time being sick instead of backpacking.

Cumberland Plateau

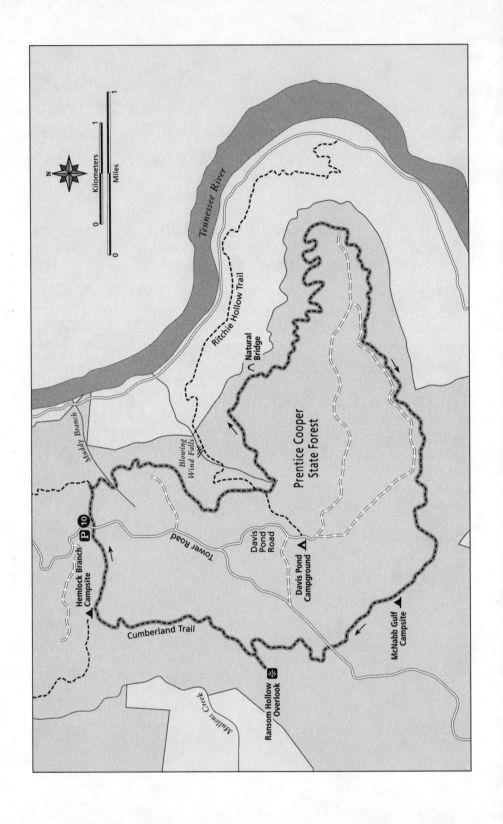

10

Pot Point Backpack

THE BACKPACK

This overnight adventure at Prentice Cooper State Forest traverses the most southerly segment of the Cumberland Trail, looping high above the Grand Canyon of the Tennessee River. Start with a sweeping view from Snoopers Rock, then visit Natural Bridge, a sturdy arch. Loop your way along the rim of the canyon to overnight at intimate McNabb Gulf campsite. After that, enjoy a superlative view from Ransom Hollow Overlook. Finally, come to Hemlock Branch campsite before returning to the trailhead.

Distance and Configuration: 12.1-mile loop
Difficulty: Moderate
Outstanding Features: Views, arch, good campsites
Elevation: 1,829 feet low point, 1,401 feet high point
Scenery: 5
Solitude: 3
Family Friendly: 3
Canine Friendly: 3
Fees/permits: None, must check state forest hunt dates
Best season: September through May
Maps: Pot Point Loop—Cumberland Trail Conference
For more info: Prentice Cooper State Forest, PO Box 160, Hixson, TN
    37343, (423) 658-5551, www.tn.gov/agriculture/forests
Finding the Trailhead: From the junction of US 27 and US 127 north-
    west of Chattanooga, take US 127 north for 1.6 miles to TN 27 west.
    Turn left on TN 27 west and follow it for 8 miles to Choctaw Trail
    and a sign for Prentice Cooper WMA. Turn left on Choctaw Trail
    and follow it for .2 mile to reach Game Reserve Road. Turn left on
    Game Reserve Road and enter Prentice Cooper State Forest, where
    it becomes Tower Road. Keep straight on gravel Tower Road for 4.6
    miles to the Cumberland Trail parking area on your left. GPS trail-
    head coordinates: 35.101617, -85.429283

Ransom Hollow Overlook is yet another highlight on this backpack.

This backpack explores the rim of the gorge of the Tennessee River in wild and magnificent Prentice Cooper State Forest, a worthy Tennessee natural resource. The loop presents two designated campsites on its length, but unfortunately they aren't well situated for a 2 night trip, being too close to one another. Overall, the trail is level more than not. More importantly: the state forest is closed to hikers during spring and fall hunt dates. Check with the state forest website for these weekends before you plan your backpack.

The parking area is popular with forest visitors who make the short jaunt to Snoopers Rock. From the trailhead kiosk follow a short connector to reach the Cumberland Trail. Here, head left toward Snoopers Rock, passing a small pond en route to the edge of Walden Ridge and a trail junction at 0.3 mile. For now, head left Snoopers Rock, crossing a small parking area to enter the terrace-like rock outcrop that is Snoopers Rock. Before you opens the Grand Canyon of the Tennessee River 900 feet below, cutting its gorge through the Cumberland Plateau. The river extends beyond sight, curving round Raccoon Mountain. What a sight!

Backtrack from Snoopers Rock and join the Cumberland Trail, southbound, toward Pot Point and the Natural Bridge. The trail winds under maples and oaks

The Grand Canyon of the Tennessee River as seen from Snoopers Rock.

along with pines along the gorge rim. Dip to hop normally clear Muddy Branch at 0.6 mile. Switchback uphill to level off in rocky woods.

At 1.2 miles, the Cumberland Trail curves into Ritchie Hollow. Bridge a tributary stream of Ritchie Hollow at 1.7 miles, then meet the Ritchie Hollow Trail at 2.0 miles. This path leads left to Blowing Wind Falls and right to Davis Pond Campground. Ahead, the Cumberland Trail bridges more small stony streamlets before returning to the rim of the Tennessee River at 2.8 miles. Stay along the

The trail takes you directly over Natural Bridge.

rim edge, passing a partial overlook before making Natural Bridge at 3.1 miles.
The path leads you atop the 70 feet long by 30 feet wide by 30 feet high thickset,
formidable arch. It is not too difficult to get a look at the span from below and is
worth the trouble. The trail is less used beyond the Natural Bridge as you trek
amidst evergreens and hardwoods and brush. Cross the stream of Blowing Springs
Hollow at 3.4 miles. Wind in and out of shallow hollows, passing the streamlet
of Chestnut Bridge Hollow at 4.1 miles. You'll reach what is left of Pot Point
Road at 5.2 miles (It is admittedly hard to distinguish this fading track amidst
other old roads in this locale). Pot Point got its name as one of the three spots
on the river below—The Pot, The Skillet and The Pan. Before the Tennessee
River was dammed 30 miles of rough waters in the river gorge wreaked havoc
on early boaters.

From Pot Point the trail arcs westerly. The terrain becomes more piney and
rocky as you traverse a south facing section of the gorge. Interestingly, you are
only about 6 miles from downtown Chattanooga as the crow flies, but a world
apart, separated by Raccoon Mountain and three bends of the Tennessee River.
The trail leads into hollows with tiny streams and big boulders divided by brushier,
more fire subject rib ridges dividing them.

At 6.6 miles, come to the spur leading left to Raccoon Mountain Overlook. The rock outcrop presents a partial vista to the south as you scan through pines. Descend a bit then fully turn into McNabb Gulf at 8.0 miles. The hollow narrows. Hemlocks and mountain laurel dominate the woods as the cool stream makes its way toward the Tennessee River. The hollow is quite narrow upon making McNabb Gulf Campsite at 8.5 miles. Three small campsites are strung along the slender but reliable stream. Tent sites are limited.

From the campsites continue up McNabb Gulf, criss-crossing rills flowing into McNabb Gulf before making Tower Drive at 9.2 miles. The Cumberland Trail continues past a trailside kiosk and travels down more than not above the Mullens Creek gorge to reach the signed spur to Ransom Hollow Overlook at 9.1 miles. Follow this side trail to reach an outcrop opening to the west and mountain-rimmed Nickajack Lake with Ransom Hollow immediately below. This is one of my favorite views in Tennessee.

Backtrack and continue the Cumberland Trail, with the maw of Mullen Creek Gulf opening to your left. Rock walls are visible as you wander north. At 10.6 miles, the trail crosses a stream just above a modest waterfall before slicing through a jumble of noteworthy boulders, actually squeezing through a slot. Keep north in rich woods, gently descending toward Hemlock Branch and a trail junction at 11.5 miles. Here, head left toward Mullen Cove Overlook to shortly reach smallish Hemlock Branch campsite, set on both sides of Hemlock Branch, bordered by rock outcrops under evergreens. To complete the loop, hike up pretty Hemlock Creek, gently rising past a tributary and into hardwoods to make Tower Road and backpack's end at 12.1 miles.

Mileages

0.0	Tower Road trailhead
0.3	Snoopers Rock
3.1	Natural Bridge
6.6	Raccoon Mountain Overlook
8.5	McNabb Gulf campsite
9.1	Ransom Hollow Overlook
11.5	Hemlock Branch campsite
12.1	Tower Road trailhead

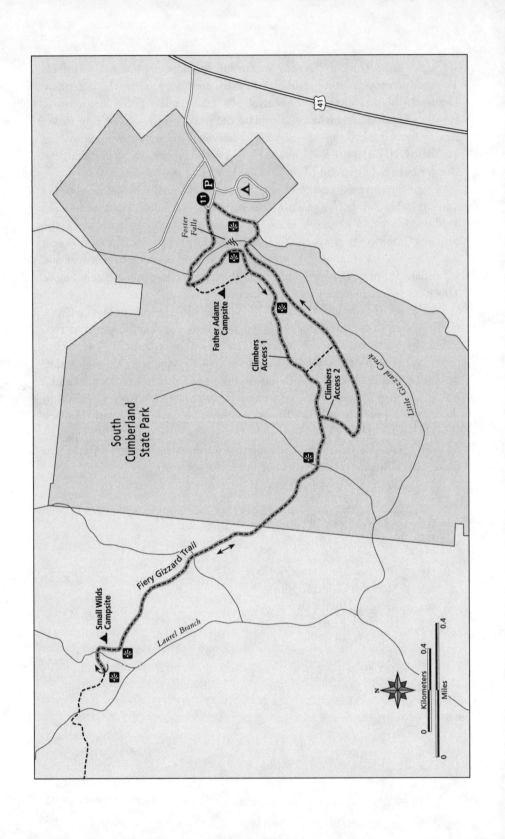

11

Foster Falls Backpack

THE BACKPACK

This fine one night backpack offers two camping areas and highlights aplenty, centered on 60-foot Foster Falls, part of South Cumberland State Park. Start your adventure by first viewing Foster Falls from atop the Cumberland Plateau, near the Father Adamz campsite. From there, cruise the rim of the Little Gizzard Creek gulf, soaking in views and other lesser cataracts. The very level hike then leads out to a view and the recommended Small Wilds campsite. Next day, backtrack then take the Climbers Access to walk the clifflines of the gulf, and reaching a view of Foster Falls from its base. Ahead, grab one more look at the big cataract before completing the backpack.

Distance and Configuration: 4.6-mile balloon loop
Difficulty: Easy
Outstanding Features: Foster Falls, gulf views, good campsites
Elevation: 1,773 feet high point, 1,585 feet low point
Scenery: 5
Solitude: 2
Family Friendly: 4
Canine Friendly: 3
Fees/permits: Fee based camping permit required
Best season: September through May
Maps: Fiery Gizzard Trail—South Cumberland State Park
For more info: South Cumberland State Park—Savage Gulf Ranger
   Station, 3157 SR 399, Palmer, TN 37365, 931-779-3532,
   www.tnstateparks.com/parks/south-cumberland
Finding the Trailhead: From exit 155 on I-24 west of Chattanooga,
   take TN 28 north for 1.5 miles, join US 41 north and follow
   US 41 through Jasper for a total of 9.5 miles on US 41 to reach
   Foster Falls Road and turn left into the park. The trailhead offers
   restrooms, water and a covered picnic shelter. Address: 498 Foster

Gazing into the gulf of Little Gizzard Creek.

Falls Road, Tracy Highway 41, Sequatchie, TN 37374. GPS
trailhead coordinates: 35.182262, -85.674003

Foster Falls takes Little Gizzard Creek 60 feet over a naked rock ledge into a
plunge pool of the first order. The greater Fiery Gizzard area was named by
master woodsman Daniel Boone himself. See, Daniel was cooking his dinner a

Daniel Boone himself named this valley Fiery Gizzard.

campfire and burned it. He got mad and threw his blackened fare into the gorge below, giving Fiery Gizzard its name. This backpack traverses the rim of Fiery Gizzard Gulf, where you can overnight at two reservable camping areas while enjoying the falls and views from stony overlooks. The walk to the two campsites is easy, as you stay on the rim of the gulf, but your return route—if you choose—can be much more challenging, while trekking through rocky, irregular terrain along clifflines used by climbers to ply their trade. You are also rewarded with a bottom up view of powerful Foster Falls and a trip over one of South Cumberland State Park's famous suspension bridges.

Leave the parking area on the Fiery Gizzard Trail, joining a wooden boardwalk that quickly opens to a power line. Head right along the powerline, crossing a small stream slavering over a rock slab. Foster Falls roars below. Turn toward Little Gizzard Creek, enshrouded in dense forest of mountain laurel, hemlock and magnolia.

Span Little Gizzard Creek on a swinging bridge then rise to reach the spur loop to the Father Adamz campsite at .3 mile. Here, 8 sites are stretched out on a loop under Plateau woods of oak, hickory, maple, holly and plenty of greenbrier. Recommended reservable sites include #2, #3, and #4. A privy serves the sites.

Bring your own water. At .5 mile, reach the top down overlook of Foster Falls, leaping into a massive plunge pool from which rise naked stone walls that echo the reverberation of the 60 foot cataract. Immerse into the view, then continue along the rim of Fiery Creek gulf. Pass the other end of the Father Adamz campsite access trail at 0.6 mile. Pines stretch off the edge of the gorge. When back from the rim you will cross wet areas on boardwalks, divided by drier forests dominated by hickory and oak. Spur trails head left to informal accesses on the rim, including a fine view at 0.7 mile down Little Gizzard Creek.

At 0.9 mile, Climbers Access 1 splits left and heads below the gorge rim. We stay above the rim on the Fiery Gizzard Trail to make signed Climbers Access 2 at 1.1 miles. After overnighting at Small Wilds Campsite, we will return this way. At 1.3 miles, bridge a perennial stream just before it makes its own difficult-to-see cataract diving from the gulf rim. Sun burnished rock opens to a view into the main chasm of Fiery Gizzard Creek, 700 feet below.

Leave the rim of the gulf, running parallel to the rim but turning into the Laurel Fork gulf. At 1.8 miles, bridge another creek. Like most small creeks hereabouts this waterway can range from a torrent to a trickle. However, the rock outcrop near the stream offers views year-round. The path continues curving into the Laurel Branch gulf. Watch for a trail leading left at 2.1 miles to a fine overlook. Just ahead reach the signed trail leading right to the Small Wilds Campsite, named when this was a Tennessee Valley Authority-owned Small Wild Area. Here, a spur passes seven campsites with water access nearby from a tributary of Laurel Branch. Recommended reservable sites include #1, #5 and #6.

After dropping your pack, cross the tributary and work your way to a view reached at 2.3 miles. Here, you can telescope down Laurel Branch gulf, up Little Gizzard Creek gulf and into the maw of Big Fiery Gizzard Creek. Stone rims are bordered by dense forests.

Next day, backtrack 1.2 miles to Climbers Access 2. Backpackers wanting lesser challenge can backtrack to the trailhead. However, I recommend taking the climbers access, dropping off the rim on steep wooden steps, viewing a rockhouse on the right. Once at the base of the cliffline, head left toward Foster Falls. The trail winds around boulders and below sheer cliffs where climbers tackle these foreboding walls. Take your time in this stony wonderland and reach Climbers Access 1 at 4.0 miles. It rises left to meet the Fiery Gizzard Trail. The main route continues along the cliffline to cross a lumpy boulder garden.

The trail leads you toward singing Little Gizzard Creek, ensconced in evergreens. Come to the suspension bridge over the stream at 4.3 miles. After crossing the bridge walk left to find the waving plunge pool of Foster Falls, its sheer stone walls rising in defiance.

Beyond the falls, climb through a continuous boulder garden for a short distance then return to the gorge rim at 4.5 miles. Head left here at the powerline cut then pass a final overlook of Foster Falls. From here, make the short backtrack to the trailhead, completing the backpacking adventure.

Mileages

0.0	Foster Falls trailhead
0.3	Spur to Father Adamz campsite
0.5	Foster Falls
2.1	Small Wilds campsite
4.6	Foster Falls trailhead

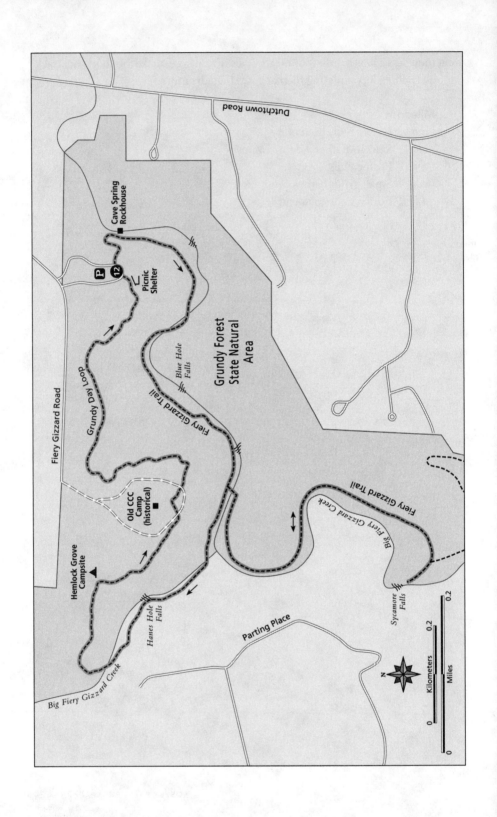

12

Grundy Forest Backpack

THE BACKPACK

This short but gorgeous overnighter may be the ideal one night backpack. Visit old growth hemlocks, four waterfalls, and a historic site at Grundy Forest State Natural Area. Follow Little Fiery Gizzard Creek into a gorge extraordinaire past Blue Hole Falls and its swimming hole, then meet Big Fiery Gizzard Creek to view wide Sycamore Falls. Backtrack, looping past the tongue-drop of Hanes Hole Falls. Rise to uplands and your campsite, not far from the historical display of the Civilian Conservation Corps Camp that developed these trails nearly a century back. Finally, trek past School Branch Falls.

Distance and Configuration: 3.5-mile loop with out-and-back
Difficulty: Easy
Outstanding Features: Old trees, geology, waterfalls, historic CCC camp
Elevation: 1,822 feet high point, 1,614 feet low point
Scenery: 5
Solitude: 2
Family Friendly: 5
Canine Friendly: 4
Fees/permits: Fee based camping permit required
Best season: September through May
Maps: Fiery Gizzard Trail—South Cumberland State Park
For more info: South Cumberland State Park—Savage Gulf Ranger Station, 3157 SR 399, Palmer, TN 37365, 931-779-3532, www.tnstateparks.com/parks/south-cumberland
Finding the Trailhead: From exit 135 on I-24 near Monteagle, join US 41 Alt south toward Tracy City for 0.5 mile to join US 41 south. Stay with US 41 south toward Tracy City. Hit your odometer as you pass the South Cumberland State Park Visitor Center on your left. Drive for 2.2 miles beyond the visitor center to turn right on 3rd

Street. Follow 3rd Street for 0.4 mile, then turn right on Marion Street. Follow Marion Street for 0.1 mile, then turn right on Fiery Gizzard Road to dead end at the trailhead, passing the overflow parking area. The trailhead offers restrooms, picnic tables and a shelter. Address: 131 Fiery Gizzard Road, Tracy City, TN 37387. GPS trailhead coordinates: 35.251828, -85.747523

Backpacker navigates a rocky section of the Fiery Gizzard Trail.

Otter eye view of Sycamore Falls.

The setting for this hike is now part of South Cumberland State Park. Before that it became one of the earliest preserved parcels on the Cumberland Plateau when the citizens of nearby Tracy City, recognizing the incredible scenery in their backyard, donated a 212 acre parcel known as Grundy Forest, which was then developed for recreation by the Civilian Conservation Corps (about which there is now a historical trailside display near the backcountry campsite here). You, too, will be impressed with the cluster of highlights on this overnight trail adventure. Elevations are not difficult and it is but a short hike to the pretty little backcountry campsite, making it an ideal family backpack or for a novice trail trekker or anyone visiting the area who wants to combine waterfalls, geology and backpacking into one fine exploit. The setting is the upper end of the Fiery Gizzard gorge, where Little Fiery Gizzard Creek and Big Fiery Gizzard Creek converge.

Start the Grundy Day Loop behind the trailhead picnic shelter. Immediately reach a trail split. Head left on the loop. Dip to Little Fiery Gizzard Creek, finding immense Cave Spring Rockhouse, next to which stands a regal hemlock, half a millennium old. Continuing down trail on a slender, rooty track you will pass another of these evergreen giants.

Trace the dancing watercourse deeper into the gorge of its making, passing eye catching patterns in the rock walls. Moss is prevalent. Bridge School Branch at 0.4 miles. Upstream, School Branch makes its own waterfall.

Come to 10-foot Blue Hole Falls at 0.5 mile. The classic pourover is best known for its shimmering pool, a popular swimming hole. Heading on, a wide slide cascade froths white, contrasting with the gorge walls. Come to the Fiery Gizzard Trail at 0.7 mile. There has been a bridge here in the past and hopefully one in the future. Here, cross Little Fiery Gizzard Creek, joining the Fiery Gizzard Trail, on the top ten all time Tennessee trail names list. Continue downstream to make the confluence of Big Fiery Gizzard Creek and Little Fiery Gizzard Creek at 0.9 mile. Just below the merging of the waters a dark slot canyon forms. This is called Black Canyon.

Trace the curves of the Big Fiery Gizzard Creek along a rocky hillside to make the columnar sandstone pillars known as the Chimney Rocks before reaching a trail intersection at 1.3 miles. Follow the blue-blazed trail leading right to Sycamore Falls. The broad cataract dives 15 feet into a massive plunge pool. Admire the falls from above and from the pool base before backtracking 0.6 mile to the Grundy Day Loop. Backpack up the Big Fiery Gizzard Creek valley to reach 10-foot Hanes Hole Falls at 2.1 miles. Its signature feature is the tongue-like stone lip over which it flows. Grab some water before climbing away from the creek at 2.2 miles. Rise into upland hardwoods mixed with pine, typical of the Cumberland Plateau, along with lots of greenbrier. At 2.4 miles, meet the spur trail leading left to the Hemlock Grove Campsite, also listed by the state park as Grundy Forest Campsite. The six camps are stretched on a spur under hardwoods, pines and a few hemlocks. Recommended reservable sites include #2 and #3. A privy is the only amenity. Bring your own water.

The Grundy Day Loop continues east and reaches the CCC Camp Tour. Take this worthwhile 0.3 mile sub-loop, exploring the extensive displays about the young men who worked to develop the very trails that we walk today. Interestingly, this used to be the site of the Grundy Forest backcountry camp before they developed the CCC site into the tour of today.

Cross a few tiny streams on boardwalks. The trail wanders easterly through woodland before bridging School Branch at 3.4 miles, just above a 20 foot sheer drop of a waterfall. Complete the adventure at 3.5 miles, one of the most highlight-heavy short backpacks in Tennessee.

Mileages

0.0	Grundy Forest picnic shelter
0.7	Join Fiery Gizzard Trail
2.1	Hanes Hole Falls
2.4	Hemlock Grove/Grundy Forest campsite
3.5	Grundy Forest picnic shelter

13

Great Stone Door Backpack

THE BACKPACK

Waterfalls and overlooks highlight this backpacking adventure at Savage Gulf State Natural Area, part of the greater South Cumberland State Park. Hike to the spectacular Stone Door Overlook then along the rim of Big Creek Gulf to a fine campsite. Next day, visit worthy Boardtree Falls and Greeter Falls before departing into rugged Big Creek Gulf to view veil-like Ranger Creek Falls and the historic Cator Savage Cabin before overnighting at Sawmill campsite. Your return trip leads you through the Stone Door, a break in the cliffline used for centuries.

Distance and Configuration: 18.9 mile balloon loop with
   out-and-backs
Difficulty: Difficult
Outstanding Features: Great Stone Door, waterfalls aplenty
Elevation: 1,850 feet high point, 997 feet low point
Scenery: 5
Solitude: 2
Family Friendly: 2
Canine Friendly: 1
Fees/permits: Fee based camping permit required
Best season: September through May
Maps: Savage Gulf—South Cumberland State Park
For more info: South Cumberland State Park—Savage Gulf Ranger
   Station, 3157 SR 399, Palmer, TN 37365, 931-779-3532,
   www.tnstateparks.com/parks/south-cumberland
Finding the Trailhead: From exit 127 on I-24 near Pelham, take TN
   50 east to Altamont. From Altamont, join TN 56 north and follow it
   5.5 miles to Stone Door Road. Turn right on Stone Door Road and
   follow it 1 mile to enter Savage Gulf, then dead end at the Stone
   Door trailhead after 0.4 more mile. GPS trailhead coordinates:
   35.446544, -85.655815

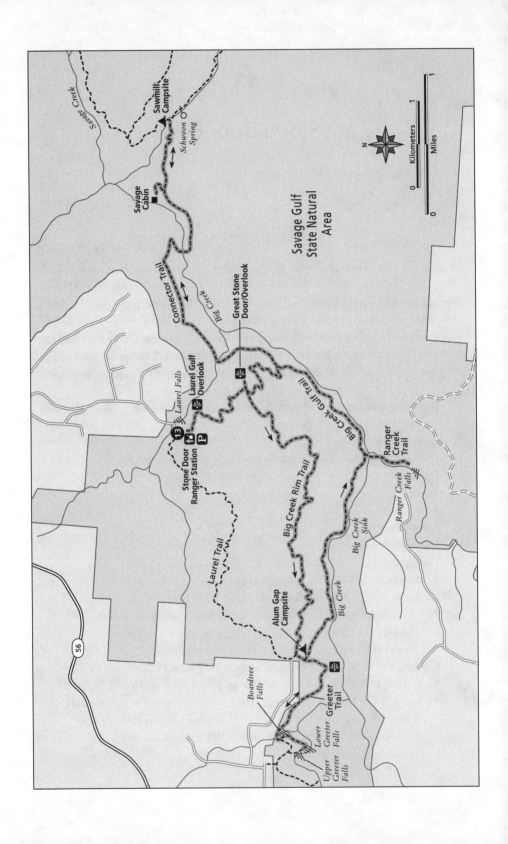

Savage Gulf
State Natural
Area

N

Kilometers
0   1

Miles
0

Sawmill
Campsite

Savage Creek

Schwoon Spring

Savage Cabin

Connector Trail

Big Creek

Great Stone
Door/Overlook

Laurel Falls

Laurel Gulf
Overlook

13

P

Stone Door
Ranger Station

Laurel Trail

56

Big Creek Gulf Trail

Big Creek Rim Trail

Ranger
Creek
Trail

Ranger Creek
Falls

Big Creek Sink

Alum Gap
Campsite

Big Creek

Boardtree Falls

Greeter Trail

Lower Greeter Falls

Upper Greeter Falls

This highlight reel of a backpack not only has spectacular sights, but also not-to-be-forgotten names—Great Stone Door, Cator Savage Cabin, Schwoon Spring . . . Names and places aside this adventure will live up to your high expectations, so raise the bar and load your pack. Along the way you will pass two campsites that pretty much set the trip, though a trailhead walk-in camping area is also available. All the campsites here are fee-based reservable sites that include a privy. Be apprised hiking through the Big Creek Gulf is slow due to endless boulder gardens, so adjust your expectations. The hiking is comparatively easy along the rim of Big Creek Gulf. Other highlights include the famed swinging bridges over major streams, Big Creek Sink and strange Schwoon Spring, a combination cave/sink/spring/rockhouse.

Leave the Stone Door Ranger Station on asphalt, quickly passing the worthy short spur to Laurel Falls, yet another highlight. The asphalt Stone Door Trail stays right. The hard footing makes an unusual backpacking start. Cumberland Plateau woodland of pine, white oak, maple, dogwood and holly border the track. At 0.2 mile, reach the Laurel Gulf Overlook. Rake your eyes southeast into the meeting of wild Collins, Big Creek and Savage Gulfs. Join a level natural surface path, aiming for the Great Stone Door.

At 1.0 mile, reach an intersection. We will go right on the Big Creek Rim Trail, but first stare down the crack of the Great Stone Door to your right. You will return up those stone steps. Visit the Great Stone Door Overlook, dead ahead. Here, a sandstone slab landscaped with straggling pines divulges fantastic vistas of the gulfs below and land beyond, where Savage Creek, Big Creek and Collins River meet, creating the massive lower Collins River Gulf. This is one of my favorite spots in the Volunteer State.

Join the Big Creek Rim Trail, winding southwesterly along the Big Creek Gulf rim, shaded by oaks, pines and mountain laurel. Ahead you will wander by three major overlooks of the narrowing chasm. Listen for Big Creek flowing below before going silent into a sink. The Big Creek Rim Trail turns away from the gorge to reach Alum Gap campsite at 4.1 miles. Individual campsites are stretched along the rim and linked by trail. Recommended sites are #4, #5 and #7. Come to a trail intersection just beyond the campsites. For the side trip to Greeter Falls, head left on the Big Creek Gulf Trail then turn right on the Greeter Trail, dipping across a small stream that is the water source for Alum Gap campsite. Keep along the rim to emerge at Big Bluff Overlook at 4.5 miles. It opens down Big Creek Gulf. Continue along the rim to cross a suspension bridge over Boardtree Creek and reach an intersection at 5.2 miles. Stay left and come to 50-foot Upper Boardtree Creek Falls. A spur trail leads to mid-fall, where you can see the stream dance down layers of rock. It then gathers briefly in a pool, then pours over a lip in a sheer drop below. Continuing on, Lower Boardtree Creek Falls is a tough access, as the Greeter Trail curves around a ridge to reach the

Morning sun illuminates the author as he looks into Big Creek Gulf.

spur to Greeter Falls at 5.6 miles. The spur itself splits. Head to Upper Greeter Falls first, where you find a wide ledge cataract dropping 20 feet, below which stands a huge boulder. The ruler-straight ledge seems almost manmade. To reach Lower Greeter Falls descend a circular silver staircase to a stone amphitheater floored with a huge pool where Lower Greeter Falls pirouettes 50 feet, making quite a splash, a physical embodiment of why Tennessee state parks exist.

Backtrack to Alum Gap campsite, picking up the Big Creek Gulf Trail at 7.0 miles as it descends a stream break in the cliffline to come within sight of splashing Big Creek at 7.4 miles, a melding of shoals and pools, bordered by bluffs, boulders and tree cover. The descent moderates as you go on and off an old jeep track amidst woods and big boulders, coming to Big Creek Sink at 8.3 miles, beyond which the stream must be high to flow on. At 8.9 miles, take the spur right to Ranger Creek Falls. Cross normally dry, bouldery Big Creek and up dry Ranger Creek. How can there be a falls with no water? Keep up the Ranger Creek vale to find out, crossing the dry streambed to reach Ranger Creek Falls at 9.3 miles. The going is slow and stony but there you arrive at the 28 foot cataract, spilling

Greeter Falls dives into its picturesque plunge pool.

over a wide ledge into a bed of rocks and seeping underground in its own sink. Savage Gulf has a peculiar plumbing system.

Backtrack, then rejoin the Big Creek Gulf Trail as it picks through the rocky lower gorge, going on and off an old jeep road, meeting the Connector Trail at 10.8 miles. Stay easterly on the Connector Trail, heading deeper into the Big Creek Gulf. Cross Laurel Creek on a swinging bridge at 11.4 miles. Ahead,

Cator Savage Cabin.

mercifully join the old Jay Hobbs Road. The walking eases a bit then drop right abruptly from the former logging grade. The trail here is rocky to the extreme. Cross normally dry, stony streambed of Big Creek on a swinging bridge at 12.6 miles. Climb to pick up another logging track and follow it to an intersection at 13.3 miles. Here, head left and descend a quarter mile to a grassy flat and the Cator Savage Cabin. Savage Gulf was named after his predecessors. The cabin is a two floor chinked wooden affair built in 1910.

Resume the Connector Trail to cross yet another swinging bridge over normally dry Collins River (It has its own upstream sink at Horsepound Falls) at 14.2 miles. Here, the Sawmill Campsite lies about 100 yards to the left. It offers 7 sites stretched along the trail, recommended sites include #5, #7 and #8, lying under sweetgum, sycamore and tulip trees. Bring a water container to distant Schwoon Spring, set on a cliffline 0.3 mile up the Collins River. The route to the spring is signed and blazed.

Your final day starts with a 2.9 mile backtrack on the Connector Trail to the Big Creek Gulf Trail. Here, wind uphill by loping switchbacks. The trail steepens before reaching the stony steps of the Great Stone Door. March through this marvelous rock passage to reach the rim. From here it is one mile of backtracking to complete the backpack at 18.8 miles.

Mileages

0.0   Stone Door Ranger Station
1.0   Great Stone Door
4.1   Alum Gap campsite
5.6   Greeter Falls
7.0   Descend Big Creek Gulf Trail
9.3   Ranger Creek Falls
10.8   Join Connector Trail
13.3   Spur left to Cator Savage Cabin
14.2   Bridge Collins River, Sawmill campsites left
17.1   Climb Big Creek Gulf Trail
17.9   Hike through Great Stone Door
18.9   Stone Door Ranger Station

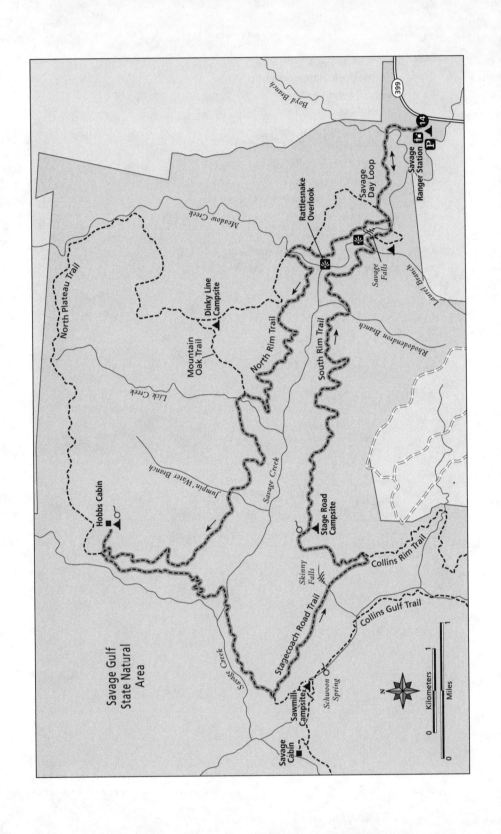

14

Savage Gulf Loop

THE BACKPACK

This spectacular loop backpack is one of Tennessee's finest treks. Explore this state natural area first by viewing Savage Falls, then visiting numerous overlooks into the chasm of Savage Gulf to overnight at Hobbs Cabin or its adjacent campsites. Drop into ultra rugged Savage Gulf before rising to its south rim via historic Stage Road Trail. Enjoy more overlooks to spend night two at Savage Falls campsite, visiting Savage Falls from its base.

Distance and Configuration: 20.0 mile balloon loop
Difficulty: Moderate-difficult, does have one rugged section
Outstanding Features: Views aplenty, Hobbs Cabin, Savage Falls
Elevation: 1,865 feet high point, 1,082 feet low point
Scenery: 5
Solitude: 2
Family Friendly: 1
Canine Friendly: 2
Fees/permits: Fee based camping permit required
Best season: September through May
Maps: Savage Gulf—South Cumberland State Park
For more info: South Cumberland State Park—Savage Gulf Ranger Station, 3157 SR 399, Palmer, TN 37365, 931-779-3532, www.tnstateparks.com/parks/south-cumberland
Finding the Trailhead: From exit 135 on I-24 near Monteagle, coming from Nashville, take US 41 alt south toward Tracy City for .5 mile to join US 41 south. Stay with US 41 south to reach Tracy City. Turn left on TN 56 north to reach TN 108. Turn right on TN 108 and follow it 7.1 miles to TN 399 east. Turn left on TN 399 and follow it 4.8 miles to Savage Gulf Ranger Station on your left. GPS trailhead coordinates: 35.434131, -85.539574

Famed backpacker Ark Evans gazes into Savage Gulf from the North Rim Trail.

Savage Gulf State Natural Area, a confluence of three gorges on the Cumberland Plateau, is a truly rugged and extremely scenic locale of which Tennesseans should be proud. Savage Gulf, part of the larger South Cumberland State Park, is 16,000 acres of craggy gulfs, tumbling falls, stunning views, and human history. The term "gulf" is local nomenclature referring to gorges cutting deep swaths into the Cumberland Plateau. This circuit passes six reservable campsites along the route—including one at the trailhead, allowing for trips of varied days and distances. Hobbs Cabin can be reserved as well. It's a four-sided shelter offering bunks and a fireplace inside, with picnic table and fire ring without. I recommend 2-3 nights to best enjoy the circuit, and trekking poles to negotiate the boulder-strewn inner gorge that you must navigate.

The first part of the hike can be busy with day hikers. Leave the rustic Savage Ranger Station on the Savage Day Loop, entering a Plateau forest of hickory, holly and oak on the Savage Day Loop. Ahead, a side trail leads left to the Savage

Hobbs Cabin.

Station campsites, more like car camping sites than backpacking. Like the other campsites at Savage Gulf, the camp is comprised of several reservable individual campsites with a common privy. Each site does have a fire ring. Come to a suspension bridge over hemlock shaded Boyd Branch at 0.4 mile. This is the first of several exciting suspension bridges you will cross. Continue west as Savage Creek begins cutting its defile to reach an intersection at 1.1 miles. Hike left toward Savage Falls, still on the Savage Day Loop. At 1.3 miles, reach another intersection, staying right with the Savage Day Loop as the South Rim Trail keeps straight. The Savage Falls campsite is only 0.4 mile down the South Rim Trail.

You can hear Savage Falls. At 1.5 miles, take the spur trail left to Savage Falls Overlook, a distant view down to the 30-foot waterfall, tumbling over a rock rim. Stay in pine-oak woods to make Rattlesnake Point Overlook, your first of many views into Savage Gulf, at 2.1 miles. At 2.2 miles, join the North Rim Trail as it leads to the swinging bridge over rhododendron-shaded Meadow Creek. At 2.6

miles, the North Plateau Trail, leading to the Dinky Line campsite with seasonal water, leaves right as we keep with the North Rim Trail. Open onto Meadow Creek Overlook at 2.9 miles, where rock, rim and forest spread below. More tempting overlooks open as you alternately hike the rim's edge then through nearly level hickory-oak forests. The rim is broken by little seasonal rills, bordered in mountain laurel, dropping off the rim edge. The trail turns into the Lick Creek Gulf to intersect the Mountain Oak Trail at 5.0 miles. The North Rim Trail bridges perennial Lick Creek at 5.0 miles and returns to widening Savage Gulf and more overlooks draped in sparkleberry and shortleaf pines, revealing a decidedly greater chasm.

The trail continues working out to the rim and into little creek valleys, then back to the rim again. At 6.5 miles, cross Jumpin' Water Branch just above a five-foot cascade. More views open ahead, including looks into Collins Gulf to the west, Big Creek Gulf to the southwest and Coppinger Gulf to the north. Turn into Coppinger Gulf at 7.2 miles, still on a mostly level track. At 8.2 miles, a spur trail leaves right to the Hobbs Cabin and campsite. A signed path drops right to a spring. If you aren't reserving the Hobbs Cabin consider one of the 8 campsites stretched on a path. Recommended sites include #1, #5 and #8.

From Hobbs Cabin, join the Connector Trail as it descends into Coppinger Gulf. The Connector Trail becomes rocky to the extreme and travel ultra slow. Watch your footing carefully. Coppinger Gulf widens as you switchback down to cross normally dry Savage Creek on a swinging bridge at 10.3 miles, a little downstream from a sink into which Savage Creek drains. The going stays slow on a north-facing slope full of tulip and beech trees. Curve into the mouth of Collins Gulf then meet the Stagecoach Road Trail and the Connector Trail at 11.5 miles. Take note, the Sawmill Campsite is 0.4 mile down the Connector Trail. If staying at Sawmill campsite, water can be had from Schwoon Spring, 0.3 mile up Collins Gulf Trail.

Our backpack rises on the Stagecoach Road Trail, an 1840s era slave-built toll road linking Chattanooga to McMinnville. The wider track seems easy even as it climbs in tall forest littered with impressive boulders. Come along a cliffline to reach 100-foot high but low flow Skinny Falls, at 12.6 miles. A bluff towers overhead as you pass a stone livestock trail climbing to the rim. Make a sharp switchback to enter a break in the bluff along which a small creek flows then reach a trail intersection at 13.0 miles.

Head left with the South Rim Trail, briefly curving atop Collins Gulf before striking through rolling hardwoods to open onto the south rim of Savage Gulf at 13.8 miles. Pass a signed spring at 14.0 miles then climb to make Stage Road Campsite at 14.1 miles. Recommended campsites are #5 and #7. Continue the South Rim Trail, cruising along the rim of the gulf then turning into a most likely

Savage Falls.

dry streambed and ambling out to the gulf edge. You will meet several blazed spur trails leading to overlooks. Don't pass these spurs by.

At 15.9 miles, bridge a small unnamed stream. The walking is easy as you roll under hickories and oaks, crossing Rhododendron Branch on a bridge at 17.0 miles. More signed overlooks lie ahead, as Savage Gulf narrows. Scan for overlooks across the gorge. Step over Laurel Branch on a narrow iron plank at

You will traverse several swinging bridges on this backpack.

18.1 miles. Reach the spur to Savage Falls campsite at 18.2 miles. Recommended sites are #1, #2, and #4.

Beyond Savage Falls campsite descend to the steps leading to the falls base. Soak in a head-on look at the shimmering plunge pool into which Savage Creek makes its 30-foot gambit over a rock ledge. Resuming toward the ranger station, pass a signed streamside moonshine still site then enjoy another suspension bridge, this one spanning Savage Creek. Ahead, you will finish the loop portion of the backpack then backtrack 1.3 miles to the Savage Ranger Station, completing your highlight-laden backpack at 20.0 miles.

Mileages

0.0	Savage Ranger Station
1.3	Begin loop
1.5	Savage Falls Overlook
2.2	Join North Rim Trail
5.0	Bridge Lick Creek
8.2	Hobbs Cabin, campsites, spring
10.3	Bridge Savage Creek
11.5	Join Stagecoach Road Trail, Sawmill campsite nearby
13.0	Join South Rim Trail
14.0	Spring, then Stage Road campsite
17.0	Bridge Rhododendron Branch
18.2	Savage Falls campsite, Savage Falls
18.7	Complete loop
20.0	Savage Ranger Station

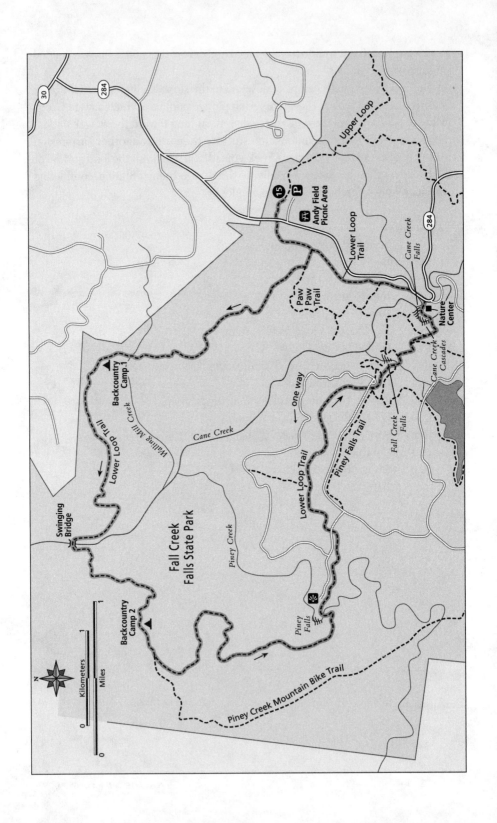

15

Fall Creek Falls Backpack

THE BACKPACK

This fun circuit visits two backcountry camps while circling the Cane Creek gorge and viewing several highlights along the way. First find Walling Mill Creek and a backcountry campsite before entering rocky Cane Creek gorge, passing a rock house and waterfall before reaching the second backcountry campsite. Meander through Plateau woods before coming to another swinging bridge and impressive Piney Creek Falls. From there, enter the main park area, viewing Fall Creek Falls, Cane Creek Cascades, Rockhouse Creek Falls and Cane Creek Falls.

Distance and Configuration: 12.1-mile loop
Difficulty: Moderate, does have one challenging segment
Outstanding Features: Waterfalls galore, swinging bridges
Elevation: 1,033 feet low point, 1,811 feet high point
Scenery: 5
Solitude: 2
Family Friendly: 3
Canine Friendly: 3
Fees/permits: Fee-based backcountry camping permit required
Best season: September through May
Maps: Fall Creek Falls State Park
For more info: Fall Creek Falls State Park, 2009 Village
 Camp Road, Spencer, TN 38585, 423-881-5708,
 www.tnstateparks.com/parks/fall-creek-falls
Finding the Trailhead: From exit 288 on I-40 near Cookeville, take
 TN 111 south to Spencer. From Spencer take TN 30 east for 10.8
 miles to TN 284 west. Turn right and take TN 284 west, entering
 the state park at 1.7 miles. Go for a total of 3.1 mile to a four-way
 stop. Turn right toward the nature center to get a backcountry
 permit. Return to TN 284, now backtracking east for 1 mile to
 pass the Andy Field Picnic Area. Turn right just north of the picnic

Fall Creek Falls makes its 256 foot dive.

area into a gravel road and maintenance area. Park at the sign
for backcountry parking. GPS trailhead coordinates: 35.675335,
-85.337428

This is one of two major backpacking loops at Fall Creek Falls State Park, among
the 56 miles of trail here. Additionally, some of the newer trails have backcountry
sites (a total of four sites) that together allow treks up to 3 nights. The Lower
Loop at 12 miles offers two backcountry camps for you to enjoy. Fall and spring
are the best times to enjoy the circuit, with an added peace of mind with the
reservable backcountry campsites. Winter presents solitude aplenty. The only
significant challenge of the trek is the trip into and out of the gulf of Cane Creek.

Rockhouse Creek Falls (*left*) and Cane Creek Falls contrast
one another as they tumble into the same pool.

Along the way you traverse three major swinging bridges. The end of the loop
reaches the heart of the park and its most popular area. Here, you enjoy highlights galore but also lose that backcountry aura, a tolerable tradeoff for even
the most jaded backpacker.

From the backcountry parking area, shortly join the Lower Loop to cross TN
284 at 0.2 mile into prototypical Plateau woods of oak, hickory, shortleaf pine,
maple and holly. At 0.5 mile, the singletrack Lower Loop Trail meets the Paw
Paw Trail. Turn right here, as the two trails run in conjunction, bridging Paw
Paw Creek. At 0.6 mile, split on the Lower Loop Trail, well back from the rim
of the Cane Creek canyon, winding northwesterly into shallow drainages divided
by low hills.

Descend to bridge Walling Mill Creek, ensconced in mountain laurel, holly
and hemlock at 2.2 miles (Get your water here if camping at Backcountry Camp
1). Rise into hardwoods to find Backcountry Camp #1 at 2.5 miles. Four camping
nodes with a fire ring are set in the forest and share a common privy.

Beyond the camp, the trail skirts the park boundary, then passes a rockhouse
at 2.8 miles before reaching the rim of the Cane Creek canyon at 3.5 miles. The

other side of the gorge is visible but you must go down to go up. Dip onto a stony slope mixed with boulders and bluffs. Bisect stands of beard cane in the lower gulf. Cross the suspension bridge over Cane Creek at 4.1 miles. This is the backpack's low point, 700 feet below the rim of the gulf. As with other Plateau streams, Cane Creek can froth white and other times nearly dry up altogether.

Now begin working your way out of the hole, traversing rhododendron thickets as well as mind-blowing boulder gardens. Trail blazes help you navigate the uber-rocky terrain. At 4.9 miles, a spur leaves left 100 yards to an overhanging rockhouse and low flow 20 foot waterfall. Keep climbing, open onto the clearing of Backcountry Camp #2 at 5.3 miles. A pump well serves the camp. Tent sites are set back in hardwoods forest beyond the main clearing.

Continuing the loop, follow a doubletrack then at 5.7 miles the Piney Creek Mountain Bike Trail splits right as we cruise Plateau lands, making for easy hiking on singletrack trail. Skirt the rim of Horsepen Branch before bridging it at 7.1 miles. Leave the sandy stream, trekking amidst oak groves on the Cumberland Plateau. Reach and cross Piney Creek on a lengthy suspension bridge at 7.7 miles. This can be a busy area but take time to view Piney Creek Falls from the short spur.

From here, the Lower Loop Trail heads east parallel with Scenic Loop Road, an auto nature trail. Cross Scenic Loop Road at 8.4 miles and stay easterly to emerge at the Falls Creek Falls ADA accessible overlook at 9.7 miles. Look down on the Cumberland Plateau's highest cataract at 256 feet, purportedly the highest free-fall drop of any waterfall east of the Mississippi River. From here, stay with the signs indicating the Lower Loop Trail as it runs in conjunction with other nature trails.

The Lower Loop then joins the busy nature trails. Circle past Coon Creek and Fall Creek to meet the Overlook Trail at 10.1 miles. Ahead, the Campground Trail leaves right but you take concrete steps to bridge Cane Creek on a long suspension bridge above 40-foot Cane Creek Cascades at 10.5 miles. Head left here, passing the revamped Betty Dunn Nature Center then come to Cane Creek Falls Overlook. Here you can see wide 85-foot Cane Creek Falls as well as rope-like 115-foot Rockhouse Creek Falls that tumbles into the same stone amphitheater as bigger Cane Creek Falls. From there, look left for the Paw Paw Trail entering woods. The Lower Loop runs in conjunction with the Paw Paw Trail. Rock hop Rockhouse Creek to find the Cable Trail at 10.8 miles. Here, you can take a steel cable over stone to the base of Cane Creek Falls, a worthy, exciting detour. At 11.0 miles, the Paw Paw Trail heads left while the Lower Loop keeps straight, running parallel to TN 284 to complete the loop portion of the hike at 11.6 miles. From here, backtrack .5 mile to the trailhead, finishing the Fall Creek Falls Backpack.

Mileages

HELPFUL HINTS FOR PHOTOGRAPHING WATERFALLS

When backpacking, I often seek out waterfalls (I have written four waterfall guides). I photograph just about every waterfall visited, digitally preserving the collection.

Getting an excellent waterfall shot takes time, effort, and luck. For the best shots, you need a tripod, a digital camera with manual settings, and early morning or late afternoon light. Capturing the personality of a waterfall may mean several visits during different times of the year.

Here are a few hints that may help you become a better waterfall photographer:

Tripod: You need a sturdy tripod because you cannot hold a camera sufficiently steady when using slow shutter speeds. Be sure the tripod is compact and lightweight so you will be willing to carry it while backpacking. Set your camera and use a timer, reducing shake caused by pressing the shutter button.

ISO Speed: The ISO setting on most modern digital cameras is designed to approximate the ISO speed of a chosen film and corresponding camera setting used in a traditional film camera. The lowest ISO number you'll find on a digital camera, usually 100 but sometimes lower, is generally the preferred setting for shooting waterfalls. This number will yield the greatest detail, sharpness, effects and color accuracy.

Shutter Speed: Slow shutter speeds give a sense of movement. So you know, movement of flowing water is completely stopped at 1/2000 second. The fastest water will soften starting at 1/60 second. At 1/15 second, water movement will be clearly seen, but not be completely blurred. Most waterfall photographs are shot at 1/8 second or slower to produce a soft quality.

Time of Day: Midday sun creates harsh lighting and shadows. Visit a waterfall at daybreak or an hour before sunset, and use the wonderful quality of the light. Cloudy days afford more photo opportunities.

Exposure: The white water of a falls will often cause underexposure of your shot, making the water gray and the foliage slightly dark. With digital cameras you can see what you just shot and adjust aperture, shutter speed or ISO setting.

Perspective: Waterfall photographs need a reference to indicate their size. To give a feeling of depth and space, use foreground elements, such as trees, rocks, and people. Try to frame the waterfall.

Position: Shoot from the top, bottom, or side of the falls. Treat the waterfall like a piece of architecture. Be creative while shooting the waterfall from different perspectives.

People: The high reflectance of water tends to underexpose people in a waterfall photograph. When positioning people consider proper lighting for both them and the waterfall.

Rainbows: If you are lucky enough to find a rainbow at the end of a waterfall, take as many pictures as you can. Shoot at different settings then delete pictures back at home.

Watch the horizon: Horizon lines should be level, and in general, not placed in the center of the composition. In the image area, look for wasted space, light and dark areas, and distracting elements.

Using the above tips will increase your chances for a spectacular waterfall photograph while backpacking Tennessee.

16

Scotts Gulf Backpack

THE BACKPACK

Make a circuit in this lesser known, lesser visited gorge of the Caney Fork River, locally known as Scotts Gulf. Here, backpack in rolling woods to the edge of Scotts Gulf to visit Screw Cliff Overlook. Run the gulf rim, dropping to the Caney Fork River. Cruise bottomlands along the wild stream, passing qualified campsites. Climb past Lower Polly Branch Falls and hike the slopes of the gorge. Rise to Joe Holloway Cave, making the uplands. Join the Yellow Bluff Trail, enjoying first rate panoramas. Pass a pond before returning to the trailhead.

Distance and Configuration: 14.6-mile loop
Difficulty: Moderate
Outstanding Features: Overlooks, waterfalls, solitude
Elevation: 1,154 feet low point, 1,797 feet high point
Scenery: 4-5
Solitude: 4
Family Friendly: 2
Canine Friendly: 3
Fees/permits: No fee or permit required
Best season: September through May
Maps: Bridgestone Firestone Centennial Wilderness
For more info: Tennessee Wildlife Resources Agency Region 3 Office, 464 Industrial Boulevard, Crossville, TN 38555, 931-484-9571, www.tn.gov/twra
Finding the Trailhead: From the intersection of US 127 and US 70 west in Crossville, take US 70 west for 16.4 miles to reach De Rossett in White County and Eastland Road. (From downtown Sparta, take US 70 east for 9.3 miles to Eastland Road.) Turn left from Crossville, right from Sparta, southbound on Eastland Road, for 5.7 miles to reach Scotts Gulf Road. Turn right on Scotts Gulf

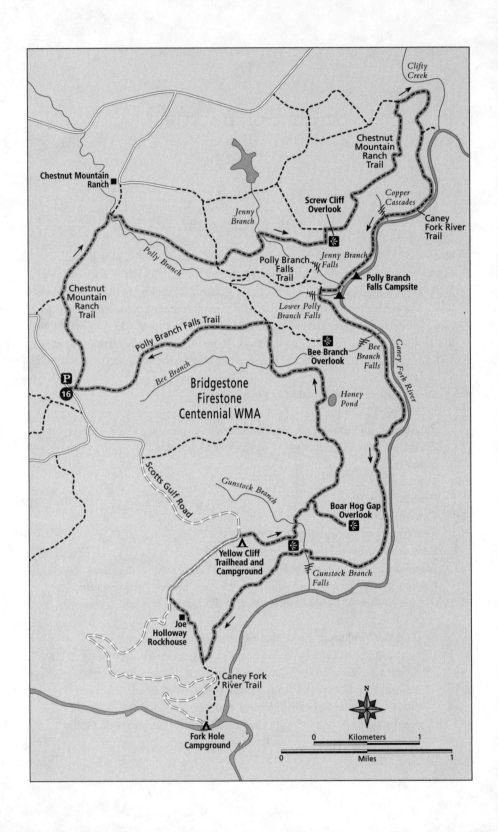

Road and follow it for 2.0 miles to the Scotts Gulf trailhead, on your left, just before reaching the popular Virgin Falls trailhead on the right. GPS trailhead coordinates: 35.856263, -85.283272

Note: Scotts Gulf, aka, Bridgestone Firestone Centennial Wilderness WMA, is closed to hikers during big game hunts. So check ahead before backpacking here. If you are looking for solitude and challenge come to this tract once owned by Firestone then Bridgestone tire companies. The 12,000-plus acre tract, now managed as a state of Tennessee wildlife management area, links to other public lands creating a huge wild land centered on the Caney Fork River gorge known as Scotts Gulf. Though there are a few established campsites, you can camp anywhere in the backcountry without penalty. Most of the trails are old doubletracks reverted to hiker only paths. Trail intersections are mostly signed. The scenery is gorgeous and incredibly rugged inside Scotts Gulf. Backpackers can easily execute a one-night adventure or a relaxing 2 night endeavor. Spring and winter are the best seasons to visit. Non-hunt times during autumn are worthy too.

Leave the Scotts Gulf parking area, heading east just a few feet before turning left on the Chestnut Mountain Ranch Trail. The trail works north in hardwood hills of hickory and oak with tulip trees and ferns in moister drainages, along with scattered hollies and pines. At 0.6 mile, top a ridge then keep north, declining for Polly Branch. Rock hop Polly Branch at 1.4 miles, then come to an intersection. Here, a signed spur trail keeps straight to Chestnut Mountain Ranch. We turn right, heading down the Polly Branch watershed. Trundle easterly, crossing feeder branches of Polly Branch. At 1.9 miles, pass a spur leading right down to Polly Branch and Upper Polly Branch Falls. Stay in uplands then step over Jenny Branch at 2.4 miles. From here, the sometimes grassy trail aims east to reach the signed spur to Screw Cliff Overlook at 2.8 miles. The partial vista opens south easterly into the Caney Fork canyon 500 feet below. From here, the trail keeps northeasterly on a wide grassy track. You enter a locale where woods and fields are mixed and old roads spur away. This is a prescribed fire demonstration area. Just keep the rim of the gorge to your right and you can't mess up. Cross a branch at 3.3 miles.

At 4.0 miles, come to a four-way signed junction. Grassy tracks leads straight and left. Turn right here, easterly, officially joining the Caney Fork River Trail, dropping sharply into thick woods, circling within earshot of Clifty Creek, passing bluffs along the way. The trail becomes rocky and slow. At 4.4 miles, a signed very rough spur leads left to the confluence of Caney Fork Clifty Creek and Caney Fork.

At 4.8 miles, watch left as the trail leaves the old roadbed and dives left as a faint singletrack toward Caney Fork, working around an incredible boulder jumble. Reach wooded bottoms suitable for camping. At 5.2 miles, rock hop

The view from Yellow Cliff Overlook.

Copper Cascades as it loudly dashes among boulders. Beyond there, admire the boulders and cataracts of Caney Fork as well. At 5.5 miles, an old jeep road fords left. Come to the hemlock shaded Polly Branch Falls Campsite to your right, backed up against a rising boulder field. At 5.7 miles, come to more campsites between Jenny Branch and Polly Branch and a signed turn. Here, the Caney Fork River Trail leaves right and climbs to reach a signed trail intersection at 5.9 miles. Here, we follow the Caney Fork River Trail left while the Polly Branch Falls Trail turns right. Quickly drop to rock hop Polly Branch just above 14-foot Lower Polly Branch Falls. This spiller dives over a stone rim then splatters onto a rock jumble before regrouping and giving its waters to Caney Fork just downstream. You are back on old doubletrack working through extremely rocky forest with plenty of beech and other hardwoods. At 6.4 miles cross Bee Branch a little downstream of 20-foot Bee Branch Falls, spilling over a stone lip then slaloming down rocks. You can hear the cataract from the stream crossing but it takes a little effort to reach this lesser visited spiller.

Close up view of Lower Polly Branch Falls.

Beyond Bee Branch the Caney Fork River Trail fights south along the waterway, crossing lesser branches. Leave the bottoms and potential camping areas at 6.9 miles. Remember, Caney Fork can run underground in dry and hot times. At 7.5 miles, saunter past massive gray boulders. The trail curves to the west with the gorge. Make an unexpected switchback climb before crossing Gunstock Branch at 8.5 miles, above Gunstock Branch Falls, disappearing over a rock rim below. Continue well above the Caney Fork, within sight of the cliffline of the gorge rim before dropping. At 9.5 miles, join old Scotts Gulf Road as it cuts acutely right and uphill and the Caney Fork River Trail keeps straight toward four-wheel-drive accessible Fork Hole campground, about a half-mile distant.

Old Scotts Gulf Road climbs the slope, breaking through a small drainage to meet the signed spur to Joe Holloway Rockhouse at 9.8 miles. The spur leads 60 yards to a low stone shelter amidst big boulders. Return to the main trail climbing to make gravel Scotts Gulf Road at 10.0 miles. Turn right here and enjoy some easy level and foot friendly walking. Pass fields en route to the Yellow Bluff Campground and trailhead, reached at 10.6 miles. Here, a designated flat area with 4-5 fine primitive sites is available for overnighting. Backpackers could cache water here before embarking, for there is no accessible aqua nearby.

Continuing the backpack, pick up the Yellow Bluff Trail, a doubletrack path that wanders through pine/oak/hickory forest to the rim of Caney Fork canyon and Yellow Bluff Overlook at 10.9 miles. And what views can be had from multiple overlooks into Scotts Gulf, Short Creek gorge and more!

From there, turn away from the rim and drop to a wetland and Gunstock Branch, still looking a little odd after heavy rains blew out a dam long ago. Stay right here as the path joins an old road. At 11.2 miles, take the spur right 0.3 mile to Boar Hog Gap Overlook. From the pine bordered cliff you can peer into Scotts Gulf and across to the outcrops of Short Creek. Continue the hike and reach an intersection at 12.3 miles. Here, a wide trail splits left 1.1 miles to Scotts Gulf Road. The Yellow Bluff Trail stays right and reaches small Honey Pond at 12.6 miles. Level spots in nearby woods make potential campsites.

The track works into the Bee Branch drainage, crossing the smallish stream at 13.1 miles. Rise to a four-way intersection. Head left here, away from ho-hum Bee Branch Overlook, on the Polly Branch Falls Trail. The walking is easy in mostly level hardwoods and you are back at the trailhead, backpack completed at 14.6 miles.

Mileages

0.0   Scotts Gulf trailhead

2.8   Screw Cliff Overlook

4.0   Join Caney Fork River Trail

5.7   Polly Branch Falls campsite
6.4   Bee Branch Falls
8.5   Gunstock Branch
9.5   Right up old Scotts Gulf Road
10.6   Yellow Bluff Campground and Trailhead
11.6   Boar Hog Gap Overlook
12.6   Honey Pond, potential camping
14.6   Scotts Gulf trailhead

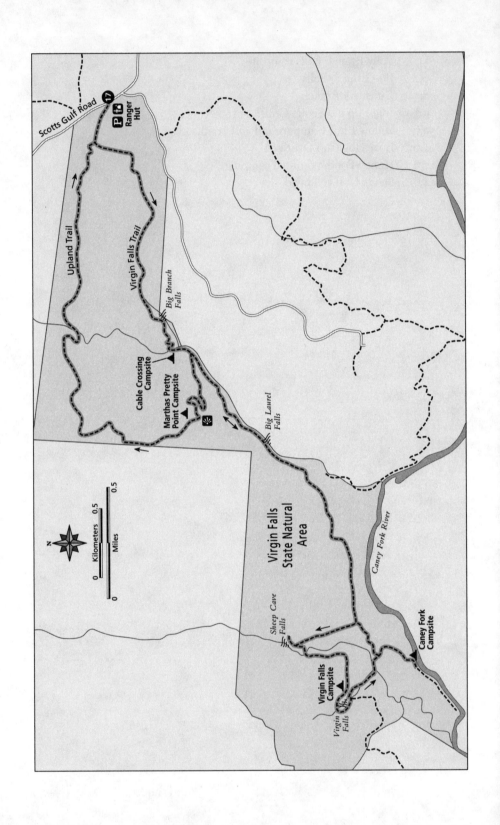

Scotts Gulf Road

17

P

Ranger Hut

Upland Trail

Virgin Falls Trail

Big Branch Falls

Cable Crossing Campsite

Marthas Pretty Point Campsite

Big Laurel Falls

Virgin Falls State Natural Area

Sheep Cave Falls

Caney Fork River

Virgin Falls Campsite

Virgin Falls

Caney Fork Campsite

N

Kilometers 0.5

0

Miles

0

0.5

17

Virgin Falls Backpack

THE BACKPACK

Overnight at an incredible—and popular—state natural area with waterfalls, overlooks and reservable backcountry campsites on the Cumberland Plateau near Sparta. First, drop into the Big Laurel Creek canyon with its waterfalls and sinks. Come along the rugged Caney Fork River before looping past Sheep Cave Falls and staggeringly superb Virgin Falls. After a backtrack, rise to the rim of Scotts Gulf to absorb a first rate panorama then return to the trailhead. Several designated backcountry campsites create varied overnighting options.

Distance and Configuration: 10.6-mile there-and-back with loops
Difficulty: Moderate
Outstanding Features: Virgin Falls, other waterfalls, Martha's Pretty Point
Elevation: 863 feet low point, 1,765 feet high point
Scenery: 5
Solitude: 2
Family Friendly: 3
Canine Friendly: 2
Fees/permits: Fee-based backcountry camping permit required
Best season: September through May
Maps: Virgin Falls State Natural Area
For more info: Fall Creek Falls State Park, 2009 Village Camp Road, Spencer, TN 38585, 423-881-5708, www.tnstateparks.com/parks/fall-creek-falls
Finding the Trailhead: From the intersection of US 127 and US 70 west in Crossville, take US 70 west for 16.4 miles to reach De Rossett in White County and Eastland Road. (From downtown Sparta, take US 70 east for 9.3 miles to Eastland Road.) Turn left from Crossville, right from Sparta, southbound on Eastland Road, for 5.7 miles to reach Scotts Gulf Road. There will be a sign here

The one and only Virgin Falls.

for Virgin Falls. Turn right on Scotts Gulf Road and follow it for 2.0 miles to Virgin Falls trailhead, on your right, just after passing the Scotts Gulf trailhead on the left. GPS trailhead coordinates: 35.854202, -85.282135

Virgin Falls deserves its status as a designated Tennessee state natural area—and then some. It's a place of highlights mixed in with everywhere-you-look beauty. Four reservable fee-based campsites are available in the backcountry, making it a fine backpacking destination. These campsites are reserved through Fall Creek Falls State Park. Do know that campsites are snapped up during predictable busy periods. Try for off-times such as during the week or winter for solitude. The trail system here continues to expand, with the addition of the Upland Trail and connections to Lost Creek State Natural Area. I believe ultimately these will also officially link up with the paths at adjacent Scotts Gulf (A backpack at Scotts Gulf is also detailed in this guide).

Leave the parking area and ranger hut, joining the Virgin Falls Trail through Plateau hickories, oaks and pines. The level track leads to an intersection at 0.2 mile. Here, the Upland Trail splits right and is your return route. For now, keep westerly, sidling alongside Big Branch. It may or may not be flowing at this point. Mountain laurel flanks the waterway. At 1.2 miles, after crossing Big Branch, reach the rim of the Caney Fork gorge and quickly find 15-foot Big Branch Falls, dropping by tiers adjacent to a small rockhouse.

The descent sharpens and you boulder hop Big Laurel Branch at 1.5 miles, with the aid of a metal cable. Your first backcountry camping opportunity is nearby. Cable Crossing Campsite presents three streamside camps—a bit close together—above Big Laurel Branch. Campsite #3 is the best. Descend the trail along Big Laurel Branch. Hemlocks and magnolias rise along the boulder strewn primitive waterway. At 1.6 miles, the other end of the Upland Trail—your return route—splits right. For now continue deeper into the gorge, traveling among sizeable boulders and beneath a regal cliffline, cheered along by continuous cascades. At 2.2 miles, look down upon Big Laurel Falls. Scramble to the base of the 40-foot curtain style cataract that pours over a stone lip then disappears into a sink. This has been a traditional camping area but is not listed in the reservable sites these days.

Keep down the Big Laurel Creek Valley, now devoid of water, traversing the ever widening chasm toward big Caney Fork below. If the water is up you may hear the river already. The Caney Fork can slow to nothing but pools, party flowing underground. The ground drops steeply below as the singletrack trail makes an intersection and the loop to Virgin Falls at 3.4 miles. Turn right toward Sheep Cave and Sheep Cave Falls, north up the valley of Little Laurel Creek.

The view from Martha's Pretty Point.

Split right at the spur trail to Sheep Cave at 3.8 miles, just after peering into the dark passage into which the stream of Sheep Cave disappears. The spur trail leads to Sheep Cave, a stone opening from which pours a lustrous little stream, then drops by tiers 90 feet, only to return underground, a brief yet scenic, yet ethereal appearance, and difficult to see in its entirety.

Backtrack, then resume the loop, stepping over very-unlikely-to-be-flowing Little Laurel Creek, then curve into the valley of Virgin Falls. Come to the three camps at Virgin Falls campsite at 4.3 miles. Campsite #10 is recommended, but overall avoid these busy sites unless you are here at off times. Reach impressive Virgin Falls at 4.7 miles. Here, you can admire big and loud Virgin Falls vaulting 110 feet over rock layers and back to the underworld. It is a real showstopper. Take the spur circling around the cataract where you can see the water emerge at Virgin Falls Cave.

After circling around the falls, meet the Lost Creek Trail coming in from your right. That path traverses a newer state natural area and provides alternate access to Virgin Falls, with an added visit to 40-foot Lost Creek Falls. Our hike continues toward Caney Fork, descending to river bottoms at 5.1 miles. For now, stay toward Caney Fork, cruising hemlock-sycamore flats to reach the Caney Fork Campsite at 5.3 miles. Here, four superior riverside reservable sites are stretched along a big pool of the Caney Fork. Campsites #11 and #14 are highly recommended.

Backtrack from the Caney Fork Campsite to continue the loop, climbing a bluff above Caney Fork. Finish the loop portion of the hike, then backtrack 1.8 miles up Big Laurel Creek, reaching the Upland Trail at 7.6 miles. Head acutely left, rising to a cliffline, then switchback past a drip (a potential water source for Martha's Pretty Point Campsite) at 7.9 miles. Climb a wooden ladder and shortly reach the rim of the gorge after tunneling amidst evergreens. Ahead, the Upland Trail passes a lesser overlook before reaching the spur to Martha's Pretty Point at 8.1 miles. Here, a flat outcrop opens down Big Laurel Fork chasm into Caney Fork gorge. What a view!

Highly recommended Martha's Pretty Point Campsite is situated in the woods just behind the overlook. Campsite #4 is close to the lookout. In foul or windy weather choose campsite #7. The path turns away from the rim of the gorge. Enjoy easy Plateau hiking. At 8.5 miles, join a jeep road. Pass through a long pine thicket then drop to rock hop gently gurgling Big Laurel Creek, a far cry from its raucous lower reaches. Keep cruising mixed woods then leave the old jeep road right at 10.1 miles. This turn is signed. Dip into a shallow vale before bridging a streambed. Ascend a bit to complete the Upland Trail at 10.4 miles. From here it is but a 0.2 mile backtrack to the trailhead, completing the backpack.

Mileages

0.0	Virgin Falls trailhead
1.5	Cable Crossing campsite
2.2	Big Laurel Falls
3.8	Sheep Cave and Sheep Cave Falls
4.3	Virgin Falls and campsite
5.3	Caney Fork campsite
7.6	Join Upland Trail
8.1	Martha's Pretty Point campsite and view
10.4	Virgin Falls trailhead

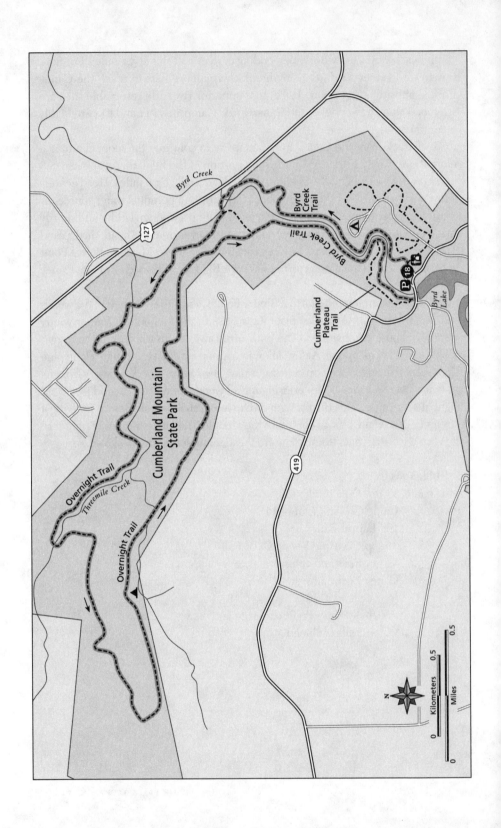

18

Cumberland Mountain Backpack

THE BACKPACK

This fun backpack explores the scenic watershed of Byrd Creek. The easy circuit runs atop the Cumberland Plateau with just under 1,000 feet elevation change over 8 miles. You'll first follow Byrd Creek under giant white pines and lush understory on a popular day use trail. Then, join the lesser used Overnight Trail, heading up the Threemile Creek valley and down another tributary, finding a primitive backcountry campsite under pines amid rock slabs. Return via Byrd Creek, soaking in more stream scenes then emerge at the historic arched bridge and dam of Byrd Lake—constructed by the Civilian Conservation Corps. Be apprised that this state park is adjacent to the town of Crossville, therefore you will hear the sounds of civilization, yet don't let that detract from this positive experience.

> **Distance and Configuration:** 8.1-mile loop
> **Difficulty:** Easy-moderate
> **Outstanding Features:** Attractive streams, family backpack
> **Elevation:** 1,918 feet high point, 1,698 feet low point
> **Scenery:** 3
> **Solitude:** 3
> **Family Friendly:** 4
> **Canine Friendly:** 3
> **Fees/permits:** Fee-based reservable campsite permit required
> **Best season:** Early fall through late spring
> **Maps:** Cumberland Mountain State Park
> **For more info:** Cumberland Mountain State Park, 24 Office Drive, Crossville, TN 38555, (931) 484-6138, www.tnstateparks.com
> **Finding the Trailhead:** From exit 322 on I-40 near Crossville, take TN 101 south to US 127. Turn left on US 127 south and follow it to the intersection with TN 68. Veer right here, still on US 127

south, driving 0.6 mile, then turn right into Cumberland Mountain State Park, on TN 419 north. Follow TN 419 north for 0.2 mile to the right turn into the park office. Park here. GPS trailhead coordinates: N35°54'02.4", W84°59'49.4"

This is a fine one night or family backpack. And having a designated backcountry campsite leaves no questions as to how far to go or where to camp. Park at the office and get your permit, too, though campsites can be reserved online. As you look out the park office door, walk away from the office, crossing the parking lot and a grassy strip to cross a second road. The signed spur to Byrd Creek Trail starts on the far side of the second road, around 100 feet from the park office. Join a single-track yellow-blazed natural surface path as it beelines for Byrd Creek. Pass under a powerline clearing then reach Byrd Creek at .1 mile. Turn right, tracing the winding mountain stream shaded by white pine, mountain laurel and rhododendron. Pine needles carpet the path under a forest primeval. Regal white pines tower over preserved hemlocks and other evergreens. The path remains streamside, allowing good looks at Byrd Creek.

Elevation change is minimal. The valley opens as you circle around a tributary at 0.9 mile. Soon return to Byrd Creek and come near US 127, bridging Byrd Creek on the paved old US 127 bridge. Leave left from the pavement back into woods and quickly reach a trail junction at 1.2 miles. Here, the Byrd Creek Trail keeps straight. However, we leave right on the much less used Overnight Trail.

The Overnight Trail ascends into scrubby hickories and oaks. Make your way downhill to span Threemile Creek on a swinging bridge at 1.8 miles. Curve around a tributary of Threemile Creek. Resume your westerly direction on the singletrack path, passing over rock slabs and amid mountain laurel, where the ecotones of moist streamside woods and xeric hillside oak forest intertwine.

At 2.9 miles, walk along an old rock fence from pre-park days. Continue up the valley, bridging Threemile Creek again at 3.3 miles. Ascend an oak ridge cresting out at 3.6 miles, resuming westerly. The odd shape of the loop you are making is constricted by the narrow park boundaries. This state park was created for residents of what was known as The Homestead. During the Great Depression 250 families were selected to settle here. They lived in Civilian Conservation Corps built houses made from nearby Crab Orchard sandstone. Back then, the size and shape of the park was irrelevant, as the whole area had few residents.

The path reaches its most westerly point at 4.4 miles. It then turns back east, reaching the backcountry campsite at 5.0 miles, located on a rock slab above a branch of Threemile Creek. The fine site is located in scrubby pines growing atop thin-soiled rock slabs. Water can be had from the creek just downhill from the camp.

Bridging Threemile Creek.

Continuing on the Overnight Trail cross the branch of Threemile Creek at 5.2 miles. Stay along the park boundary, coming near a pasture at 5.8 miles. Meet the other end of the Byrd Creek Trail at 6.9 miles. Keep straight, rejoining the Byrd Creek Trail.

Quickly span a branch on an unusual covered bridge. Come alongside alluring Byrd Creek, flanked by ferns, mountain laurel and evergreens. Meet the Cumberland Plateau Trail at 7.6 miles. Keep straight along Byrd Creek. At 8.0 miles, the park's arched stone bridge and dam come into view. This is the largest stone structure built by the entire nationwide CCC. Climb to the top and reach the park road. Carefully cross the road/dam, gaining views of Byrd Lake. Beyond the bridge, the park office comes into view. Walk to the park office, completing the loop.

Enjoying a cool afternoon at camp with coffee and fire.

Mileages

0.0	Join the spur to Byrd Creek Trail near park office
1.2	Right on Overnight Trail
3.6	Reach high point above Threemile Creek
5.0	Backcountry campsite
6.9	Rejoin Byrd Creek Trail
7.6	Stay left on Cumberland Plateau Trail
8.1	Return to park office, completing the backpack

ABOUT OUTDOOR SLEEPING ARRANGEMENTS

One winter night I was on Paint Creek in Greene County. My friend John Cox and I were on the first night of a three night trip. The next two nights we were heading to trail shelters, so we didn't bring a tent for this first night of backpacking.

While lying in the open, under star-filled clear skies, snug in my bag, the wind began to blow, increasing so fiercely I could feel the cold air push into my sleeping bag. I began to chill, then get colder and colder, until by dawn it seemed as if I was sleeping in the open without a bag. What a long night.

Having the proper sleeping bag can mean the difference between a good night's rest and a miserable night followed by an exhausted next day. The primary concerns for backpackers when choosing a sleeping bag are warmth, space and weight. Match your sleeping bag to the season and situation.

For example, use a fairly warm sleeping bag on a backpacking trip in the lofty and cool Smokies high country. If you are trekking along the Duck River at Henry Horton State Park in summer, choose the lightest bag possible.

For all but the warmest times I recommend a sleeping bag comfort rated to around 40°. These can handle local cold fronts in spring and cool Appalachian mountain nights, without weighing too much. If the temperature dips, just put on more clothes and you'll be fine. In warm, summertime conditions use a simple zippered fleece blanket—one item you can get cheaply.

When going on one-night trips, backpackers can worry less about weight and space of the sleeping bag. However, take note that many modern down-filled sleeping bags can compress to the size of a water bottle.

For additional comfort consider carrying a small camp pillow or bundle your clothes up under your head. Don't underestimate the importance of a pillow.

Sleeping pads are every bit as critical to a good night's rest as is a sleeping bag. For quality sleeping while backpacking, I combine a simple closed cell foam pad, 6 feet in length, with a lightweight, three-quarter length 48" self-inflating air mattress on top of it. The lighter model air mattresses come in under a pound each. Full-length air mattresses don't weigh much and are more comfortable. These are rising in popularity as they better hold warmth.

A closed cell foam pad can not only be used under you while sleeping but can also be used around the campsite and will prevent popping a hole in your air mattress should you use it sitting around camp or by the fire. The foam pad eases things while perched on a hard rock or lying on wet ground. By the way, a thin ground sheet cut a little larger than the size of your sleeping pad helps keep you and your stuff dry from ground moisture.

Hammock campers have the advantage of not having to find an acceptable flat spot to overnight, but do need two properly placed trees to string up their haven. Sleeping in a hammock can be comfortable—but cold—the sleeper is exposed to the air all around their body. Therefore, consider using an "underquilt" a down blanket of sorts that warms your underside. Hammocks perform best in mild conditions.

Whether you are sleeping under the stars, in a tent or in a hammock—or even a trail shelter—proper sleeping arrangements can enhance or diminish your backpacking experience.

19

Obed River Backpack

THE BACKPACK

Hike a section of Tennessee's own Cumberland Trail through the rugged Obed River gorge. Leave attractive Rock Creek Campground then trek along a cliff-line with rock shelters above the Emory River. Trace the Cumberland Trail to the Obed River, traversing the slopes of the gorge to make Alley Ford, a highly recommended camping area along the Obed. Enjoy overnighting in the wooded flat before returning to the trailhead. You can extend the hike beyond Alley Ford by taking the "Trail of a Thousand Steps" to a panorama atop Breakaway Bluff.

Distance and Configuration: 4.8-mile there-and-back
Difficulty: Easy-moderate
Outstanding Features: Bluffs, great campsite, rivers
Elevation: 888 feet low point, 1,210 feet high point
Scenery: 4
Solitude: 4
Family Friendly: 3
Canine Friendly: 3
Fees/permits: No permit required
Best season: September through mid-June
Maps: Obed National Wild and Scenic River; Cumberland Trail: Obed Wild and Scenic River Segment—Devils Breakfast Table to Nemo Bridge
For more info: Obed Wild and Scenic River, 208 N. Maiden Street, Wartburg, TN 37887, (423) 346-6294, www.nps.gov/obed
Finding the Trailhead: From the Obed Visitor Center, located next to the courthouse in downtown Wartburg, take Maiden Street west two blocks to Catoosa Road. Turn right on Catoosa Road and follow it 6 miles to Rock Creek Campground, which is on the right just after the bridge over the Emory River. Park near campsite #1 and the pay station. GPS trailhead coordinates: 36.069653, -84.663469

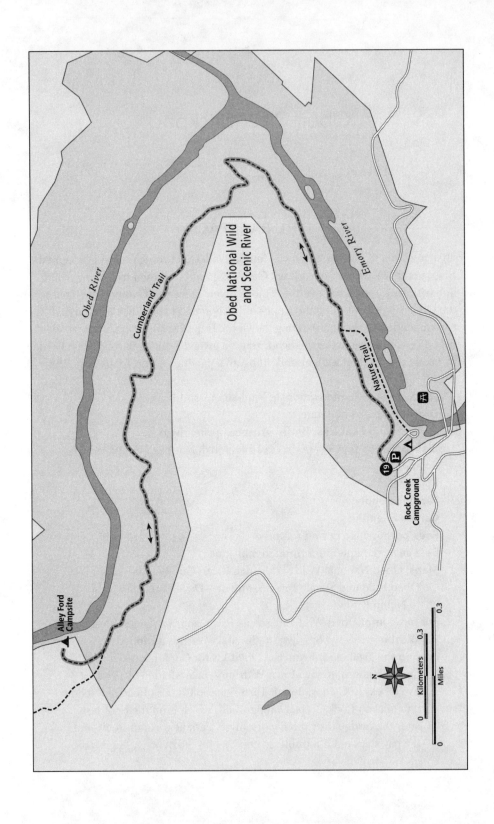

The Cumberland Trail leads you along these trailside cliffs.

This backpacking adventure is as much about the camping part as the hiking part. The flats of old Alley Ford along the Obed River fashion a fine place to overnight in the backcountry. And the National Park Service's Obed National Wild and Scenic River protects a gorgeous parcel of the Cumberlands. The Cumberland Trail has been routed through the park, linking it with adjacent Catoosa Wildlife Management Area. It is but 2.4 miles to the campsite from the trailhead, making it doable by novice backpackers. This hike is a great place to initiate a newbie backpacker. The scenery is wonderful; the trail presents enough challenges without being arduous, and the Alley Ford area features plenty of fine campsites. Bring along water or treat it from the Obed River.

The backpack begins at Rock Creek Campground, an intimate little auto accessible camp ideal for late night arrivals. Join the singletrack Cumberland Trail as it dives into woods of Virginia pine, holly, oak and beech. The campground is

The Emory River flows by Alley Ford Campsite.

visible just below you until the mountain laurel bordered trail turns northeast into the valley of the Emory River. Reach the first of a line of cliffs along which the Cumberland Trail runs. Overhangs create rock houses amidst fallen boulders littering the base of the 100 foot precipices, against which the rapids of the Emory River echo.

At 0.4 mile, the Emory River Nature Trail splits right and returns to the campground after running along the Emory River. Add this trail for new mileage on your return trip. For now, keep straight, leaving the clifflines at 0.8 mile, after passing a deeply overhung rock house. Rise along a hillside covered in oaks, hickory and pine. Switchback uphill above the confluence of the Emory River and the Obed River. The path turns into the Obed River Valley and at 1.1 miles you join an old woods road under north facing woods of hemlock, beech and maple.

At 1.3 miles, the trail comes to an old strip mine operation—but you can barely tell. Only the slightly unnatural dip in the hillside gives it away. The Cumberland Trail treads a berm above the old strip, now more resembling a sunken road grown over with trees. Breaks in the berm allow water to flow out from the dip. You will cross these outflows on little trail bridges.

Leave the old coal seam at 2.0 miles to bridge a seasonal stream cascading abruptly toward the Obed River. The hillside you are on steepens before reaching a trail junction at 2.3 miles. Here, the Cumberland Trail stays left, but we descend right on the old Alley Ford road downhill to the Obed River. This crossing has been used by peoples of the Cumberland Plateau as long as there have been peoples of the Cumberland Plateau. Follow the rocky, eroded track down to find a flat extending upriver at 2.4 miles, with campsites shaded by beech and pine. Trails lead down to sandy accesses reaching the Obed River, here flowing placidly under a long low bluff rising across the river.

Enjoy this favored locale, practicing the fine art of backpack camping. If you want to extend your hike, simply follow the Cumberland Trail 1.7 miles to a view from atop Breakaway Bluff, up the Obed River Valley. Be prepared for myriad rocky steps amidst boulder fields to reach where Obed views extend deep into the gorge with rising sandstone bluffs, affirming the waterway's designation as a national wild and scenic river. Or you could simply lounge away at Alley Ford to savor backpacking in Tennessee.

Mileages

0.0   Rock Creek Campground
0.8   Leave clifflines
2.3   Right to Alley Ford
2.4   Alley Ford campsite
4.8   Rock Creek Campground

BACKPACKER PHILOSOPHIES DIFFER

Backpacking enthusiasts run the gamut in their methodology. On one end are the so-called backpacking purists. They generally have the best gear and are always on the lookout for the latest in high tech offerings by the outdoor outfitting industry. And they are willing to pay for it.

Their fare usually consists of fancy freeze-dried food. Gore-Tex fabric and name brand labels are prominently displayed on their clothing. They have the latest phone loaded with outdoor related apps. Always prepared and ready to help the ill prepared, they rarely get in over their heads, saving taxpayer dollars and ranger headaches from having to rescue them.

At the other end of the spectrum is the make-do backpacker. He or she probably borrowed half the equipment on their back and will not hesitate to tote a cast iron skillet to fry some bacon at the campsite. They can be spotted on the trail invariably wearing tight jeans and combat boots. They would not be caught dead with a trail map in their hands.

At camp, make-do hikers try to think of ways to use that big knife in that leather case attached to their belt. An oversized cheap tent invariably pops up wherever they are. They are learning and some will eventually move across and find their own place on the spectrum.

Two other subcategories exist, the minimalists and the gearheads. Minimalists become overly obsessed with weight, paring their gear down to such a degree that much enjoyment is lost from their wilderness experience and evolves into a sheer survival test.

I once stayed with some women at a backcountry shelter who drank hot water for breakfast; they felt the weight of coffee did not justify its extravagance. Others become so concerned with pack weight they will cut off the ends of their toothbrush to save one-tenth of an ounce. However, when they tell about how much weight they save while around the campfire they are in hog heaven!

The gearhead has it all, literally, and it is in his pack. Around the fire, you grumble about losing a tiny screw from your fishing reel, ten minutes later he proudly returns with the exact size screw you needed. It is a good thing he has a hot water bottle because he is going to need it to soothe those back muscles that are cramping from carrying all that extra equipment on his back.

Pack weight has always been the source of spirited backpacker discussions. As a general guide, backpackers should carry no more than 15% their body weight. Nevertheless, wilderness adventuring has no commandments. Each person literally carries his or her own weight—and lives with their choices. "Hike you own hike," the saying goes.

While out there, I relish the opportunities to see how others conduct business on the trails. With an open mind, I usually learn something, even if it is what not to do. To think my way as the only way merely restricts my growth as an outdoorsman.

So the next time you see somebody backpacking down the trail, they are not merely putting one foot in front of the other. There is likely a philosophy in there somewhere.

20

Frozen Head Backpack

THE BACKPACK

Make a rewarding circuit hike at mountainous Frozen Head State Park. This loop is but one of many backpacking possibilities at this large preserve near Wartburg. First, climb to the crest of Bird Mountain, traversing a high rocky ridge to soak in views from the tower atop 3,324 foot Frozen Head Mountain. Complete the circuit with a trip to Chimney Top, where more views await. Six backcountry campsites are available along the rewarding route.

Distance and Configuration: 18.2-mile loop

Difficulty: Moderate-difficult

Outstanding Features: Frozen Head tower, wildflowers in season, campsites

Elevation: 1,306 feet low point, 3,324 feet high point

Scenery: 4

Solitude: 3

Family Friendly: 2

Canine Friendly: 2

Fees/permits: Fee-based backcountry camping permit required

Best season: September through May

Maps: Frozen Head State Park

For more info: Frozen Head State Park, 964 Flat Fork Road, Wartburg, TN 37887, 423-346-3318, www.tnstateparks.com/parks/frozen-head

Finding the Trailhead: From Oliver Springs, follow TN 62 west 13 miles to turn right onto Flat Fork Road. A sign for Morgan County Regional Correctional Facility and Frozen Head State Park alerts you to the right turn. Follow Flat Fork Road 4 miles to the entrance of Frozen Head State Park. The park visitor center is on your right. The backpack starts here. GPS trailhead coordinates: 36.125246, -84.504230

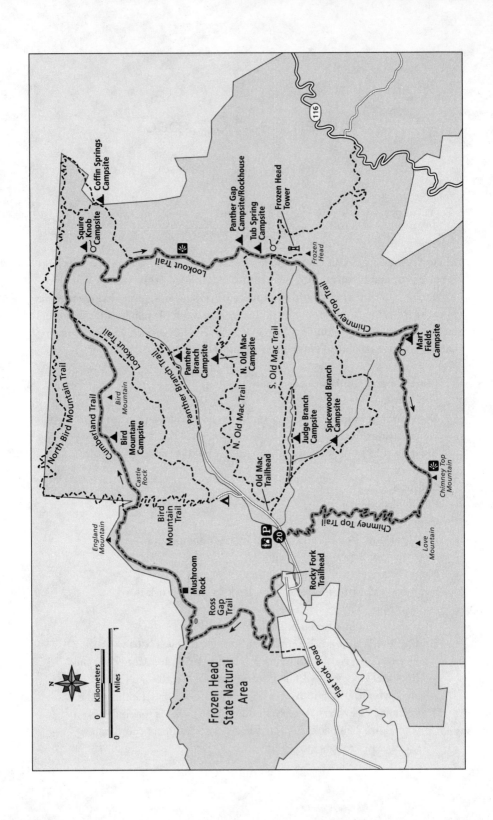

Frozen Head
State Natural
Area

Viewing an old pond atop Bird Mountain.

With over 56 miles of trails and 10 designated backcountry campsites among 24,000 acres of mountainous land carved from the Cumberland Plateau, Frozen Head State Park is a backpacker's paradise. This loop is but one of many combinations of overnight adventures that you can fashion. Originally developed by the Civilian Conservation Corps in the 1930s as part of Morgan State Forest, the rugged land also housed famed Brushy Mountain State Prison. In the 1970s the state forest was conferred to the state park system and in 1988 all but 330 acres of Frozen Head was declared a state natural area. Today, the park is one Tennessee's premier backpacking destinations.

The park trail system uses a combination of rugged rocky singletrack paths and doubletrack former logging and mining roads. Each backcountry campsite is single occupancy—if you reserve the site it is for you and your party alone. All sites have springs or other nearby water sources, but they can dry up. Call ahead to inquire about the water situation. Spring is ideal for wildflowers, for which Frozen Head is known. Fall reveals clear skies and fine views. Winter offers solitude and a chance to admire the geological wonders of the preserve.

The backpack starts with a road walk from the visitor center. Follow Flat Fork Road west back toward the park entrance, bridging Flat Fork then reaching

This tower presents 360 degree views from atop Frozen Head Mountain.

Rocky Fork field. Walk to the northeast corner of the field, making the Rocky Fork trailhead at 0.7 mile. Here, join the Ross Gap Trail that soon splits left as a trail keeps straight toward the park office but has no bridge over Flat Fork. The Ross Gap Trail works northwest in and out of drainages flowing off Bird Mountain under a mantle of oaks, beech and maple. Stone steps aid your passage across wet weather drainages on the ferny forest floor amidst hemlock and mountain laurel.

At 1.4 miles, join an old westbound jeep track, traveling the mid-slope of Bird Mountain through bouldery woods. At 1.7 miles, the Ross Gap Trail makes a signed right turn onto another old jeep road. The climbing begins in earnest under regal oak halls broken with stone sentinels rising mutely on the mountainside. Angle up the south slope of Bird Mountain, reaching an intersection just below the actual Ross Gap at 3.0 miles. Here, head right on Tennessee's master path, the Cumberland Trail, climbing to the mountain crest and a mining retention pond at 3.3 miles. This part of Bird Mountain was long ago strip mined. Swing past the pond to enter pine thickets growing from the former extraction strip.

The Cumberland Trail climbs beyond the strip atop the nose of Bird Mountain, breaking the 3,000 foot barrier on singletrack trail. You will be around or above 3,000 feet for the balance of the backpack. Make Mushroom Rock at 2.7 miles. Note the wide top and narrowed base of this trailside geological wonder, set amid cherry-rich hardwoods. The Cumberland Trail takes you along and even atop other stone outcrops.

At 4.9 miles, the trail slices south through a break in the cliffline. Hike beneath a rock shelter, then at 5.0 miles the challenging North Bird Mountain Trail drops left in switchbacks toward the Emory River. We stay with the Cumberland Trail, to go just a few feet then stay left for Castle Rock as the Bird Mountain Trail drops right to auto-accessible Big Cove Campground.

Skirt around the south side of a knob to the angular citadel of Castle Rock. Return to the crest of Bird Mountain and reach Bird Mountain campsite at 5.9 miles. Here, find a flat spot with fire ring and a table with benches, backed against a hill from which emanates a reliable spring. Note: the terrain around the spring can be mucky.

Climb away from the campsite in switchbacks. Roll over a pair of knobs as the slope drops sharply on both sides. Meet the Lookout Trail at 7.4 miles. For the next several miles you will be on a maintained doubletrack, availing good footing. At 7.5 miles, the Cumberland Trail splits left as the Lookout Trail eases around the south side of Bald Knob to Emory Gap. Turn more southerly then meet the acute left spur to Squire Knob campsite at 8.1 miles. It offers a level wooded spot with fire ring, bear food storage locker, table and a covered spring south of the campsite, all on a shoulder below Squire Knob.

The Lookout Trail continues south atop the Tennessee Valley Divide, skirting the headwaters of Flat Fork to your right that ultimately flow into the Tennessee River, with the New River to your left, feeding the Cumberland River. These headwaters, so close together now, will split then merge hundreds of miles later at the Tennessee and Cumberland Rivers confluence near Land Between The Lakes, flowing as one to the Mississippi River and the Gulf.

At 8.9 miles, at Peach Orchard Gap, a spur trail goes left 0.7 mile to Coffin Springs campsite. The Lookout Trail rolls southerly in measured ups and downs. At 10.2 miles, come to Panther Gap and the Panther Gap Rockhouse and campsite. This is one of the few rockhouses in the Cumberlands that legally allow camping under its stone shelter. The only level area is under the rockhouse with drips for water (or nearby Tub Spring). I have stayed here and find it a fine experience, especially in a rain. At 10.3 miles, the North Old Mac Trail comes in on your right. Enter a much busier section of the park.

At 10.5 miles, popular Tub Spring campsite stands on a knoll to your left. It has a fire ring remade from an old chimney, picnic tables, and food storage locker. Just ahead, reach a major trail intersection. Here, the Lookout Trail goes left toward Tub Spring and Armes Gap, with South Old Mac and Chimney Top Trails ahead. But we take still another signed track to the top of Frozen Head Mountain, named for its propensity to be snowy while the lower elevation lands remain snowless. The half-mile trail rises steadily to make the now-truncated fire tower topped with a fine observation platform. Views stretch as far as the horizon allows. To the west stands Lone Mountain and the balance of the Cumberland Plateau. To the east the Smokies rise above the valley of the Tennessee River. Scan for the TVA windmills atop Buffalo Mountain. Infamous Brushy Mountain State Prison, now a tourist destination, lies below to the south.

Return from the tower to join the Chimney Top Trail at 11.5 miles, continuing our loop in hardwoods circling the Flat Fork valley. Enjoy some more jeep trail walking then meet the Spicewood Trail at 12.4 miles. Stay left with the Chimney Top Trail, now on challenging, rocky, slender singletrack that accompanies you the rest of the backpack.

Continue among maples, oaks and tulip trees beneath striking stone citadels. At 13.3 miles, the trail abruptly cuts right, angling through rock ramparts to crest out and turn north, reaching the flat of Mart Fields campsite at 13.5 miles. The now-wooded former field offers a fire ring, homemade stone table, and a rock enclosed spring about 100 yards down trail.

Just ahead, pass the chimney of an old cabin and the original location of the Mart Fields campsite. You are now heading west, joining Chimney Top Mountain, making a sharp quarter mile drop, then level off among rock outcrops, hickories and oaks. The going is slow. At 15.0 miles, reach the base of the Chimney Top. The official trail goes right around the stone protrusion and comes alongside a smallish rockhouse and now-closed campsite. An unofficial trail going left scrambles through rocks and brush to reach the level top of Chimney Top. Push through brush to a northern outcrop and view from 3,083 feet. The Morgan County Correctional Complex and Wartburg are easily identifiable, with distant ridges beyond.

Scramble from the lookout and resume the official trail as it passes the rockhouse then plunges north, losing 400 feet in 0.4 mile! Switchback into the tulip tree rich Rocky Fork Branch valley, rock hopping the stream at 16.4 miles, 1,200 feet below Chimney Top. The challenge isn't over. Now, make the 300-foot ascent—eased by switchbacks—surmounting chestnut oak, blueberry and mountain laurel rich Rough Ridge.

Now the narrow, single-track switchbacks down the north side of Rough Ridge, passing through grapevine strewn hardwoods in places. At 18.2 miles, emerge at the rear of the park visitor center, completing the challenging and rewarding Frozen Head Backpack.

Mileages

0.0	Visitor center
3.0	Ross Gap
5.9	Bird Mountain campsite
8.1	Squire Knob campsite
8.9	Spur trail 0.7 mile to Coffin Spring campsite
10.2	Panther Gap Rockhouse/campsite
10.5	Tub Spring campsite
11.0	Frozen Head Tower
13.5	Mart Field campsite
15.0	Chimney Top
18.2	Visitor center

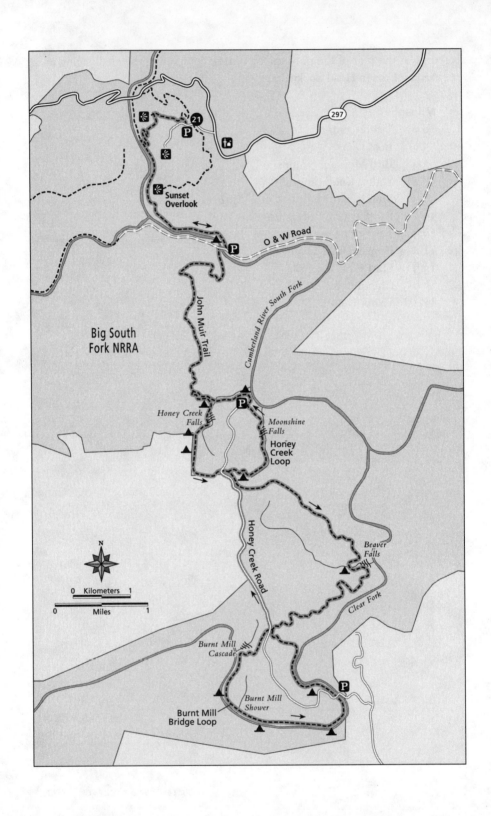

Big South
Fork NRRA

297

Sunset
Overlook

O & W Road

John Muir Trail

Cumberland River South Fork

Honey Creek
Falls

Moonshine
Falls

Honey
Creek
Loop

Beaver
Falls

Honey Creek Road

Clear Fork

Burnt Mill
Cascade

Burnt Mill
Shower

Burnt Mill
Bridge Loop

N

0   Kilometers   1

0   Miles   1

21

Honey Creek Backpack

THE BACKPACK

This adventure in the Big South Fork National River and Recreation Area incorporates the famed Honey Creek Loop, with its waterfalls, boulder scrambles, clifflines and additional geological wonderments. First, enjoy a view, then drop to the Big South Fork on the John Muir Trail to climb past waterfalls and the Devils Den. Join the ultra scenic Honey Creek Loop before traversing uplands to Clear Fork and the Burnt Mill Bridge Loop, with its fine campsites. Return to Honey Creek and more superlative scenery, including a ladder climb to a stunning vista, before finally backtracking to the trailhead. Take note: This backpack can be shortened/altered by starting at alternate trailheads.

Distance and Configuration: 28.0-mile double balloon loop
Difficulty: Difficult due to irregular terrain in places
Outstanding Features: Geology of Honey Creek, waterfalls, views, campsites, streams
Elevation: 1,556 high point, 889 low point
Scenery: 5
Solitude: 3 (Honey Creek area can be busy)
Family Friendly: 1
Canine Friendly: 1
Fees/permits: Fee based permit required
Best season: Late summer through spring
Maps: National Geographic #241 Big South Fork National River and Recreation Area
For more info: Big South Fork National River and Recreation Area, 4564 Leatherwood Road, Oneida, TN 37841; 423-286-7275; www.nps.gov/biso
Finding the Trailhead: From the intersection of US 27 and TN 297 in Oneida, take TN 297 west for 10.3 miles, to turn left toward East

View of the Big South Fork from the O and W Bridge.

Rim Overlook. Follow the road for 0.3 mile to the parking area on the right, facing a field. GPS trailhead coordinates: 36.472646, -84.656643

This highlight reel of a backpack—including a trip through Honey Creek is a true adventure punctuated with scenes that will stay in your mind long after the quest is completed. Though it doesn't have the climbs and descents found in the mountains farther east, the backpack makes up for it with distance and the sheer challenge of the Honey Creek Loop, especially when toting a fully loaded backpack amidst the streams, boulders and clifflines. The recommended overnighter can be done in 2-4 nights. Campsites are plentiful, and alternate parking areas allow you to change the backpack's length. I recommend the whole adventure but you could shorten it by doing the Honey Creek and Burnt Mill Bridge loops and the connector linking them. The Burnt Mill Bridge Trail curves along Clear Fork, with its sandbars, boulders overlooking the stream and fine campsites. It is as easy on the feet as Honey Creek is difficult. Yet both deliver a rewarding experience.

Start your adventure near the park headquarters near East Rim Overlook, taking the Leatherwood Loop Trail into woods of pine and sweetgum. At 0.2 mile, reach the actual loop of Leatherwood Loop and stay left, westerly, toward the Big South Fork, in mountain laurel. At 0.5 mile, stay straight for the River Overlook, enjoying a view into the Big South Fork gorge. Continue the loop, actively descending the gorge rim via switchbacks to make yet another intersection at 1.7 miles, now deep in the Big South Fork gorge. Head left here on the John Muir Trail (JMT), cruising south on a level track with the brawling Big South Fork flowing amidst boulders to your right. Keep in the riparian zone, rich with sycamores, climbing a bit before returning to river level at 2.8 miles.

At 3.2 miles, cross a branch strewn with massive boulders. Just ahead, in the flats on trail right you will find a small but level camping area. The JMT comes on gravel O and W Road, an auto accessible campsite and the O and W Bridge at 3.4 miles. This is also an alternate starting point to shorten this backpack. Now, cross the O and W Bridge, absorbing fine looks up and down the river and up at tan bluffs. The JMT leaves left beyond the bridge, climbing thickly wooded hillside to cross a stream and find Jakes Falls, a 30-foot spiller twinkling down layered rock.

The highlights continue beyond the cataract as you ascend to reach signed Devils Den Cave at 4.0 miles, a level shelter with a wider-than-high arched rock roof, a prototypical Big South Fork rockhouse. Climb a bit more and you are once again atop the Plateau, reaching a picnic table/campsite at 4.2 miles. Level tent sites can be found in the nearby woods.

Beaver Falls.

From here, the JMT heads south in the greater Hurricane Ridge pine and oak lands, laced with unofficial equestrian trails. Fear not as major intersections and turns are signed and blazed, making a sharp left turn at 4.6 miles. Curve south and make another left at an intersection with a fence nearby at 5.1 miles, then split right away from the equestrian trails at 5.3 miles, aiming south for North Fork Honey Creek, reaching the Honey Creek Loop at 6.2 miles. Stay right here, working along the creek rim, before dipping to view a huge, rock-littered rockhouse. At 6.5 miles, pass a campsite below the trail.

Ahead, make a squeeze through a boulder jumble after turning up Honey Creek, then passing the side trail to vegetation-shrouded 20-foot Secluded Falls. Come to Ice Castle Falls, a low flow, 38-foot cataract known for freezing in place in winter at 6.8 miles. A small campsite faces this spiller. Continue up Honey Creek, dropping to a bridge. Cross the span to find a small but level waterside campsite on your right at 7.1 miles. Here, the Honey Creek Loop turns downstream and at 7.2 miles, a spur splits left to 20-foot Honey Creek Falls, best known for its long plunge pool. The trail then curves away from Honey Creek, back toward it then away yet again, eventually heading south along a tributary, passing a small trailside campsite at 7.8 miles. The tributary, mere feet away, marks the park boundary, and you look on woods.

The Honey Creek Loop gently rises to reach the Honey Creek Loop parking area at 8.4 miles. Keep straight here, splitting right with the signed hiking trail, once again atop the Plateau. At 8.5 miles, stay right with the JMT, as the Honey Creek Loop splits left. You will return here later. For now, skirt southeast with the JMT in oak-dominated forest. At 8.8 miles, the JMT stays left at a signed intersection with an old road. Stay with the blazed JMT, undulating a ridgetop before dipping to a recommended streamside campsite along a tributary of nearby Clear Fork at 10.7 miles. The JMT then turns down this unnamed tributary. At 10.8 miles, you can hear gorgeous Beaver Falls making its 24-foot pirouette over a stone lip below, with a huge complementary rockhouse rising beside an impossibly colored greenish-blue plunge pool. The view of this scenic but lesser visited falls is worth the scramble.

From there, the JMT curves along the rim of Clear Fork, roaring down below, as you work around small side hollows to reach a trail intersection near Honey Creek Road at 12.7 miles. Here, cross Honey Creek Road, beginning a counterclockwise circuit of the Burnt Mill Bridge Loop as it circles a narrow neck of Clear Fork. Pass an oft-missed, seldom-used dry campsite on trail left at 13.0 miles before dropping into a hollow, where you find low flow Burnt Mill Cascade, dropping 12 feet, first over a lip then onto a boulder. Dip into evergreen thickets as the path turns alongside rocky, noisy Clear Fork, where the trail leads through a rich riparian zone, with sandbars, boulders, and flood-bent vegetation. The setting is first rate. At 14.0 miles, reach the first of several fine campsites

Ladders lead to this view of the Big South Fork.

in the flats overlooking Clear Fork. At 14.3 miles, 26-foot high faucet waterfall known as Burnt Mill Shower noisily spills to your left.

Reach more campsites in streamside flats, backed against a low bluff, at 14.5 miles. The scenery remains fine. Pass another campsite at 15.4 miles. At 15.7 miles, reach Burnt Mill Bridge parking area, with restrooms and picnic tables. To continue the trail walk toward the newer bridge here, then drop back to the river on a footpath, venturing amidst very fine streamside scenery, to pass a shaded, bluff-bordered campsite at 16.0 miles. The Burnt Mill Bridge Loop works between Clear Fork and stone bluffs, turning away from Clear Fork at 16.6 miles. Criss-cross a Clear Fork tributary to complete the Burnt Mill Bridge Loop at 17.1 miles. Here, you can either backtrack on the JMT for 4.2 miles or follow gravel/dirt Honey Creek Road north for 1.9 miles, ultimately returning to the Honey Creek Loop parking area.

Assuming you take Honey Creek Road, arrive at the Honey Creek parking area trailhead at 19.0 miles. Once again head east on the Honey Creek Loop, returning to the trail intersection where Honey Creek Loop and the JMT split. Stay left this time and resume the Honey Creek Loop, passing a small, sloped campsite at 19.3, just before descending along an unnamed intimate tributary of the Big South Fork. The creek cuts its own gorge with rockhouses. Squeeze through a cliff and boulders before coming to pretty Moonshine Falls, making a wide, 10 foot curtain style drop at 20.1 miles.

Continue down trail, entering a rugged segment with slick open rock faces and some creek walking. Open onto a massive elongated cliffline with tall, echoing rockhouses as the Big South Fork flows below. Admire the geology of this mother of all clifflines. At 20.8 miles, take the trail leading left along the cliffline to reach a pair of metal ladders that lead up to a first rate view down the Big South Fork gorge. This overlook is accessible from the end of Honey Creek Road and is thus auto-accessible, but don't pass by the views. The ladder climbs are fun!

Backtrack to the Honey Creek Loop, descending toward the Big South Fork. At 21.1 miles, a spur leads right steeply down to a pair of bigger campsites on either side of Honey Creek where it enters the main river. From there, the Honey Creek Loop makes its final challenging run up Honey Creek, squeezing through more boulder jumbles and at times going directly up the creek. Cross Honey Creek at 21.4 miles, continuing up North Honey Creek. Ahead, pass by a huge rockhouse with an optional ladder climb then stomach slither behind a rockfall arch.

At 21.8 miles, complete the Honey Creek Loop. You did it! From here, the backpack backtracks north 6.2 miles on the John Muir Trail and Leatherwood Loop, returning to the East Rim trailhead at 28.0 miles.

Mileages

0.0	East Rim trailhead
0.5	River overlook
1.7	Left on John Muir Trail
3.2	Campsite past bouldery creek
3.4	Auto accessible campsite, alternate trailhead at O and W Road
4.0	Devils Den Cave after Jakes Falls
4.2	Picnic table, campsite
6.2	Right on Honey Creek Loop
6.5	Campsite
6.8	Ice Castle Falls, small campsite
7.1	Waterside campsite, spur left ahead to Honey Creek Falls
7.8	Small trailside campsite
8.4	Honey Creek Loop parking area, ahead, right on John Muir Trail
10.7	Recommended creekside campsite, Beaver Falls .1 mile ahead
12.7	Cross Honey Creek Road on Burnt Mill Bridge Loop
13.0	Seldom used campsite
14.0	First campsite along Clear Fork
14.3	Burnt Mill Shower

14.5	Campsites
15.4	Campsite
15.7	Burnt Mill Bridge parking area
16.0	Campsite
17.1	Complete Burnt Mill Bridge Loop, north on Honey Creek Road
19.0	Return to Honey Creek Loop parking, resume counterclockwise on Honey Creek Loop
19.3	Small sloped campsite
20.1	Moonshine Falls
20.8	Left at intersection, climbing ladders to stellar vista
21.1	Spur drops right to large campsites along Honey Creek near Big South Fork
21.8	Complete Honey Creek Loop, backtrack
28.0	Return to East Rim trailhead, completing the backpack

BE WEATHERWISE WHEN BACKPACKING

Ominous April clouds rolled in overhead, darkening by the moment. I was backpacking the John Muir Trail. The Big South Fork National River and Recreation Area offered Plateau scenery towering over lesser hollows. By now, the western sky had turned nearly black, so I pulled out my weather radio from my pack. The monotonous computer voice delivered ominous warnings of heavy storms accompanied by heavier rain and copious lightning.

I needed to find a camp—and fast! While hiking down trail I scanned each potential campsite closely, looking for signs of ponding on the ground to avoid and high spots on which to pitch my tarp.

I spotted a likely site and dropped my pack. The lesser-used locale offered a mound slightly higher than the surrounding terrain. Tarp drainage. I pitched the tarp and called it camp. Noting the potential high winds, I looked overhead for dead standing trees, known as "widow-makers" for their propensity to tumble on unsuspecting campers, then took extra care in battening down my plastic enclave, despite peals of lightning shooting sideways across the sky.

A line of strong showers rushed toward me in a low rumble. I dove under the low-slung tarp and prepared for the aquatic siege. Soon, rain pelted the plastic, which flapped wildly with each punishing gust. Lightning repeatedly illuminated my shelter, followed by ground-shaking thunder enough to wake the dead—or at least a Big South Fork backpacker. Next day, I found out the area had received over 3 inches of rain! Water puddled in places, yet my judicious choice of campsites kept me mostly dry.

Backpackers live and die with the weather and the seasons. Reveling in the changes, we wait with anticipation as each season unfolds, along with its unique conditions, each potentially threatening in its own way—the storms of spring, the heat and lightning of summer, the first cold blasts of fall, the snows and frigid temperatures of winter.

Knowing the weather when backpacking is paramount. Having an idea of what to expect you can bring gear and clothing appropriate for the predicted situations—or call it off altogether. However, try to play the weather cards you are dealt. Avoid becoming a slave to the weather forecasts, reacting to their declarations as a servant to its master. I call it "weather paralysis," not knowing a course of action when the weather is iffy.

After all, what do you do when there's a 50% chance of rain?

Avoid weather paralysis, but be prepared and informed. Know the possibilities and have not only the clothing and gear contingencies covered, but also alternate plans if the weather gets dangerous.

Phones can offer instant weather predictions and real time radar but reception is not guaranteed, therefore I recommend bringing a portable weather radio. They come in small backpacking sizes and weights, often with AM/FM radio bands included. Weather radio broadcasts originate from the National Oceanic and Atmospheric Administration (NOAA), with over 1,000 transmitters stretching throughout the United States. NOAA not only predicts forthcoming weather, but it also gives short term forecasts, which can be helpful during strong, potentially life-threatening storms.

No matter what, check the weather before leaving home. Furthermore, learn weather averages well before embarking to a distant destination, so you can get an idea of typical temperatures and precipitation of the area during the time you plan to backpack. That way you will be weatherwise when embarking on your adventure.

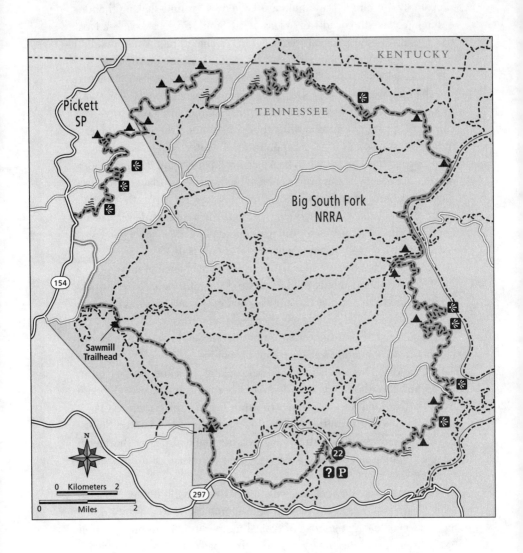

22

Big South Fork Loop

THE BACKPACK

This grand circuit has it all—including distance. A full 50 plus miles, make a tour de force of the Big South Fork National River and Recreation Area, a land of overlooks, cliffs, waterfalls, arches, deep forests, rockhouses and plenty of room to roam. Leave developed Bandy Creek area, then hike the rim of the Big South Fork before dropping along the river itself. Climb to uplands then heading upstream along superlative Rock Creek and Thompson Creek then finally returning to the trailhead via Salt Pine Ridge.

Distance and Configuration: 55.3-mile loop

Difficulty: Difficult due to distance

Outstanding Features: Multi-day trip, views, waterfalls, geology, challenge

Elevation: 1,690 high point, 840 low point

Scenery: 5

Solitude: 4 (a few sections busy)

Family Friendly: 1

Canine Friendly: 1

Fees/permits: Fee based permit required

Best season: Early fall through spring

Maps: National Geographic #241 Big South Fork National River and Recreation Area

For more info: Big South Fork National River and Recreation Area, 4564 Leatherwood Road, Oneida, TN 37841; 423-286-7275; www.nps.gov/biso

Finding the Trailhead: From the intersection of US 27 and TN 297 in Oneida, take TN 297 west for 14 miles, coming to the turn to Bandy Creek Visitor Center and campground. Turn right and follow the East Bandy Creek Road for 1.6 miles, reaching

At John Muir Overlook.

the left turn to the visitor center and the right turn into Bandy
Creek Campground. Turn right into the campground, passing the
entrance station. Turn left immediately past the entrance station,
coming to the pool on your left. Park here. In summer you may
have to park at nearby visitor center. GPS trailhead coordinates:
36.490139, -84.698111

The 125,000-acre Big South Fork National River and Recreation Area (shared
with Kentucky) is one of the best places to backpack in the Volunteer State.
Situated on the Cumberland Plateau, the Big South Fork offers not only its own
geological wonderment but also contrast to the Southern Appalachians farther
east. Once hardscrabble farmlands and later coal country, the Big South Fork
NRRA was established in the 1970s and has come unto its own.

Best hiked from fall through spring, this exciting circuit offers low elevations and is thus a great winter choice. It also presents lesser vertical challenge than do the eastern highlands, yet it has plenty of its own trials—fords aplenty, rocky trails, hiking along clifflines and more. In spring you will have roaring waterfalls but deeper fords. Conversely, in autumn, the fords will be a breeze and waterfalls but a trickle. Most major crossings are bridged, leaving but 4 necessary stream fords—Tacket Creek, two on Rock Creek and one on Laurel Fork. There are lots of smaller unbridged stream crossings that shouldn't pose a problem.

Trails in the Big South Fork are well maintained and signed. The circuit also loops through Scott State Forest, as well as Pickett State Park and Forest. Absolutely bring the recommended National Geographic map, in case you need to shortcut or otherwise alter the trip.

And it is a long adventure, one of those to which we backpackers aspire. Established campsites are located all along the circuit. Almost all are along streams, so if desiring to camp in the uplands, bring a water vessel.

The backpack starts at Bandy Creek, with its recommended car campground as well as visitor center, where you can obtain you required backcountry permit. From there the circuit takes the John Litton Farm Loop east, soon coming along the first of many clifflines, and Fall Branch Falls, the first of several cataracts. Beyond there, join the revered John Muir Trail (JMT), a path worthy of being named for the famed naturalist. Cruise along the Big South Fork gorge rim, enjoying looks deep into the canyon. Next, the JMT leads along the Big South Fork, allowing closer looks at this brawling watercourse rushing among massive boulders and flood thrown brush.

The circuit next heads into historic No Business Creek, where you will see old homesites before rising to grand John Muir Overlook. From there, head west in rich hardwood uplands before tracing an old railroad grade down Massey Branch, with its cataracts, majestic rockhouses and cliffs. Then turn up the ultra-attractive Rock Creek valley, with its everywhere-you-look rugged beauty leading into Pickett State Park and Forest. Leave the JMT for the Hidden Passage Trail where overlooks, waterfalls, arches and rockhouses will astonish. Beyond there, a little road walk is in order before taking the doubletrack Salt Pine Ridge Trail down to Laurel Fork, avoiding several fords on Laurel Fork. Finally, climb into the maze of trails around Bandy Creek, finishing with more melding of water and geology that make the Big South Fork so special.

Mileages

0.0   Leave from the Bandy Creek pool parking area on the singletrack John Litton Farm Loop, first north along Duncan Hollow Road, then east along Fall Branch

1.9   Fall Branch Falls, small, heavily used campsite

Massey Branch Falls.

2.8   John Litton Farm Loop leaves left, right on Fall Branch Trail, small campsite ahead on right, pass by large rockhouse

3.1   Small dry campsite on trail right atop gorge rim, easy level hiking

3.8   Overlook down Fall Branch valley into Big South Fork gorge

4.2   Good, larger campsite on trail curve above tributary of Fall Branch; second campsite directly along tributary; bridge tributary and climb

4.7   Trail intersection with Grand Gap Loop; stay left on JMT, crossing Alfred Smith Road; pass second intersection with Grand Gap Loop, stay left with JMT

5.3   Pass by overlook above Big South Fork as the river makes a big bend

7.2   Descend short ladder

7.7   Spur trail goes right to overlook; another spur to view in 0.8 mile

9.1	Bridge sandy creek with trail sign on bridge
9.5	Small campsite in small hollow to left of trail, water available from creekbed crossing
11.0	Small overlook on right
12.6	Bicycle trail climbs left, JMT descends right toward Laurel Fork, passing clifflines
14.4	Campsite and bridge over Laurel Fork, head right beyond bridge
14.5	Cross Station Camp Creek on hiker bridge, continue down Station Camp Creek
15.0	Campsite above Station Camp Creek, continue downstream on wide doubletrack
15.2	Split left onto hiker only JMT at homesite, run parallel to equestrian trail; pass intersection with right spur to Station Camp crossing of Big South Fork; at this point JMT and equestrian trail repeatedly merge and diverge
16.3	Bridge Parch Corn Creek, stay right
16.8	Bridge Harvey Branch; look for piled rocks indicating former farmland
18.3	Bridge Big Branch, small campsite, stay left with JMT up Big Branch
19.3	Split gap near Maude's Crack and big bluff, descend toward No Business Creek through Betty Branch valley
20.3	Bridge Betty Branch and No Business Creek, campsite beside No Business Creek, head upstream in bottomland, pass spur right to Big Island, stay left
20.8	Pass homesite on trail left, scan for other homesites amid briers
21.5	Cross Tacket Creek; no bridge, campsite in nearby flats up Tacket Creek
21.7	Split right with JMT, climb via switchbacks up Chestnut Ridge
22.9	John Muir Overlook, gaze upstream on No Business Creek. Look for chimney in the valley below; continue along scenic rock slab and pine ridge
23.5	Chestnut Ridge Trail leaves right, stay left, westerly, easy hiking ahead, working along Plateau rim with feeder branches of No Business Creek crossing trail
28.8	Descend long wood stairwell to pass 18-foot wet weather waterfall and walkway along bluff; more seasonal waterfalls ahead
30.2	Reach and cross gravel Divide Road, descend through hardwoods

30.6	Bridge Massey Branch, Rock Creek Loop heads left, stay right with JMT on old railroad grade, enter gorge with rockhouses and cliffs
30.8	Pass 16-foot Massey Branch Falls on right; huge rockhouse below falls
31.8	Drop right off railroad grade to reach intersection, stay left with JMT up Rock Creek, begin rolling through bouldery hills alternating with wooded flats
31.9	Campsite in flat, pick up railroad grade again, lose it again, beech trees galore
32.8	Campsite directly beside Rock Creek in big flat
33.2	Campsite, continue up remote gorgeous valley replete with geological wonder
35.0	Campsite in flat beside trail on right
35.2	Pass partly embedded old rails, Rock Creek Loop enters on left, Stay right with JMT as it crosses Rock Creek at a curve; sure-fire ford, keep upstream along the right bank of Rock Creek, navigating washed out trail sections, gorgeous valley
35.4	Confluence of Rock Creek and Thompson Branch, old trail once went left here, now abandoned; keep straight along blue-green Rock Creek below ever-present clifflines
36.3	Ford Rock Creek, small campsite. Here, climb then split right with Tunnel Trail, ascending from Rock Creek as JMT goes left through old railroad tunnel, pass column arches
36.7	Meet Hidden Passage Trail, head left, descend to cross creek just upstream of difficult-to-see waterfall, walk along sheer cliffline
37.8	Reach doubletrack ranger road and Thompson Overlook just ahead, views, keep along cliffline of Thompson Overlook ignoring ranger road
38.1	Pass .6 mile spur trail left to Double Falls, good campsite near falls, rockhouses ahead
39.5	View, pass under powerlines, continue in young fire affected woods, more rockhouses, Cumberland sandwort habitat
41.5	Spur leads left to base of 35-foot Crystal Falls, first a slide then veil drop; just ahead cut under rockhouse, making the Hidden Passage that is technically an arch; ahead stay left as other end of Hidden Passage Loop comes in from the right
42.3	Reach TN 154 trailhead after staying right, as side trail goes left into Pickett State Park network. Walk south along paved TN 154

42.6	Turn left on Watson Branch Road, just across from Pickett State Park office. Watson Branch Road quickly becomes gravel. Cross shallow Watson Branch (no bridge)
43.8	Reach gravel Divide Road. Turn right, southbound on ridge-running road
44.7	Left on Fork Ridge Road
45.5	Pass Middle Creek equestrian trailhead. Keep straight, now on Fork Ridge Road and Trail, open to bicyclers, equestrians, hikers and vehicles.
46.0	Pass Sawmill trailhead after passing Slave Falls Loop
46.5	Pass another leg of Slave Falls Loop, then pass Yellow Cliff Trail entering on right
47.1	Leave right on doubletrack Salt Pine Ridge Trail, can have muddy segments
48.5	Top out on a knob, slowly descend
49.7	Reach Laurel Fork. Left on Laurel Fork Trail, campsites ahead
50.1	Ford Laurel Fork, join hiker-only West Entrance Trail after ford, climb
51.7	Cross paved West Bandy Creek Road at West Entrance trailhead, join Collier Ridge Trail/West Entrance Trail, eastbound
52.2	Collier Ridge Trail splits, stay left with West Entrance Trail
52.5	Split right with hiker-only West Entrance Trail, descend to tributary of Bandy Creek, enter and exit Scott State Forest
53.9	Cross Collier Ridge Trail
54.1	Blevins Farm Loop goes left; we turn right to bridge Bandy Creek, campsite on right just beyond bridge over Bandy Creek, climb past rockhouse up Muleshoe Hollow
54.7	Pass 12 foot Muleshoe Hollow Falls on right while climbing steps
54.7	Blevins Farm Loop goes left, stay right on West Entrance Trail, cross a horse trail
55.1	Emerge near large parking area with a house-looking bathroom. Head toward the bathroom and keep east crossing field toward pool parking area
55.3	Reach pool parking area, completing the backpack

NIGHT HIKING IS A VIABLE OPTION

A gust of wind blustered through Laurel Fork valley as I sat before the flickering flames of the evening fire. Fallen leaves scattered across my Big South Fork campsite. Concerned about a change in already sullen early winter skies, I turned on my weather radio. It predicted showers moving in around daybreak. I was hiking out the next day and amended my plan in order to beat the rain back to the car.

The new plan: night hiking. Yep, walking in the dark, strolling under the stars, trudging in the blackness. I broke camp at 5 a.m., strapped on my pack and logged over 3 miles before dawn lightened the skies, making the trailhead just as heavy rain reached my neck of the woods.

As fall progresses and winter approaches we have fewer hours of daylight. Hikers should consider adapting to increased darkness. Using the hours after sunset or before sunrise for backpacking in Tennessee can make more trips happen. And isn't that what it's all about—making trips happen? On the above example I used night hiking simply to escape inclement weather. Consider adding night hiking to your backpacking arsenal.

Most night hiking is done after sunset, rather than before sunrise. Most night hiking is done on Friday evenings, when just-off-work backpackers race to the wilderness, hike to a given point and set up camp under cover of darkness. Even if you have the car packed, the pack loaded, and the grub bought, it's just hard to get out of work and to your destination before the sun drops in winter. There's the invariable last minute stop, the wrong turn and your sidekick being late again.

So what are the advantages of a night hiking? First, you can simply travel when you want 24 hours a day, even if getting a late start, avoiding a rainstorm or covering more miles than there is daylight. Night hiking presents a completely different experience—an often eerie one. Your auditory senses rise. Every sound of the woodlands seems amplified and takes on more meaning. Was that crack of a breaking stick or a bear coming? Was that rushing sound moving water or an unseen stranger talking? Is that loud splash a beaver or someone coming to get you?

Since your range of light is limited you more closely notice that which is near—the shape of the rocks on the trail, tree limbs reaching for your pack, or that pair of eyes reflecting just beyond.

Night hiking has plenty of disadvantages. First, you simply can't see as much of what you came to see. Also, you may miss landmarks, campsites or trail junctions. Furthermore, there is simply an increased risk of taking a spill.

Travel by night has a way of seeming slow. Maybe because can't tell where you are most of the time. When embarking on your first night hike, go somewhere with which you are already familiar. Get the feel of what it is like without bad consequences. Avoid rain and fog if you can. And make absolutely sure you have fresh batteries in your headlamp. In the final benefit vs. risk analysis, I will continue to use night hiking to enjoy more trails that lace the Volunteer State, especially in fall and winter.

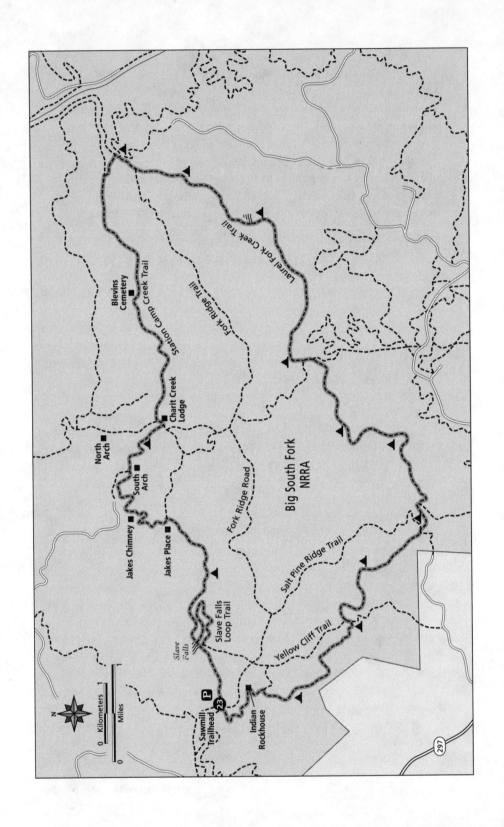

N

0   Kilometers   1

0   Miles

Sawmill
Trailhead

Slave
Falls

Slave Falls
Loop Trail

Indian
Rockhouse

Jakes Chimney ■

Jakes Place ■

South
Arch ■

North ■
Arch

Charit Creek
Lodge

Station Camp Creek Trail

Blevins ■
Cemetery

Fork Ridge Trail

Fork Ridge Road

Laurel Fork Creek Trail

Big South Fork
NRRA

Salt Pine Ridge Trail

Yellow Cliff Trail

P

23

297

23

Twin Arches Backpack

THE BACKPACK

This backpack combines incredible geology, attractive waterways and history on one fine loop at the Big South Fork NRRA. Leave Sawmill trailhead, descending to view Needle Arch then Slave Falls before reaching the homestead of Jakes Place. From there, climb to massive Twin Arches, the biggest pair of natural spans in the East, then drop to Charit Creek Lodge, offering rustic overnight lodgings. Push down Charit Creek before turning up Laurel Fork, with its unending splendor in a deep valley primeval. Follow the stream 10 miles toward its headwaters to visit regal Indian Rockhouse before returning to the trailhead. Campsites are plentiful plus most of the trails here are hiker only.

Distance and Configuration: 21.7-mile loop
Difficulty: Difficult, does have numerous fords last 8 miles
Outstanding Features: Twin Arches, Needle Arch, Slave Falls, Laurel Fork Creek
Elevation: 1,575 high point, 850 low point
Scenery: 5
Solitude: 3 (Twin Arches area can be busy)
Family Friendly: 2-3
Canine Friendly: 2
Fees/permits: Fee based permit required
Best season: Year-round, summer can be hot
Maps: National Geographic #241 Big South Fork National River and Recreation Area
For more info: Big South Fork National River and Recreation Area, 4564 Leatherwood Road, Oneida, TN 37841; 423-286-7275; www.nps.gov/biso
Finding the Trailhead: From Jamestown, take US 127 north for 2 miles to TN 154. Turn right on TN 154 north and follow it for 10.1 miles to Divide Road. Turn right on Divide Road and follow it for

1.0 miles to the signed right turn for Middle Creek trailhead and Charit Creek. Follow this road for 0.6 mile reaching the Middle Creek equestrian trailhead. Keep straight, joining the Fork Ridge Road and Trail for .5 mile farther to the Sawmill trailhead, on your left. GPS trailhead coordinates: 36.526522, -84.779386

If you like rich geology, attractive streams and an opportunity to overnight in a backcountry lodge, this is your backpack. Even if a backcountry lodge holds no interest for you, this circuit presents plenty of campsites for a 2-3 night backpack. And the Twin Arches are a Tennessee marvel with bragging rights as the largest pair of natural arches in the East. Make sure and factor in the fords on this backpack. The first 13.8 miles you can keep your feet dry but the upper segment of Laurel Fork necessitates over a dozen fords. All but two of the fords can be avoided at the expense of missing the scenery and solitude of upper Laurel Fork by using the Black House Branch Trail and Fork Ridge Road and Trail on the final leg of the backpack.

This backpack takes you by Needle Arch.

The overnight adventure starts by leaving Sawmill Trailhead on the Slave Falls Loop Trail, briefly paralleling the entrance road before coming to the loop portion of the Slave Falls Loop, heading right, east, toward Slave Falls. Enter a draw and by 0.9 mile you are on the rim above Slave Falls, but can only hear the cataract, not see it. At 1.0 mile, keep straight toward Needle Arch, as the Slave Falls Loop heads right. Just ahead, a spur leads left .2 mile to Slave Falls but hold your fire and keep straight again toward Needle Arch. At 1.2 miles you will reach Needle Arch, the astounding, delicate stone span measuring 35 feet long, formed when a rock shelter behind it collapsed.

From Needle Arch the trail curves into the Mill Creek watershed, passing a rockhouse with a chimney hole before crossing the stream of Slave Falls at 1.8 miles. Quickly reach an intersection and head left 0.2 mile via switchbacks for a view of the cataract as it makes a 70-foot dive from an overhanging cavernous ledge. Backtrack, then head down Mill Creek on the singletrack Slave Falls-to-Charit Creek Trail, officially inside the Twin Arches State Natural Area in rich evergreen woods mixed with beech and tulip trees. At 3.0 miles, pass a large streamside campsite, then quickly pass a second smaller site.

The valley widens. Boardwalks get you over mucky spots. Bridge Middle Creek to reach Jakes Place and a trail intersection at 3.9 miles. This is a popular camping spot, in broken woods dominated by cedar beside a growing over field, nearby which the crumbled remains of Jake Blevins chimney stand. Several streams come together in these flats. Our backpack heads left toward the Twin Arches, on the Twin Arches Loop Trail. Cross Andy Creek then climb by switchbacks into mesic woods rich in mountain laurel and oaks. At 4.8 miles, come along a rockhouse where you may spot a circular hole in the roof known as Jakes Chimney. Ahead, pass a colossal cliffline with monumental rockhouses, another reason why this is a designated state natural area.

Reach North Arch, the first of the Twin Arches, at 5.5 miles. It is 62 feet high with span of 93 feet. A spur trail goes left to the Twin Arches Road parking lot and another path to the top of the arch but we keep toward Charit Creek Lodge and soon reach the spur to the South Arch. The official figure states, "The South Arch is the tallest at 103 feet high. It has a clearance inside the arch of 70 feet and its span is 135 feet between the inside base of the feet." Wow. From here, stay with the Twin Arches Loop Trail, descending in long switchbacks to reach Charit Creek and a decent campsite at 6.4 miles.

Pop out at Charit Creek Lodge at 6.7 miles. The retreat offers varied services from private cabins to bunkhouses with meals to showers. Please visit their website at www.ccl-bsf.com for the latest information. Here, you head left past the lodge and the Charit Creek Lodge Connector on a gravel doubletrack that is the Station Camp Creek Trail, a wide path shared with equestrians loping along the north side of Station Camp Creek. The walking is easy while keeping east

The Big South Fork is known for its trailside clifflines.

toward the Big South Fork River. At times the trail nears clear and inviting Station Camp Creek. At 8.3 miles, a short spur heads left to the Blevins Cemetery, where Tennessee pioneer Jonathan Blevins (1780-1863) is buried. He was one of the first, if not the first, white settler to farm what is now the Big South Fork National River and Recreation Area.

The creek and valley widen. At 9.9 miles, reach an intersection. Here, head right toward Bandy Creek Campground, fording Station Camp Creek (though you can use a hiker bridge over Station Camp Creek by going straight here, then curving back up Station Camp Creek). At 10.0 miles come to Laurel Fork and the Laurel Fork Creek Trail in a sandy, muddy, riparian area. Head right here on the Laurel Fork Trail, passing the hiker bridge over Laurel Fork, on the other side of which stands a heavily used campsite. The track is wide, passing through bottoms, until 10.3 miles, where the Fork Ridge Trail rises right while the hiker-only Laurel Fork Trail keeps straight, bisecting a horse-blocking fence. Rise well above the creek in beech, holly, tulip and cedar trees, as beaver-dammed ponds form in spots below.

The North Arch of the Twin Arches.

At 10.8 miles, a spur drops left to the creek and a streamside campsite. The stream is gorgeous, with big boulders, pools, and white rapids. At 11.8 miles, a roaring cascade can be heard from the trail as Laurel Fork crashes through a boulder garden. At 12.0 miles, find a recommended campsite below the trail left, facing a massive boulder. A huge swimming pool lies below the campsite. Ahead, the Laurel Fork Trail shortcuts a stream bend then heads more westerly, winding through wooded boulder fields, encountering more and more evergreen thickets. At 13.8 miles, come to your first inevitable ford. Enter a wooded flat and a pair of good campsites before fording the stream a second time at 13.9 miles.

Meet the Black House Branch Trail at 14.0 miles. Stay left up the creek then come to another intersection, as Jacks Ridge Loop fords Laurel Fork, while you resume a hiker-only portion of the Laurel Fork Creek Trail, entering regal forests with big beech trees rising skyward. The stream is less raucous here, with many a bend and frequent sandbars, as well as frequent fords. At 15.8 miles, ford over to the right hand bank and come to a campsite. Continue frequent wet crossings. At 16.8 miles, the signed West Entrance Trail climbs left while you stay right, making yet another ford, passing a campsite in the evergreen rich flats ahead.

At 17.1 miles, meet the Salt Pine Ridge Trail, dropping sharply. Head left here, fording Laurel Fork with the horse trail, and then split right ahead as the Laurel Fork Creek Trail once again becomes hiker only, though this segment illegally used by horseback riders, mucking up the track in places. Stream crossings continue repeatedly as you work up the striking valley, the most scenic stream in the Big South Fork NRRA. Laurel Fork continues to get smaller as it loses tributaries, since we are heading upstream.

Reach another campsite after fording to the right hand bank at 18.0 miles. Wind through a curving section of the stream then meet the Yellow Cliff Trail at 18.9 miles. Head to and ford Laurel Fork yet again, coming to a good campsite and trail intersection. Here the Yellow Cliff Trail leaves south, straight, while the Laurel Fork Creek Trail keeps right, passing around a fence to continue the upstream sojourn, continuing the frequent stream crossings. At 20.2 miles, the trail fords to the right hand bank and comes to a campsite, the final one along the stream. Here, the Laurel Fork Creek Trail crosses Ben Creek then climbs, including a segment with carved stone steps to make a trail intersection at 20.7 miles. Here, head left with the Slave Falls Loop Trail, cruising hardwood dominated uplands, passing a final geological feature, big Indian Rockhouse (There are several Indian Rockhouses along Tennessee's Cumberland Plateau) at 20.9 miles. Ahead, stay right at a junction as the Middle Creek Trail leaves left then you return to the Sawmill trailhead at 21.7 miles, completing the backpack.

Mileages

0.0	Sawmill trailhead
1.2	Needle Arch
1.8	Left on 2nd spur to Slave Falls, backtrack
3.0	Campsites on Charit Creek
3.9	Jakes Place, campsite
5.5	First of the Twin Arches
6.4	Campsite
6.7	Charit Creek Lodge, left on Station Camp Creek Trail
8.3	Left spur to Blevins Cemetery
9.9	Right toward Laurel Fork
10.0	Campsite on other side of hiker bridge on Laurel Fork
10.3	Fork Ridge Trail leaves right
10.8	Left spur to streamside campsite
12.0	Recommended campsite by huge boulder
13.8	First inevitable ford, campsites .1 mile ahead

14.0	Black House Branch Trail leaves right, ahead Jacks Ridge Loop leaves left
15.8	Campsite after ford to right bank
16.8	West Entrance Trail leaves left, ford, campsite ahead
17.1	Meet Salt Pine Ridge Trail, ford left, then right again up Laurel Fork
18.0	Campsite after ford to right bank
18.9	Meet Yellow Cliff Trail, ford, campsite
20.2	Last campsite after ford to right bank
20.7	Left on Slave Falls Trail, Indian Rockhouse ahead
21.7	Return to Sawmill trailhead, completing the backpack

East Tennessee and
the Appalachian Mountains

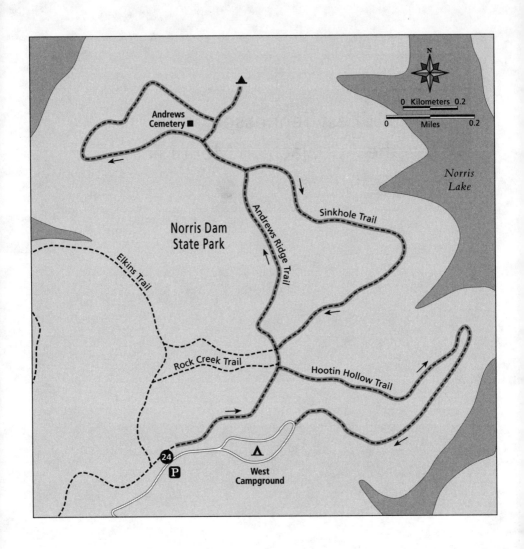

Andrews Cemetery

Norris Dam State Park

Norris Lake

Andrews Ridge Trail

Sinkhole Trail

Elkins Trail

Rock Creek Trail

Hootin Hollow Trail

24

West Campground

24

Norris Dam Backpack

THE BACKPACK

This easy yet rewarding overnighter explores a once populated ridgeline near Norris Lake. The Andrews Ridge Trail traces old roads, rolls under hardwoods, and passes homesites before reaching a designated backcountry campsite. Your return route takes the Sinkhole Trail and Hootin Holler Trail, adding new mileage and scenery.

Distance and Configuration: 4.4-mile triple loop
Difficulty: Easy
Outstanding Features: Historic trails, easy trek, good family trip
Elevation: 1,429 feet high point, 1210 feet low point
Scenery: 3
Solitude: 3
Family Friendly: 5
Canine Friendly: 5
Fees/permits: Fee-based reservable campsite permit required
Best season: Early fall through late spring
Maps: Norris Dam State Park
For more info: Norris Dam State Park, 125 Village Green Circle, Rocky Top, TN 37769, 865-425-4500, www.tnstateparks.com
Finding the Trailhead: From Exit 128, Lake City, on I-75, take US 441 south for 2.8 miles to the entrance of Norris Dam State Park. Turn left into the entrance and follow it for 0.3 mile and a road split. Head left for the West Campground and hiking trails. Drive for 1.3 miles to campground entrance station with across from an RV dump station. There are several parking spots here. Please do not block the dump station road. GPS trailhead coordinates: 36.241599, -84.124048

Backpacker checking out the Andrews Cemetery.

Looking for a fun and easy initiation trip for the newbie backpacker? Look no further, for Norris Dam State Park offers a short but satisfying trek to a designated backcountry campsite. There's only one catch—you must tote your own water from the trailhead to the camp. But it is less than two miles to your overnight destination, with only moderate hills to surmount.

Before TVA came to this part of East Tennessee, the Andrews clan and neighbors carved out a subsistence existence in the hillers and hollers of the Clinch River valley. The land eventually became part of Norris Dam State Park. The area of our hike—Andrews Ridge—is bordered on three sides by the Cove Creek arm of Norris Lake. What once were fields, gardens, and pasture have now reverted to towering hardwoods of maple, beech and tulip trees rising above wildflowers. Yet, relics remain, including the Andrews Cemetery, home foundations, bricks, and metal scraps, adding a historic bent to the trek. The campsite isn't bad either. Two sites are set on a flat part of the ridge, denoted simply with fire rings.

After parking near the West Campground's RV dump station, join the double-track Andrews Ridge Trail, northeast, as the Chuckamore Trail heads southwest. The walking is easy. Drop to a gap at 0.4 mile. Here, the Hootin Hollow Trail leaves right—your return route. For now, pass two arms of the Rock Creek Trail

At the backcountry campsite.

and the Sinkhole Trail, while rising on a south face of Andrews Ridge where sourwood, sassafras, dogwood and black gum flourish. At 0.8 mile, meet the other end of the Sinkhole Trail. For now keep straight, still on Andrews Ridge Trail, passing a large sinkhole to your right At 1.0 mile, reach the loop part of the Andrews Ridge Trail. Note foundations of a homesite here to the right of the intersection. Stay left here and ahead you will find the small Andrews Cemetery, just on the east side of a hill, where exotic periwinkle covers the ground. Continue circling around the relatively flat ridgetop, from which the land drops 300 feet down to Norris Lake, visible through the trees, especially in leafless winter.

At 1.7 miles, come to the backcountry campsite spur trail. Head left here and quickly drop to the main campsite, set in a hardwood shaded gap with a fire ring. The other campsite is about 30 yards north, to the right of the continuation of the backcountry campsite access trail, which eventually peters out. Remember, no water is available at the campsite; you must bring your own.

After camping out, continue your circuit back to the trailhead by finishing the loop portion of the Andrews Ridge Trail. Backtrack to meet the Sinkhole Trail at 2.1 miles. Here, dip to a flat then cruise with the contours, where the land dives toward Norris Lake. At 3.0 miles, return to the gap where many trails converge. Backtrack south then head left on the Hootin Holler Trail. It takes you out a ridge to reveal more lake views before rising to reach the state park's West Campground near campsite #26 at 4.1 miles. Join the paved campground road, touring the auto-accessible campsites to return to the trailhead at 4.4 miles, completing the backpack.

Mileages
0.0	Trailhead
0.4	Multiple trail junction
0.9	Loop portion of Andrews Ridge Trail
1.7	Backcountry campsite spur, backcountry campsite
2.1	Left on Sinkhole Trail
3.0	Left on Hootin Holler Trail
4.4	Trailhead

BACKPACKERS HAVE FOOD CHOICES

Inquisitive outdoor enthusiasts often ask me, "What do you eat while backpacking?" The answer: "It depends." What type of trip am I going on? How long is it? I want foods to have as little water weight as possible, are packaged for travel, are nutritious (or at least filling), and easy to make. Place a grain of salt in your pack when you read this and don't blame me for food poisoning.

When I started backpacking, I tried freeze-dried meals. Generally coming in foil pouches to which you add boiling water and wait, freeze-dried meals are tastier than they used to be, but are pricey and no fun to cook. After questioning the freeze dried status quo, I brought my indoor pantry outdoors.

First, why the paranoia on spoiled food? If it smells bad, don't eat it. Few backpacking trips last longer than a week, and most trips just a weekend. So why eat like an Appalachian Trail thru-hiker?

Breakfast. Simple Quaker oats are light and filling. Traditional long-cooking oats taste better and are more nutritious than individual packets. Raisins lend flavor and add some nutritious fruit to your wilderness diet. Other lightweight breakfasts include country ham, bagels and cream cheese. Make your own cereal and mix it with reconstituted dried milk.

The base of my lunches: flat flour tortillas. Think of tortillas as pre-smashed bread. Other packable breads include bagels, English muffins and pita bread. Add peanut butter and fruit preserves to make a roll-up sandwich. You have to work to get fruit into an outback diet. Or put in smoked oysters then add mozzarella slices to munch a nice greasy filling lunch.

To meat or not to meat? (If you are vegetarian, skip to the next paragraph.) Even on the trail, my first night's fare features heavy perishables to cook over hot coals, such as hamburgers, chicken breasts, or steak and whole baked potatoes or baked onions. Microwave the taters or onions at home, then wrap in foil after smearing them with butter and spices. Reheat in coals. If you are suspicious about meat going bad do this: Freeze it at home, wrap it in foil and it will be thawed by the time you arrive at camp.

Spam and Vienna sausages are no-brainers, so let's skip to hot dogs, kielbasa and other pre-cooked links. You would think that kielbasa and dogs are for the first or second night, but they will keep to up to a week. Salami and summer sausages are good choices that don't require refrigeration.

Cheese: My tests show that cream cheese keeps well not refrigerated. Regular cheese keeps pretty good too. It might get a little greasy or malformed in warmer weather, but it neither scares me nor makes me sick. Also consider string cheese or wax covered cheese.

Snacks: trail mix, dried fruit, nuts, or sardines. Don't forget the bars—candy, granola, nutrition or energy bars. Other standards, like jerky and dried fruit, are standards for a reason. They work. They're light.

Backpackers carry easy dinners—macaroni and cheese, instant mashed potatoes, couscous, stuffing, rice, Ramen noodles (or Remain noodles, since they remain in your pack until all else is gone). The most important thing is your backcountry experience. There's no reason you can't enjoy what you normally eat, and even look to it as a reward at the end of a hard day. After all, "an army travels on its stomach" . . . well, so does a backpacker.

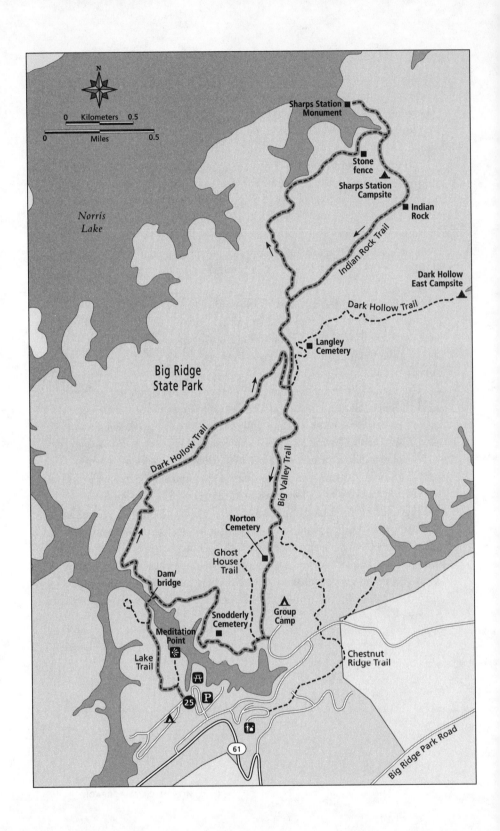

25

Big Ridge Backpack

THE BACKPACK

This overnight adventure, a great family, novice or casual backpack, explores the greater peninsula of Big Ridge State Park, passing a pair of backcountry campsites with an option for another. Walk the shores of Big Ridge Lake before reaching Dark Hollow and your first campsite. Pass old homesites then climb Big Ridge before dropping to Sharps Station and another camp. Return via Indian Rock and the Ghost House Trail, enjoying more lake views and scads of East Tennessee history.

Distance and Configuration: 9.3-mile figure-eight loop
Difficulty: Easy-moderate
Outstanding Features: Lake views, history, designated campsites
Elevation: 1,476 feet high point, 1,027 feet low point
Scenery: 3
Solitude: 3
Family Friendly: 4
Canine Friendly: 4
Fees/permits: Fee-based reservable campsite permit required
Best season: Early fall through late spring
Maps: Big Ridge State Park
For more info: Big Ridge State Park, 1015 Big Ridge Park Road, Maynardville, TN 37807, 865-992-5523, www.tnstateparks.com
Finding the Trailhead: From Knoxville, take TN 33 north to TN 61. Follow TN 61 west as it winds through hills to reach the state park after 6.3 miles to enter the state park, on your right. Enter the park and drive a short distance to turn left at the old entrance station. The park office is to your left and offers maps. Continue downhill to park near the park lake. The Lake Trail starts on the road to the campground. GPS trailhead coordinates: 36.243203, -83.931581

Toting the pack uphill on the Dark Hollow Trail.

Big Ridge State Park, developed by the Civilian Conservation Corps and set in hilly terrain of Tennessee's ridge and province country, surrounded on three sides by Norris Lake, is an often overlooked backpacking destination. Fact is, this is but one of 17 Tennessee state parks with designated backcountry campsites, yet another reason why our state is so special when it comes to backpacking opportunities. Here, you can tackle fairly easy trails yet pitch your tent at designated reservable sites. The closest campsite—Dark Hollow West—is but 1.5 miles from the trailhead.

The backpack traces what was a Union County road before Norris Lake was impounded. The old road makes for easy walking as you near several former homesites. Our chosen route then climbs over Big Ridge before dropping to Sharps Station, one of what become East Tennessee's earliest settlements, along what was the Clinch River, later dammed as Norris Lake. Explore the state park's isolated northern reaches, where Sharps Station Campsite presents another overnighting opportunity. Return past historic sites such as Indian Rock and pre-park pioneer cemeteries, as well as Big Ridge Lake. Backpackers also can opt for Dark Hollow East Campsite, on a dead end trail.

The hike starts on the Lake Trail. Climb into forest on the natural surface track, at 0.1 mile passing the spur trail to Meditation Point. Keep north under pine, hickory and oak, passing a covered bench then a spur to Loyston Overlook before descending to Big Ridge Lake and the dam/bridge dividing Big Ridge Lake from Norris Lake.

Cross the dam and reach a trail intersection at 0.6 mile. Here, head left on the singletrack Dark Hollow Trail under cedar, pine and mountain laurel, while cruising the sloped shoreline, the Bryant Fork arm of Norris Lake. Enter the embayment of Dark Hollow then bridge its sycamore-shaded stream of Dark Hollow West to arrive at Dark Hollow West Campsite at 1.5 miles. The smallish, slightly sloped site is set in a side hollow under trees. Water can be had from the stream of Dark Hollow.

From there, trace what once was a county road with homesites. Look for exotic vegetation, piled rocks, and flats while gently climbing to make a four-way trail junction at 2.6 miles. The Dark Hollow Trail continues straight, easterly, for 1.3 miles to reach Dark Hollow East Campsite. The stream of this site can run dry so make sure you have water or be prepared to make your way down to Norris Lake for aqua.

The main backpack route heads left here, northbound, joining the Big Valley Trail. The path leads through the small Langley Cemetery at 2.8 miles. Keep climbing, angling up Big Ridge in big woods to reach a trail intersection at 3.0 miles. Pick up the Indian Rock Trail as it makes a loop. Keep left here on a much fainter path, descending very sharply down Big Ridge. Trekking poles will come in handy at this juncture. Drop 400 feet in 0.4 mile, easing off in thickly wooded bottoms as you curve east. The trail comes along Norris Lake at 3.6 miles, allowing looks into the main reservoir from a cove. Travel a remote part of the park, yet formerly settled, as evidenced by a stone fence at 4.1 miles.

Reach a trail intersection at 4.3 miles. Head left here, crossing an intermittent stream just above a 7-foot wet weather waterfall, and aim for Sharps Station, one of the earliest white settlements in what became East Tennessee. Sharps Station became a backwater, then was literally flooded by Norris Lake, and now a monument stands in the state park, as well as a small obscure graveyard, in memorial. From there backtrack and continue the Indian Rock Trail as it climbs south from Norris Lake. At 5.0 miles, the rib ridge you are climbing briefly flattens out. Here you find the Sharps Station Campsite, a smallish spot underneath tall hardwoods. The mostly level spot is large enough for a fire ring and a tent, and a few backpackers. Bring your own water.

Beyond the campsite, the Indian Rock Trail makes an outrageous but short ascent to crest out on Big Ridge then reach signed Indian Rock at 5.2 miles. The rock was named for Indians who hid there while ambushing an early settler named Peter Graves who was hunting. The natives' turkey call brought in Graves

Looking out on Big Ridge Lake.

who was then murdered and scalped. Keep west, winding among trees in rock woods, undulating atop Big Ridge to complete the Indian Rock Trail loop at 5.9 miles. From here, backtrack to the Dark Hollow Trail at 6.3 miles. Here is your last chance for backcountry camping by heading 1.3 miles to Dark Hollow East campsite. Otherwise, keep straight, south, down the Big Valley Trail, crossing Pinnacle Ridge, then descending through pines to an intersection at 7.1 miles. There, head right on the Ghost House Trail. Keep left as the Ghost House Trail splits. Here, you pass a purportedly haunted homesite. Look for the root cellar, cistern—and maybe a ghost. From there, continue to the relatively large Norton Cemetery, with better tended graves, interring locals from 1907-1928.

At 7.7 miles, pass the other end of the Ghost House Trail, then split right onto the Lake Trail. Enjoy easy but sometimes mucky walking in flats near Big Ridge Lake. Pass the spur to the Snodderly Cemetery at 8.1 miles. Curve along the shore of Big Ridge Lake before reaching the dam/bridge where you were earlier at 8.7 miles. From here, it is a 0.6 mile backtrack and you complete the backpacking adventure at 9.3 miles.

Mileages

0.0	Lake Trail
0.6	Bridge/dam dividing Big Ridge Lake and Norris Lake
1.5	Dark Hollow West Campsite
3.0	Indian Rock Trail
5.0	Sharps Station Campsite
6.3	Spur 1.3 miles to Dark Hollow East Campsite
7.7	Rejoin Lake Trail
8.7	Bridge/dam dividing Big Ridge Lake and Norris Lake
9.3	Trailhead

TENT OR TARP OR UNDER THE STARS WHILE BACKPACKING?

Whenever possible I sleep out in the open, under the stars, partly because I am lazy and do not want to carry, set up or take down a tent. On short trips with a reliable weather forecast, I bring no shelter at all, saving weight and space, and get to backpack, camp—and sleep—in the great outdoors. However, on longer trips or with rain in the forecast I bring a tarp.

Nevertheless, tents are the time-honored shelter of choice for backpackers. Before pitching a tent ask yourself why are you staying in a nylon bubble? There are five primary reasons for taking a tent with you: Bugs, precipitation, cold, wind and privacy. A tent will keep the bugs out, the rain away, make it a little warmer and will block the wind.

It also allows for privacy when at crowded campsites. However, a tent is an *enclosure* that divides you from the outdoors. Why not sleep in nature if you can, under the stars? If taking a neophyte backpacker I do recommend a tent. Tents can provide mental protection as well as physical shelter for first time greenhorn campers.

Backpackers have to consider a smaller tent, sacrificing tent space for weight. Be prepared for a tight squeeze when sharing a tent that weighs under five pounds, but don't bring a heavier one since you are carrying the tent on your back. Ultralight tents cost a pretty penny, but there are also some adequately performing mid-price tents out there. Do stay away from low-end tents found at mega stores. They have questionable waterproofness, limited life span and cab be downright heavy.

Consider a tarp. Tarps can be used as your primary shelter if not in bug country. I exclusively use a tarp in the mountains of Tennessee. Today's silicon impregnated nylon tarps can be 6' x 8' and weigh as little as a pound. Larger size tarps (I use a 10' x 12' tarp) allow extra room for you and your gear. Tarps can be configured in a variety of ways. If the wind is high and rain is coming set your tarp low. Otherwise, you can set one end low with the other end a little higher, allowing you to get under the shelter more easily.

Tarps allow you to have shelter yet still enjoy nature. Tarps can also be used for sun protection when at camp. Bring plenty of cord to string up your tarp—at least 12 feet for each corner to be on the safe side, with a separate 40 foot cord to string a main line between trees.

Backpackers have a weight saving option while in places where mosquitoes can be a problem: a tarp and bug screen combination. A single person bug screen weighs mere ounces. Add an ultra lightweight tarp. This entire setup is very small, packable and can weigh less than 1.5 pounds. If there is no rain set up the bug screen by itself. If rain is a possibility set up the bug screen under the tarp.

Next time you are considering your backpacking shelter think outside the tent.

26

Big Frog Wilderness

THE BACKPACK

This exciting backpack takes place in the extreme southeast corner of Tennessee, within the 8,000-plus acres of the Big Frog Wilderness. Make your way to the top of Big Frog Mountain via West Fork Rough Creek and Fork Ridge. Revel in this westernmost peak above 4,000 feet in the Southern Appalachians before looping back to the trailhead on Wolf Ridge and the seldom trod Grassy Gap Trail. Overall, campsites are abundant and the trails better maintained than most wilderness trails of the Cherokee National Forest.

Distance and Configuration: 17.9-mile balloon loop
Difficulty: Moderate-difficult due to distance
Outstanding Features: Big Frog Mountain, views, cascades
Elevation: 1,630 feet low point, 4,224 feet high point
Scenery: 4
Solitude: 4, 3 atop Big Frog Mountain
Family Friendly: 1
Canine Friendly: 3
Fees/permits: No fees or permits required
Best season: Early fall through late spring
Maps: National Geographic #781 Tellico and Ocoee Rivers, Cherokee National Forest
For more info: Cherokee National Forest, Cherokee National Forest, Ocoee Ranger District, 3171 Highway 64, Benton TN 37307, (423) 338-3300, www.fs.usda.gov/cherokee
Finding the Trailhead: From the junction of US 64 and US 64 Bypass, just east of Cleveland, Tennessee, take US 64 east for 26 miles to the right turn at Ocoee Dam #3 and Thunder Rock Campground. Turn right and cross the dam, immediately passing Thunder Rock Campground. Join gravel Forest Road 45 and follow it for 2.7 miles

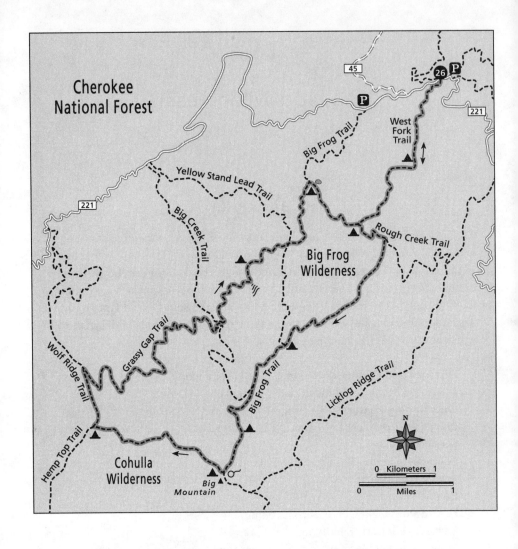

to Forest Road 221. Turn left on FR 221 and follow it for 0.4 mile to the signed West Fork Trail, on your right. Parking is limited to the shoulder here, where you will also see the Chestnut Mountain Trail and the Quartzite Loop Trail, both mountain biking trails. GPS trailhead coordinates: 35.059306, -84.487556

The top of Big Frog Mountain should be a part of every backpack in this wilderness. Linked to the Cohutta Wilderness to the south (You will straddle the two wild areas on this backpack), Big Frog and Cohutta create a contiguous federally designated wilderness of over 35,000 acres, the largest in the Southern Appalachians. Most of the Cohutta is in Georgia. Additionally, Big Frog Mountain owns the superlative of being the westernmost peak above 4,000 feet in the entire Appalachian range. In fact, you have to travel west to far western Oklahoma to reach the next high point above 4,000 feet.

Campsite atop Big Frog Mountain.

And you can camp atop Big Frog, with level sites and a fine spring nearby. Backpackers in the wilderness have many other sites from which to choose. I hazard against coming here in summer, as most trails will be overgrown. Our adventure starts north of Big Frog Mountain on FR 221 and the West Fork Trail. The Benton MacKaye Trail runs in conjunction with the initial part of the backpack all the way to Big Frog. Join West Fork Trail heading south, tracing an old forest road in pine, oak, mountain laurel woods with above average numbers of magnolia. At 0.5 mile, the trail cuts through a gap then becomes a singletrack path diving into a hollow parallel to a rhododendron-choked tributary of West Fork. At 1.0 mile, reach West Fork and an old forest road then turn right up the valley, officially entering the Big Frog Wilderness. West Fork tumbles to your left. At 1.1 miles, a spur trail leads left to a streamside flat and campsite. Continue up the valley on an easy track, despite fallen hemlocks as the woods transition away from this diseased evergreen that once dominated moist creekside woods such as this.

At 1.6 miles, step over a tributary then immediately cross West Fork at an old bridge site. Head up the left bank to cross the stream again at 1.7 miles. Depending on time of year these may be rock hops or fords. Continue upstream to meet the Rough Creek Trail at 2.3 miles. West Fork Trail ends here. Your return route comes in from the right. We stay straight on the Rough Creek Trail, passing a small campsite before crossing West Fork a final time. Climb a side hollow along a small feeder branch before leveling out on Fork Ridge at 2.8 miles. Here, the Rough Creek Trail plummets into East Fork but we head right, rising on the Fork Ridge Trail in pine, oak and sassafras with an understory of blueberry. The singletrack path is well graded and not too taxing. Licklog Ridge stands out to the east, across the gulf of East Fork Rough Creek.

At 3.8 miles, reach the crest of Fork Ridge. Continue a steady but moderate uptick, alternating with the side of the ridge and the ridgetop. At 4.7 miles, intersect and join the well-used Big Frog Trail. Keep straight here, still ascending on a sometimes slender ridgeline. At 4.8 miles, pass a small, level trailside campsite. At 5.4 miles on a slender part of the ridge, the often-bypassed Big Creek Trail leaves right. It is marked with a pair of rock cairns. We stay straight with the Big Frog Trail as it soon burrows through a rhododendron tunnel while working around a knob. The trees up here are showing effects of elevation and winds, with their wind pruned branches. At 6.1 miles, pass a large flat campsite under stunted hardwoods. Note the cool climate specialist yellow birch.

Continuing on you reach Big Frog, a trail intersection and campsite at 6.7 miles. A short trail goes acutely right a short distance to the summit and another campsite where a fire tower once stood. A reliable spring awaits about 60 yards down the Licklog Ridge Trail. This is a spot to linger or camp. Winter views are numerous in all directions.

The backpack continues by heading west on the Hemp Top Trail, where the ridge becomes narrow and rocky before widening out. The path straddles the Cohutta Wilderness to the left and the Big Frog Wilderness Trail to the right. At 8.4 miles, come to a campsite and a hard-to-find trail intersection in a narrow flat. Here are the intersection coordinates: 35.007000, -84.554000. At this point, the Wolf Ridge Trail cuts acutely right as a slender track, while the Hemp Top Trail keeps straight, aiming 1.9 miles for FR 62. Head northeast on the Wolf Ridge Trail and gain the ridgecrest, descending through pines and oaks to reach Grassy Gap at 9.0 miles. Here, the Wolf Ridge Trail keeps straight while our loop heads right on the Grassy Gap Trail. This historic contoured trail was built by the Civilian Conservation Corps back in the 1930s.

For the next almost 5 miles, the trail never strays more than 150 feet in elevation from the 2,350 feet mark, winding in and out of smallish drainages, divided by rib ridges running down Big Frog Mountain. The footbed is very narrow. Rock hop rocky Peter Camp Branch at 9.9 miles. Ahead, cross a couple of sloped, wet rock slabs—watch your footing—before rock hopping Penitentiary Branch at 10.5 miles. Circle in and out of hollows before crossing Big Creek at 12.0 miles. Continue northeast until reaching a tributary of Big Creek and meeting the Big Creek Trail, marked by rock cairns, at 12.2 miles. You can go left down the Big Creek Trail to flatter terrain and potential campsites.

Keep straight on the Grassy Gap Trail, crossing the tributary of Big Creek. Continue the hollow/rib ridge pattern, coming to a desiccated hollow at 13.0 miles, where a curtain-style waterfall tumbles below the trail about 10 feet, then follows with a 35 foot plunge. This seasonal cataract is very difficult to access due to steep terrain. At 13.3 miles, a campsite can be found to the left of the trail in pines. A little more hiking leads you to Low Gap and an intersection at 13.8 miles. Here, the Yellow Stand Lead Trail leaves left while we stay straight with the Big Frog Trail. The well-maintained track is almost level and very easy. At 14.8 miles, come to yet another trail junction. Here, we join the Rough Creek Trail splitting right. A campsite lies nearby. Just ahead pass a pond dug in the 1970s to access water for helicopter firefighting. The Rough Creek Trail descends easterly in pine/oak/mountain laurel woods. West Fork is soon singing in your ears and at 15.6 miles you reach the stream and the West Fork Trail. From here it is a 2.3 mile backtrack to complete the backpacking adventure.

Mileages

0.0	West Fork/Benton MacKaye trailhead
1.0	Reach West Fork Rough Creek
1.1	Campsite in flat to left of trail
1.6	First of two consecutive West Fork crossings
2.3	Meet Rough Creek Trail, cross West Fork

2.8	Right on Fork Ridge Trail
4.7	Straight on Big Frog Trail, campsite ahead
5.4	Big Creek Trail drops right
6.1	Dry campsite in large flat
6.7	Big Frog summit, campsite, spring nearby, join Hemp Top Trail
8.4	Campsite, right on Wolf Ridge Trail
9.0	Grassy Gap, right on Grassy Gap Trail
12.2	Intersect middle of Big Creek Trail
13.0	Wet weather waterfall below trail
13.3	Dry campsite to left of trail
13.8	Join Big Frog Trail
14.8	Right on Rough Creek Trail, campsite, pond
15.6	Left on West Fork Trail, backtrack
17.9	West Fork trailhead

27

Upper Bald River Wilderness

THE BACKPACK

This overnight circuit backpack explores one of Tennessee's newer wilderness lands on a classic loop that includes mountains and waters high and low. Follow scenic Bald River past a striking falls before turning up wildflower rich Brookshire Creek. Traverse a remote section of the state line using the Benton MacKaye Trail (BMT) before descending to the archetypal mountain stream of Kirkland Creek. Trail grades are relatively moderate and campsites are more than adequate.

Distance and Configuration: 17.4-mile loop
Difficulty: Moderate, does have many fords
Outstanding Features: Upper Bald River Falls, newer wilderness area
Elevation: 2,123 feet low point, 4,031 feet high point
Scenery: 4
Solitude: 4
Family Friendly: 2
Canine Friendly: 3
Fees/permits: No fees or permits required
Best season: Mid-March through May, September through November
Maps: National Geographic #781 Tellico and Ocoee Rivers, Cherokee National Forest
For more info: Cherokee National Forest, Tellico Ranger District, 250 Ranger Station Road, Tellico Plains TN 37385, (423) 397-8455, www.fs.usda.gov/cherokee
Finding the Trailhead: From Tellico Plains, drive east on TN 165, Cherohala Skyway, for 5.3 miles. Turn right on paved Forest Road 210. Follow it for 13.9 miles to Forest Road 126, located just past Sourwood Campground. Turn right on gravel Forest Road 126 and follow it for 5.1 miles to the Brookshire Creek trailhead on your left, at Bald River Camping Area #11. If you reach Holly Flats Campground, you have gone too far. GPS trailhead coordinates: 35°17'03.6"N 84°09'59.3"W

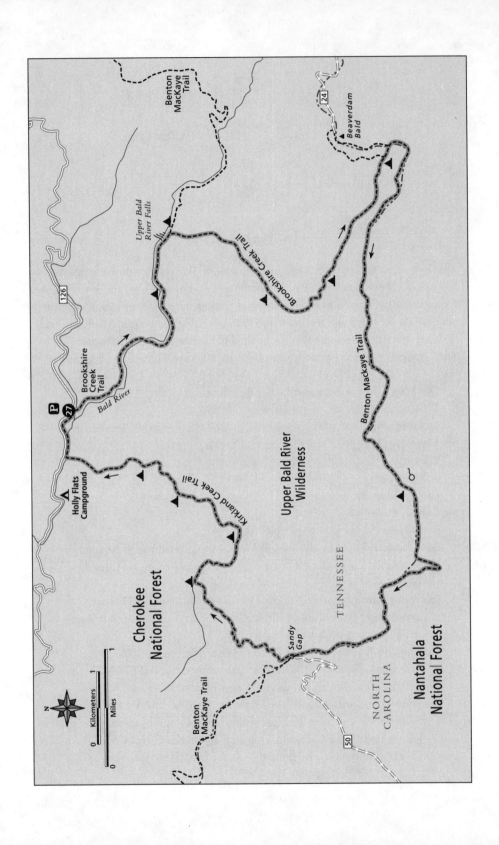

This backpack takes you by Upper Bald River Falls.

If you are looking for a good introductory wilderness backpacking trip, this is it. Upper Bald River Wilderness, 9,038 acres, was established in 2018, and is the newest federally designated untamed area in Tennessee. Deserving of its status, this Cherokee National Forest watershed harbors native brook trout, a host of wildflowers and clear, clean highland waters flowing off the Unicoi Mountains, forming the divide between Tennessee and North Carolina. The trails are in pretty good shape for a Cherokee National Forest wilderness. Kirkland Creek and Brookshire Creek Trails, divided by Indian Ridge, have been enjoyed by anglers and outdoor enthusiasts for generations. Today, the Benton MacKaye Trail links the two trails. The whole package forms a recommended 2-3 night circuit, especially if you like to fish or linger at camp. Wear long pant in summer, as the trails can become briery. Over a dozen creek crossings, especially along Kirkland Creek, make it an unwise winter choice, better for late spring and early autumn.

Holly Flats Campground and a dispersed trailhead campsite make ideal night-before-the-backpack camping. The backpack leaves Bald River Camping Area

Painted trillium graces Brookshire Creek flats.

#11 on the Brookshire Creek Trail #180, to immediately cross Henderson Branch, usually a rock hop. Begin tracing an old logging grade under black birch, pine, oaks and doghobble, moderately rising alongside the Bald River, flowing 15-20 feet wide to your right. Look for old railroad ties in mucky areas. At 1.1 miles, come to a crossing of Bald River. There has been a log bridge here in the past and may be one in the future. If not, it is an easy wade.

You are now on the right bank. At 1.4 miles, bridge Service Branch by culvert. At 1.8 miles pass a fine campsite on your left, complete with a small, shaded but deep pool. Continue uptrail, rising gently as the stream comes in and out of view amidst rhododendron thickets. At 2.4 miles, you won't miss wide, 16-foot Upper Bald River Falls, tumbling over a ledge into a plunge pool. A short trail drops to the base of the cataract. Come to a trail intersection just ahead. Here, the Benton MacKaye Trail heads straight to a good campsite just across Brookshire Creek. Our hike heads right, up along lively Brookshire Creek. The gradient increases. Mountain flats open and close in the wildflower heavy vale. At 2.8 miles, cross over to the left hand bank of Brookshire Creek, a ford in spring and a rock hop in fall. Cove hardwoods such as buckeye, cherry and tulip trees shade the track. At 3.6 miles, a small campsite lies below the trail on an old logging grade.

Beyond the camp, the path curves through a narrow hollow where Brookshire Creek noisily drops in continuous cascades, then curves east into a perched valley, where the ascent eases. At 4.4 miles, pass a sloped campsite beside the trail. At 4.9 miles, look also to the right of the trail for a crumbled chimney of a cabin. At 5.2 miles rock hop the stream twice in succession. At 5.8 miles, come to a campsite and remains of another cabin across the now tiny creek. Check out the laid stones to prevent the stream from flooding the cabin site.

Reach a trail intersection just ahead. Here, the Brookshire Creek Trail heads left to the east shoulder of auto-accessible Beaverdam Bald, now a mown area with limited summer views. Our backpack heads straight on the Benton MacKaye Trail, rising to reach Sled Runner Gap and the North Carolina state line at 6.0 miles. Here, another trail goes left a half-mile to Beaverdam Bald. We head right, south, still on the BMT, climbing to Rocky Top (not THE Rocky Top of Tennessee Vols fame), briefly breaking the 4,000 foot barrier before turning west and running parallel to Brookshire Creek, which you can hear below. The BMT moderately undulates along the state line in hardwoods and occasional evergreen thickets.

Cross Round Top at 8.5 miles, then skirt the south side of Nit Top at 9.1 miles. Drop to reach a gap and small but attractive campsite at 9.7 miles. Here, a blue-blazed spur trail drops about 100 yards to a reliable spring on the North Carolina side. From the campsite, rise to surmount Hazelnut Knob at 10.0 miles, only to descend and switchback acutely right at Moss Gap. Continue downhill more than not, weaving through piney segments, eventually joining an old logging road as well as coming near other dirt roads accessing a private inholding. Stay with the diamond-blazed BMT.

Reach Sandy Gap at 12.4 miles. Here, Forest Road 50 drops acutely left and the BMT keeps straight, but we angle right, joining the signed Kirkland Creek Trail #180. The hiking remains easy as it cruises an old forest road, passing a headwater of Kirkland Creek at 12.6 miles. Keep north in piney woods, circling around more headwaters. Split a gap at 13.5 miles and continue on a ridge in pines before diving left from the ridge at 13.9 miles. Reach clear and fast Waucheesi Creek at 14.0 miles. A recommended, big campsite stands just across the stream. The Kirkland Creek Trail turns down Waucheesi Creek before the stream crossing, wandering amid wet weather stream braids and mucky sections amid junglesque Southern Appalachian thickets in a narrow hollow. Ahead, you will criss-cross the twisting, tumbling creek, the first of many fords. At 14.8 miles, pass a small campsite to the left of the trail.

Turn down Kirkland Creek at 14.9 miles. Begin crossing it multiple times as well, giving up any hope of keeping your feet dry. Pass a campsite at 15.6 miles just after crossing over to the left hand bank. At 16.0 miles, the trail fords Kirkland Creek at an irregular-bottomed stream section as the waterway drops in tiers. You are now on the right hand bank. At this point, the path tunnels through rhododendron.

At 16.1 miles, look left in pines and holly trees for a relatively big campsite. From here on out, the path traces the right hand bank of Kirkland Creek as the stream pours over rocks and slows in pools, aiming for Bald River. Reach Bald River and your final ford of the backpacking adventure at 16.9 miles. Once across, turn right on Forest Road 126, returning to the Brookshire Creek trailhead at 17.4 miles, completing the trip.

Mileages

0.0	Brookshire Creek trailhead
1.1	Cross Bald River
1.8	Campsite
2.4	Upper Bald River Falls
2.5	Right on Brookshire Creek Trail; campsite ahead on BMT across Brookshire Creek
3.6	Campsite on right below trail
5.8	Campsite, cabin site, straight on BMT just ahead
6.0	Sled Runner Gap, right on BMT
8.5	Round Top
9.7	Campsite in unnamed gap, side trail down to water
12.4	Sandy Gap, right on Kirkland Creek Trail
14.0	Waucheesi Creek, campsite across creek
14.8	Small campsite to left of trail, shortly turn down Kirkland Creek
15.6	Campsite just after crossing to left hand bank
16.0	Noteworthy ford, join right hand bank
16.1	Campsite in holly-pine stand
16.9	Ford Bald River, right on FR 126
17.4	Return to Brookshire Creek trailhead, completing backpack

SET UP YOUR BACKPACK CAMP LIKE HOME

Setting up a backcountry camp is like setting up your home. Think of your campsite as having a bedroom, kitchen, living room and bathroom. Each area has its own distinctive characteristics that you will be emulating.

When setting up your sleeping quarters, whether they are in the open, under a tarp or in a tent, try to find level ground that is not subject to water flow from uphill. Look on the ground where you plan to sleep. Do you see evidence of water running through that spot? If so find another location. Also look for a layer of natural duff, such as leaves or pine needles that indicates water not running through it—running water scours the ground. Duff pads your bedroom. Do not clear the ground before setting up your bedroom, but do look for sticks, rocks, and other obstructions that might interrupt your sleep. Hammock campers simply need two conveniently located trees.

If you like to cook over a fire as I do, your kitchen will be located near the fire ring. I will have my grill and stove—if I bring it—located in one general area. My food will be nearby while in camp but if I leave, it will be hung up away from critters.

Backpackers expect a spartan living room. This may merely amount to a backpack leaning against a tree with a sleeping pad to sit on. That is one of the reasons I carry a closed cell sleeping pad, because I can use it when sitting around the fire and don't have to worry about it popping as I do an air mattress.

Additional comforts will be found in your "camp furniture." Backpackers have to take what they can find in the natural surroundings for their camp furniture, though ultralight folding camp chairs are carried by backpackers these days. At already established sites, you often find a combination of logs and rocks centered on the fire ring. Sometimes, logs are placed over rocks located at either end, creating a bench of sorts.

When looking for a campsite, consider the camp furniture, not only for yourself, but also your belongings. Satellite boulders and rocks can act as tables for your cook set and other gear you might prefer not to set on the ground.

The campsite bathroom should be well away from the other parts of camp. When using the bathroom, head away from camp and away from water, then find a concealed location. Dig a hole using a stick or the heel of your shoe, preferably 6 inches deep, do your business, burn your toilet paper, and then cover it up.

Backpackers should consider whether to set up a base camp or keep moving day-to-day. A base camp frees you from the chores of setting up and breaking down camp on a daily basis, availing more free time and fewer camp chores.

The advantage of moving camp on a daily basis is that you will be setting up in new surroundings every day. This allows for convenient sightseeing from each campsite. If you are going on a long backpacking adventure, I suggest staying at one camp for two nights during the middle of the trip just to free you from the daily making/breaking camp ritual. So whether you stay one night or ten, make your backpacking camp like home.

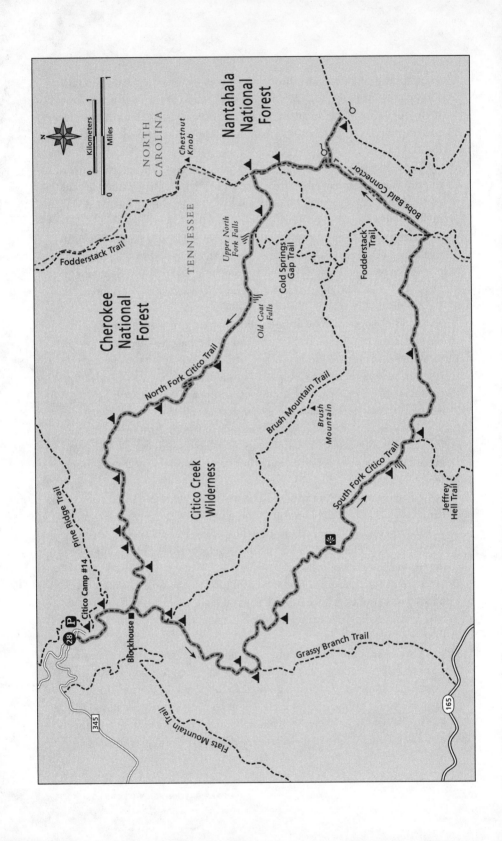

28

Citico Creek Wilderness

THE BACKPACK

This is the classic circuit backpack at one of Tennessee's premier wilderness areas. Prepare for challenge while first hiking up South Fork Citico Creek in a remote mountain valley with everywhere-you-look beauty. Join an old railroad grade then make the upper valley before climbing into the high country to Bobs Bald. From there, traverse the state line, then descend North Fork Citico Creek past waterfalls aplenty on a very rugged route that seems an obstacle course at times. Campsites are spread throughout. Be prepared for stream fords, trail navigation, a nearly 3,600 foot climb and incredible beauty exuding the very essence of Tennessee wilderness.

Distance and Configuration: 17.7-mile loop
Difficulty: Difficult due to rugged conditions and elevation change
Outstanding Features: Gorgeous streams, waterfalls,
    views from Bobs Bald
Elevation: 1,708 feet low point, 5,260 feet high point
Scenery: 5
Solitude: 3
Family Friendly: 1
Canine Friendly: 1
Fees/permits: No fees or permits required
Best season: March through October
Maps: National Geographic #781 Tellico and Ocoee Rivers,
    Cherokee National Forest
For more info: Cherokee National Forest, Tellico Ranger District,
    250 Ranger Station Road, Tellico Plains TN 37385, (423) 397-8455,
    www.fs.usda.gov/cherokee
Finding the Trailhead: From Tellico Plains, drive east on TN 165,
    Cherohala Skyway, for 14 miles to Forest Road 345 at the signed
    left turn for Indian Boundary Recreation Area. After 1.2 miles,

The South Fork Trail.

pass the turn into Indian Boundary. Stay straight as FR 345 turns to gravel. Continue for 2.5 more miles, then turn right at the concrete ford across Citico Creek as the forest road makes a hard left. This is the best parking area, though there is room for 2 cars at the actual start of the South Fork Citico Creek Trail. GPS trailhead coordinates: 35.405639, -84.079976

A backpacking adventure on the forks of Citico Creek and Bobs Bald makes for a trip to remember. The unending beauty and challenge will make an impression long after your muscles have recovered from the trek. The first part of the circuit on South Fork seems easy enough, mostly tracing an old railroad logging grade upstream before crossing the creek and climbing to a higher grade, entering a perched valley of northern hardwoods. The final 1,500 foot climb from South Fork to Bobs Bald will exercise your lungs but reward you with views from this field just over the North Carolina state line. From there, trail conditions deteriorate as you sharply descend a faint trail to drop into North Fork, where the path seems

Looking down from Bobs Bald.

more an obstacle course for Marines, testing your endurance and agility, rather than a backpacking pathway. Walk down and through creeks, above waterfalls, and in dense evergreen thickets. Waterfalls galore are part of your reward however, including crashing 40-foot Old Goat Falls. The last half of North Fork calms down, with mere straightforward stream crossings. You can make the trip in 1-3 nights, though I recommend at least 2 nights out. Multiple fords are inevitable, especially on North Fork. Trekking poles come in handy for creek crossings and balance on the irregular trail surfaces. Finally, expect to do some route finding. The trails are primitive but signed at intersections.

Start your backpack on the South Fork Citico Creek Trail #105. Hike around the vehicle barriers as the trail soon narrows, passing along a steep bluff above the creek. Descend to the scenic waterway, coming to a Citico Wilderness sign and a campsite on your left at 0.6 mile. Join an old logging railroad grade bordered with doghobble and rhododendron. Overhead rise sycamore, red maple and sweetgum.

At 0.8 mile, come to a trail intersection and a concrete building foundation, a

South Fork Citico Creek is one of Tennessee's most picturesque streams.

relic of the logging community of Jeffrey that timbered the watershed a century back. Here, your return route, the North Fork Citico Trail #98, leaves left while the backpack continues straight on the South Fork Trail, Trail #105. Walk astride the glistening, surging South Fork, challenged in beauty only by the mountain streams of the Smokies. At 1.2 miles, Ike Camp Branch enters on your left and just ahead the Brush Mountain Trail fords South Fork to reach a large campsite then continue toward the state line.

Carry on up the valley, passing a streamside campsite at 1.5 miles. Cool climate specialist yellow birch rises in the valley, even here at 2,000 feet. The stream occasionally splits around islands then merges together again. At 2.0 miles, come to an old ford. However, the trail cuts acutely right and up along a bluff, returning to the grade at 2.3 miles. Pass another campsite at 2.4 miles, then reach the big ford of South Fork over a bottom of irregular depth. Use trekking poles and acumen on the crossing. Come to a sloped campsite on the left bank just after the ford. At 2.6 miles, the signed Grassy Branch Trail leaves right up to the Cherohala Skyway.

The South Fork continues a big bend. At 3.4 miles, the trail reaches a very small campsite then abruptly climbs left uphill as a singletrack path, coming along and crossing a streamlet, then meeting a mountainside railroad grade at 3.8 miles. You just climbed 400 feet in 0.4 mile! This grade was blasted from the mountainside, leaving crumbling rocks around which to walk. Other areas are rich in viney woods, while clear tributaries dance down mountainside coves. At 4.5 miles, a brushy, viney area opens an elevated view of the watershed. Ahead, look for coils of metal cable, relics from the logging days.

By 5.3 miles, you are directly along the stream, now at 3,200 feet in northern hardwood forest of birch, cherry and maple rising above a sea of rhododendron. Look for more metal relics. At 5.7 miles, pass a sloped streamside campsite on trail right, just downstream of an 8-foot waterfall and a sizeable plunge pool. At 6.0 miles, reach a signed intersection. Here, the Jeffrey Hell Trail leaves right for the Cherohala Skyway. We stay straight on the South Fork Trail, passing a small but level campsite at 6.1 miles. This upper valley widens, feeding many tributaries into South Fork Citico Creek. At 6.8 miles, cross now small South Fork. The grade keeps arrow straight. At 7.1 miles, a spur trail drops left to a campsite in a wide valley where a logging camp once stood. Metal relics can be found hereabouts.

Uptrail, the trail leaves the grade right at 7.6 miles, beginning the mostly steep 700-foot ascent to reach Cold Springs Gap at 8.3 miles. Here, the Fodderstack Trail traces a gated gravel road right 2 miles to the Cherohala Skyway and heads left on an old roadbed towards Fodderstack Mountain. You can avoid the climb to Bobs Bald by heading north on Fodderstack Trail, but you miss the views.

I recommend taking the Bobs Bald Connector up the Tennessee-North Carolina state line on a well-used trail. Walk betwixt wind pruned yellow birch and beech trees amid upthrust rocks to make a trail intersection at 9.3 miles. You will return to this intersection to complete the circuit, but for now, make a side foray to Bobs Bald by keeping straight on the Stratton Bald Trail #54. Pass by a piped spring at 9.4 miles, continuing an uptick before topping out on Bobs Bald at 9.8 miles, an ascent of just under 3,600 feet from the trailhead. The clearing is kept open by mowing and offers views aplenty, especially to the south and east. Campsites can be found where the trees and meadows merge as well as east in a stand of planted evergreens. Another spring can be found south below the evergreens.

To continue the loop, backtrack to the Bob Bald Connector then head north, descending a much less used track along the state line, switchbacking to mitigate the steep descent. Pass some huge yellow birch trees, Fraser magnolia and other hardwoods. At 10.9 miles, reach a trail intersection and a fine, level but waterless campsite. Here the Fodderstack Trail comes in from your left. Keep straight, rolling on the stateline ridge to make Cherry Log Gap and a small, dry campsite at 11.2 miles.

Turn left on the North Fork Citico Trail #98. Get your mojo on, your navigational prowess ready and tackle the forthcoming challenge. Start with a diving descent into Tennessee, coming to tributaries feeding North Fork under hardwoods. At times you will be walking down the streambeds, not just across them. Pass a bad sloped campsite to the left of the trail at 11.7 miles. At 11.9 miles, the Cold Springs Gap Trail leaves left. We keep descending along, in, around and through braids of the North Fork.

Continue downstream, then negotiate a slick stone slab with footholds cut into it at 12.0 miles. Cross North Fork below the first of many waterfalls. At 12.1 miles, cross the creek just above 15-foot Upper North Fork Falls. Be careful! Continue criss-crossing the stream, on hints of a grade in some places and irregular footing in others. North Fork is crashing all around you in a rugged gorge. At 12.6 miles, cross over to the right bank, climb over a rock ledge then descend sharply. To your left a faint trail tunnels through rhododendron to 40-foot Old Goat Falls, a two tiered flume diving from a stone face. Don't pass it by!

The path remains steep, amid towering cliffs in a crazy rugged gorge. Tulip trees are appearing. North Fork has gained steam. At 13.2 miles, cross an unnamed but significant tributary before it flows into North Fork. Beyond here, the obstacle course eases. Join a railroad grade and at 13.4 miles, a spur trail drops from the grade to a fine campsite in the large flat below. At 13.7 miles, the trail makes a switchback, returning creekside. Squeeze past a steep hill astride the bouldery, handsome stream. At 14.3 miles, ford North Fork then reach a good campsite on the left hand bank heading downstream.

Continue downstream, negotiating places where the grade has been washed out to bedrock. Pass a decent campsite at 14.8 miles. At 15.2 miles, the trail squeezes along a bluff. At 15.3 miles, the old railroad grade crosses the creek while the official trail stays left and climbs as a singletrack path, avoiding two fords. A campsite is located across the creek along the grade. Dip to the streamside grade at 15.5 miles. A tributary comes in here. Resume downstream, passing along another bluff and a couple of campsites before fording to the right hand bank of North Fork at 16.3 miles and coming to a small campsite. Quickly ford to the left hand bank, as the stream squeezes through a mini-gorge riddled with large boulders.

At 16.6 miles, pass an old dam, then bridge the South Fork. Here, the wooden span uses the old railroad grade abutments. A sloped campsite is located at the convergence of the North Fork and South Fork. At 16.9 miles, return to the

South Fork Trail. From here it is a 0.8 mile backtrack, completing the challenging wilderness backpack.

Mileages

0.0	South Fork Citico Creek Trail trailhead
0.6	Campsite, officially enter Citico Wilderness
0.8	North Fork Trail leave left
1.2	Brush Mountain Trail leaves left, campsite across creek
1.5	Campsite
2.0	Trail climbs bluff, avoids two fords
2.4	Campsite, ford ahead
2.6	Grassy Branch Trail leaves right
3.4	Campsite, trail leaves grade, climbs
4.5	View
5.7	Campsite, waterfall ahead
6.0	Jeffrey Hell Trail leaves right, campsite 0.1 mile ahead
6.8	Cross South Fork, campsite 0.3 mile ahead
8.3	Cold Springs Gap, join Bobs Bald Connector
9.4	Right on Stratton Bald Trail, spring ahead
9.8	Bobs Bald, campsites, backtrack
10.2	Right on Bobs Bald Connector, descend
10.9	Good campsite, Fodderstack Trail enters
11.2	Cherry Log Gap, left on North Fork Citico Creek Trail
11.7	Bad, sloped campsite, Cold Springs Gap Trail leaves left 0.2 mile ahead
12.1	Upper North Fork Falls
12.6	Old Goat Falls
13.4	Good campsite in flat below
14.3	Ford North Fork to left hand bank, good campsite
14.8	Campsite
15.3	Campsite across creek
16.3	Small campsite between two fords
16.9	Bridge over South Fork, sloped campsite before backtracking down South Fork
17.7	South Fork Trailhead

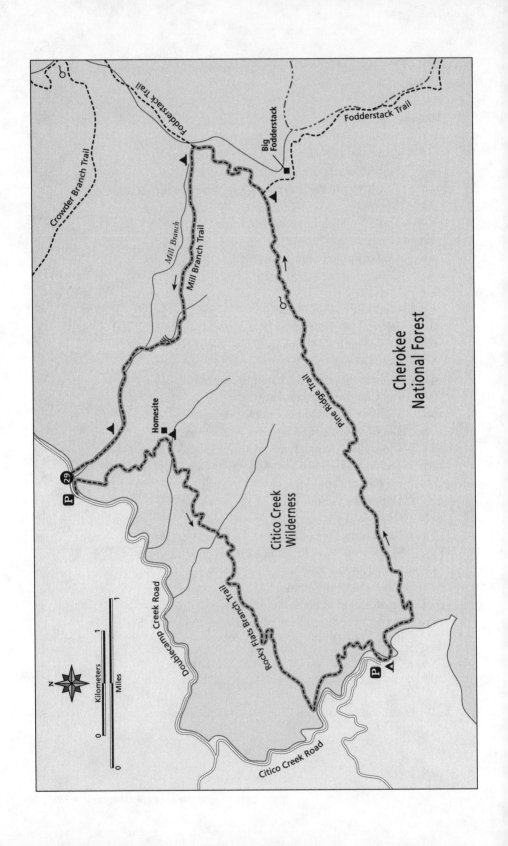

Cherokee
National Forest

Citico Creek
Wilderness

Crowder Branch Trail

Fodderstack Trail

Fodderstack Trail

Big
Fodderstack

Mill Branch

Mill Branch Trail

Homesite

Pine Ridge Trail

Doublecamp Creek Road

Rocky Flats Branch Trail

Citico Creek Road

29

N

Kilometers

Miles

29

Rocky Flats Backpack

THE BACKPACK

This overnight adventure takes place inside the Citico Wilderness on lesser used, challenging trails. Start on the Rocky Flats Branch Trail, passing a homesite and crossing streams flowing off Pine Ridge to traverse a bluff above Citico Creek. From there, make the steady ascent on Pine Ridge, rising to Big Fodderstack. Cruise the mountainside down to Big Stack Gap and descend on the seldom trod Mill Branch Trail, with its copious cascades. You can make this a one- or two-night adventure. Remember the challenges entail faint, overgrown trails, multiple crossings of small but lively creeks, plus the 2,300-foot ascent along Pine Ridge.

Distance and Configuration: 11.7-mile loop
Difficulty: Moderate-difficult due to faint trails and elevation changes
Outstanding Features: Rocky Flats homesite, Citico Creek gorge, views
Elevation: 1,616 feet low point, 3,985 feet high point
Scenery: 4
Solitude: 4
Family Friendly: 1
Canine Friendly: 2
Fees/permits: No fees or permits required
Best season: Early fall through late spring
Maps: National Geographic #781 Tellico and Ocoee Rivers, Cherokee National Forest
For more info: Cherokee National Forest, Tellico Ranger District, 250 Ranger Station Road, Tellico Plains TN 37385, (423) 397-8455, www.fs.usda.gov/cherokee
Finding the Trailhead: From the intersection of TN 360 and US 411 in Vonore, take TN 360 south for 12 miles to turn left onto Chestnut Valley Road and follow it for 1.6 miles, then veer left at a road split on Buck Highway toward Citico Creek and staying with it for 3.4 more miles to reach Citico Road, FR 35-1. Turn right on Citico

Road and follow it for 6.6 miles, then turn left onto Doublecamp Creek Road, FR 2659, and travel for 2.5 miles to the Rocky Flats Branch trailhead, with the trail on your right and parking and a dispersed campsite to the left. GPS trailhead coordinates: 35.430750, -84.061194

Citico Wilderness is one of Tennessee's premier untamed areas, and this trek makes a testing circuit within its uninhabited confines. The trails as a whole can be overgrown, somewhat faint in places and challenging to follow. The seemingly innocuous Rocky Flats Branch Trail is your initial conduit. Leading to a homesite—about your only camping opportunity on this stretch—the faint path winds up and down, in and out of drainages before emerging at Citico Creek, at an auto-accessible camping area. From there, the extended climb up the south side of Pine Ridge will tax your lungs and legs. Like elsewhere, that path can be overgrown but the well graded track leads to the shoulder of Big Fodderstack Mountain. Briefly enjoy the well maintained Fodderstack Trail to reach Big Stack Gap. Here, descend into scenic Mill Branch, reaching a highland camp before working down the flowery vale, passing a waterfall while crossing plentiful tributaries. Hike's end flattens before returning to the trailhead.

This chimney is all that remains of a trailside homesite.

Backpacker crosses one of several spirited streams along the loop.

Though the mileage may seem short, it makes a good two-night endeavor. Rocky Flats homesite makes an easy short first day. Consider reversing the loop as well. Either direction you can make a night down low and another up high. Just don't come here during summer, much of the trek will be overgrown and steamy. No matter what time of year, wear long pants and expect to work around blown down trees.

A roadside campsite at the trailhead is good for late arrivals. The Rocky Flats Branch Trail leaves Doublecamp Creek Road, tracing a former logging track under white pine, maple, sweetgum and oaks, lulling you into thinking the path is going to be easy. Come near Mill Creek then gently ascend a ridge. Turn into the Rocky Flats Branch drainage, reaching the stream at 1.0 mile. Here, the trail turns downhill. A flat to your right next to a crumbled chimney provides a tent site. A fire ring will be found at the standing rock chimney down trail. Imagine this locale cleared and the centerpiece of a mountain farm.

Leaving the homesite, the now-narrow trail turns down and crosses Rocky Flats Branch then winds along hollows with small drainages divided by rib ridges, punctuated with short but steep ups and downs. Along the streams young brushy woods rise where hemlocks have fallen. At 1.9 miles, step over Laurel Branch, flowing into Doublecamp Creek. Continue working on the north slope of Pine Ridge. At 3.0 miles, turn down a bounding tributary of Citico Creek. Trace the rill through a narrow, wildflower and rhododendron-rich hollow, criss-crossing the waterway on an indistinct track. At 3.6 miles, the faint trail crosses left over the creek then abruptly climbs a rocky wooded bluff above Citico Creek, its white noise rising to your ears. Enjoy craggy stream looks from the outcrops then turn into and out of small, sloped, wooded coves before dropping out at 4.5 miles at a dispersed campsite and trailhead, divided from Citico Creek Road by a concrete ford with a deep pool below it. Campsites here are auto accessible.

Leave Citico Creek by staying left in the camping flat, passing between a pair of auto blocking boulders then splitting left on the signed Pine Ridge Trail. Come along a bluff above Citico Creek with a fine stream view. Ahead, rock hop a tributary. You might be able to work up a campsite in the streamside flats below the path here. Campsites are scarce along Pine Ridge Trail. Start ascending the south slope of Pine Ridge on a consistent grade, leaving water noise behind as you hike beneath pines, oaks, sassafras and flame azaleas. By 6.1 miles, briefly crest out in a gap, then resume the uptick, working around normally dry draws on the rocky south slope of Pine Ridge. At 7.5 miles, pass a small spring. Continue working up through thick tree cover and brush. At 8.2 miles, meet the Fodderstack Trail and a small, flat but fine campsite. Congratulations, you just climbed 2,300 feet. Enjoy the views north toward the Smokies and the Tennessee Valley.

From here, head left on the Fodderstack Trail, as it descends the west slope of Big Fodderstack, reaching the small saddle of Big Stack Gap at 9.0 miles. If you want to extend your trip, continue north on the Fodderstack Trail a mile, then head left down Crowder Branch, camping either along the Fodderstack Trail near its junction with Crowder Branch Trail or at Crowder Place, a small campsite/homesite, with a fine spring, then hike 2.6 miles down Crowder Branch Trail to Doublecamp Creek Road, followed by a mile road walk back to the Rocky Flats Branch trailhead. This option adds about 2 miles to the backpack.

Our loop heads left on the Mill Branch Trail. A fine but slightly sloped campsite with water lies but 0.1 mile down the path. Beyond the campsite, the Mill Branch Trail winds through evergreen thickets, crossing several wide, rocky and shallow branches feeding Mill Branch. At 9.6 miles, pass through an old logging camp in a semi-flat. Look for old metal logging cable and other relics. Beyond the logging camp, the trail and Mill Branch separate, as Mill Branch Falls steeply away. The path cuts through a gap then dramatically descends along a tributary of Mill Branch. Watch carefully as the trail follows a reroute right at 10.2 miles, staying well above the tributary. At 10.5 miles, pass a fifteen foot tiered cascade to your left, a standout among several cataracts along this tributary of Mill Branch. Return to and cross Mill Branch at 10.6 miles. Continue down the valley, staying above the stream. At 11.2 miles, pass a campsite. Here, the valley flattens and the walking is easy. Reach Doublecamp Creek Road at 11.6 miles. From here it is 0.1 mile left to the Rocky Gap Branch trailhead and backpack's end.

Mileages

0.0	Rocky Flats Branch trailhead
1.0	Rocky Flats Branch/homesite/chimney/campsite
3.6	Bluff above Citico Creek
4.5	Citico Creek auto accessible campsite/Pine Ridge Trail
7.5	Trailside spring
8.2	Fodderstack Trail/campsite
9.0	Left on Mill Branch Trail
9.1	Campsite/water
10.5	Tiered 15 foot waterfall on tributary
10.6	Cross Mill Branch
11.2	Campsite in streamside flat
11.6	Left on Doublecamp Creek Road
11.7	Rocky Flats Branch trailhead

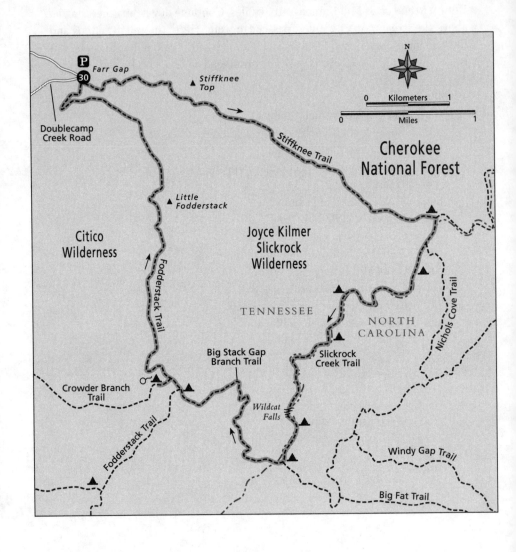

Cherokee
National Forest

N

0   Kilometers   1

0   Miles   1

Farr Gap

Stiffknee
Top

Stiffknee Trail

Doublecamp
Creek Road

Little
Fodderstack

Citico
Wilderness

Joyce Kilmer
Slickrock
Wilderness

Fodderstack Trail

TENNESSEE

NORTH
CAROLINA

Nichols Cove Trail

Big Stack Gap
Branch Trail

Slickrock
Creek Trail

Crowder Branch
Trail

Wildcat
Falls

Fodderstack Trail

Windy Gap Trail

Big Fat Trail

30

Joyce Kilmer Slickrock Wilderness

THE BACKPACK

Enjoy one of the most scenic streams in the Southern Appalachians on this loop backpack in the Joyce Kilmer Slickrock Wilderness. Start up high enjoying views of the Smokies then drop to Slickrock Creek, forming the Tennessee-North Carolina state line. Head upstream, passing big Wildcat Falls amidst everywhere-you-look beauty. The many creekside camps provide an ideal way to laze away a summer day. From Slickrock Creek climb to the crest of the Unicoi Mountains. Stop by the Crowder Place homesite before closing the circuit on this surprisingly gentle segment of the Fodderstack Trail. Be apprised the loop requires 8 sure fords of Slickrock Creek.

Distance and Configuration: 11.8-mile loop
Difficulty: Moderate, does have 8 fords
Outstanding Features: Views, swimming, fishing, Wildcat Falls
Elevation: 1,388 feet low point, 3,589 feet high point
Scenery: 5
Solitude: 3
Family Friendly: 1
Canine Friendly: 3
Fees/permits: No fees or permits required
Best season: Spring through late fall
Maps: National Geographic #781 Tellico and Ocoee Rivers, Cherokee National Forest
For more info: Cherokee National Forest, Tellico Ranger District, 250 Ranger Station Road, Tellico Plains TN 37385, (423) 397-8455, www.fs.usda.gov/cherokee
Finding the Trailhead: From the intersection of TN 360 and US 411 in Vonore, take TN 360 south for 12 miles to turn left onto Chestnut Valley Road and follow it for 1.6 miles, then veer left a road split on Buck Highway toward Citico Creek and staying with it for 3.4 more

Looking north toward the Smokies from the Stiffknee Trail.

miles to reach Citico Road, FR 35-1. Turn right on Citico Road and follow it for 6.6 miles, then turn left onto Doublecamp Creek Road, FR 2659, and travel for 6.3 miles to Farr Gap and the Fodderstack Trail trailhead. GPS trailhead coordinates: 35.463306, -84.027472

Located just south of the Great Smoky Mountains, Joyce Kilmer-Slickrock Wilderness comprises 19,000 plus acres of wildland straddling the Tennessee-North Carolina state line in the Cherokee and Nantahala National Forests. An extensive trail network makes extended trips viable, especially when considering much of Joyce Kilmer Slickrock Wilderness abuts 16,000-acre Citico Wilderness, located entirely within the Volunteer State. Both wildernesses are characterized by faint, barely maintained trails that will tax the backpacker, yet will reward them with a truly scenic and primitive natural experience.

This particular adventure will give you a taste of Joyce Kilmer and whet your appetite for more. I recommend this as a summertime experience to best enjoy Slickrock Creek. You must consider the 8 fords required to make the loop. Doing this in winter would be an ordeal. Ideal times are from late spring through fall. If you come to the first ford and it is too difficult, turn back. It's not worth

Wildcat Falls and its big plunge pool.

it. Heavy rains can trap you between fords. Once, I was stuck at a campsite here between fords for three days as a tropical storm pushed through and raised Slickrock Creek to levels unsafe for crossing. That said, in normal years fording should be no problem from June through September.

Start this backpacking adventure high in the Unicoi Mountains at Farr Gap. Walk around wooden barriers then reach a signboard and trail split. Head left with the interestingly named Stiffknee Trail, eastbound. The north slope of the highlands falls away, allowing wintertime views of the Great Smoky Mountains across the Little Tennessee River valley. Cross uppermost Tallassee Creek at 0.2 mile. Ahead, the path descends sharply using switchbacks and at 0.9 mile you cut through a gap to enter the Slickrock Creek watershed. Step over Little Slickrock Creek at 1.1 miles, crossing other headwaters in a forest transitioning away from hemlock dominated woods, now rising with fire cherry, black birch, sweetgum and tulip trees, as well as white pines. Bisect rhododendron and doghobble thickets, sometimes cutting through overflow stream braids. At 2.4 miles, make the first of six crossings of Little Slickrock Creek, all of which are possible fords. At 3.0 miles, pass through a rocky flat with old bricks and other evidence of habitation.

At 3.4 miles, you are on the left hand bank descending. Reach desirable campsites at the confluence of Slickrock and Little Slickrock Creeks, as well as the intersection with the Slickrock Creek Trail. Here, our hike goes right on the Slickrock Creek Trail, immediately crossing Little Slickrock Creek one last time. Head up Slickrock Creek in junglesque woods. Come to your first ford of Slickrock Creek at 3.5 miles. Use hiking poles or a wood staff to aid your passage. If you can make this you should be fine the rest of the way. Cross over to the North Carolina side of the stream and at 3.6 miles, intersect the Nichols Cove Trail. It can be used to bypass most of the Slickrock Creek fords. However, our adventure stays straight along more heavily used Slickrock Creek Trail, tracing an old logging railroad grade that once stripped this land a century back but has recovered nicely. Unfortunately, the forest is transitioning again, as diseased hemlocks are being replaced.

Slickrock Creek is normally clear as air, with tropical colorations in its chilly depths, where feisty trout lurk. Notice blasted low bluffs, cleared when the logging trains ran through. Pass a small campsite at 3.8 miles, then ford Slickrock Creek at 3.9 miles, back in Tennessee. Cascades and pools are breathtakingly beautiful. Expect to navigate bare rock in washed out trail sections. At 4.8 miles, step over small Wildcat Branch then pass through a campsite. At 5.1 miles, make a couple of switchbacks, working around a washed out section. Descend back to the creek and pass through a campsite at 5.2 miles. At 5.5 miles, the fords come fast and furious. Walk through Slickrock Creek at 5.5, 5.7, 5.8 and 5.9 miles.

You are now on the Tennessee side of the creek, rising. At 6.0 miles, big, tiered Wildcat Falls comes into view. Here, Slickrock Creek tumbles 45 feet in multiple stages, ending in a plunge pool of the first order. You will see the roaring white cataract before coming to a rock outcrop that you have to squeeze around, then ford Slickrock Creek at 6.1 miles, a little above Wildcat Falls. Enter a large, level camping area with multiple sites. At 6.4 miles, make your final ford of Slickrock Creek, returning to Tennessee. Here, meet the Big Stack Gap Branch Trail at a small campsite.

Start heading up narrow, lesser-trod Big Stack Gap Branch Trail, entering brushy thickets to cross Big Stack Gap Branch at 6.7 miles. Begin climbing upstream then turn away from the branch. Start angling up a ridge amid oaks, pines, mountain laurel and blueberry bushes. At 7.7 miles, reach the nose of a ridge and a sharp turn to the left, westerly. Here, partial views open to the north and east of the wilderness in the near and the Smokies beyond. The climbing eases before you step over a small spring branch at 8.1 miles. Continue up the streamlet then open to a wooded cove before meeting the Fodderstack Trail at a fine, grassy campsite at 8.2 miles.

From here, head right, north, along the wide and easy Fodderstack Trail, drift down to meet the Crowder Branch Trail at 8.3 miles. Even if you aren't camping, take the Crowder Branch Trail 0.1 mile through a small cove to Crowder Place, where a tumbled chimney, metal relics and tin roofed spring mark the former dwelling. After backtracking to the Fodderstack Trail, continue northbound, climbing a wide clear track in pines and oaks. Look back south at the sharp peak of Hangover Lead. Curve to a knob then begin gently undulating in oak dominated forest. Reach a high point at 9.7 miles. It's almost all downhill from here, on a well-used and maintained trail. At 10.0, pass a small, dry campsite. At 10.2 miles, swing around the west side of Little Fodderstack, eventually to curve west. Make a hard switchback to the right at 11.5 miles. Continue descending to pass the Stiffknee Trail and reach the trailhead at 11.8 miles, completing the backpack.

Mileages

0.0	Farr Gap trailhead
0.9	Enter Little Slickrock Creek watershed
3.4	Campsites, right on Slickrock Creek Trail
3.6	Intersect Nichols Cove Trail
4.8	Wildcat Branch/campsite
5.5	First of four consecutive Slickrock Creek fords
6.0	Wildcat Falls
6.1	Ford, large campsite
6.4	Eighth and final ford, campsite, join Big Stack Gap Branch Trail
7.7	Ridgetop views, head west
8.1	Cross spring branch
8.2	Fodderstack Trail, campsite
8.3	Crowder Branch Trail, left to Crowder Place
8.4	Crowder Place homesite/campsite/spring; backtrack
10.0	Small dry campsite on Fodderstack Trail
11.8	Farr Gap, backpack's end

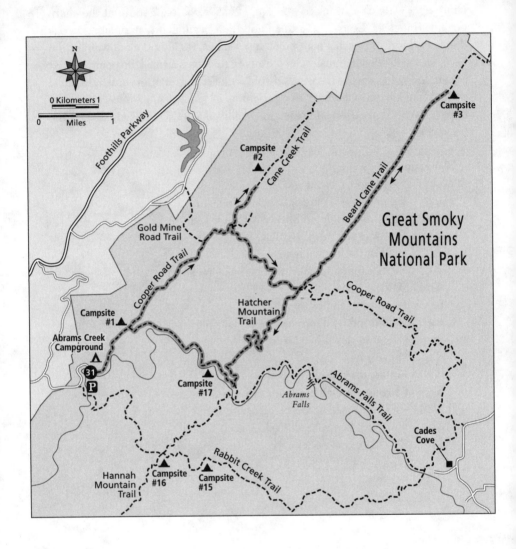

Great Smoky Mountains National Park

N

0 Kilometers 1

0 Miles 1

Foothills Parkway

Gold Mine Road Trail

Cane Creek Trail

Campsite #2

Campsite #3

Beard Cane Trail

Cooper Road Trail

Cooper Road Trail

Hatcher Mountain Trail

Campsite #1

Abrams Creek Campground

31

P

Campsite #17

Abrams Falls

Abrams Falls Trail

Cades Cove

Hannah Mountain Trail

Campsite #16

Campsite #15

Rabbit Creek Trail

31

Abrams Creek Backpack

THE BACKPACK

This Great Smoky Mountains backpacking trip takes you through the park's lesser trod western lowlands, cut by scenic creeks beneath piney ridges. Start on the Cooper Road Trail astride fabled Abrams Creek to reach formerly settled but now remote Cane Creek. Next make your way to seldom visited Hesse Creek via incised Beard Cane Creek valley. Finally return to Abrams Creek, the grand stream of the area. Elevations are low for the Smokies, and the trek is also without long climbs or descents. Along the way you'll pass several designated backcountry campsites, most of which are lightly used.

Distance and Configuration: 19.7-mile loop
Difficulty: Moderate
Outstanding Features: Streams, remoteness, Smokies history
Elevation: 1,099 feet low point, 2,038 feet high point
Scenery: 4
Solitude: 3
Family Friendly: 4
Canine Friendly: 0 (Dogs not allowed)
Fees/permits: Fee-based permit required
Best season: Year-round, late spring and early fall best
Maps: National Geographic #229 Great Smoky Mountains National Park
For more info: Great Smoky Mountains National Park, 107 Park Headquarters Road, Gatlinburg, TN 37738; (865) 436-1200; nps.gov/grsm
Finding the Trailhead: From Maryville, take US 129 south, Alcoa Highway, on to Chilhowee Lake. Once at Chilhowee Lake, continue to the intersection with the Foothills Parkway. From there, keep south on US 129 for .5 mile farther to Happy Valley Road. Turn left on Happy Valley Road, following it 6 miles to Abrams Creek Road. Turn right on Abrams Creek Road and drive

At remote Cane Creek campsite.

0.7 mile, passing the ranger station. The parking area is on the
right just after the ranger station. Cooper Road Trail starts at the
rear of the campground. Park your car in the designated area near
the ranger station. Do not park in the campground, which is gated
during the cold season. GPS trailhead coordinates: 35.609021,
-83.935234

The Abrams Creek area of the Smokies has long been a favorite backpacking
area of mine. The combination of cool mountain streams, low but stately ridges,
fine backcountry campsites and settler history construct a winning combination.
Harboring the park's lowest elevations, this locale offers excellent year-round
backpacking. In summer you can take a dip to cool off, autumn is ideal with clear
warm days and crisp cool nights, winter is much more tolerable than the high
country, and spring can be a wildflower extravaganza. Views of nearby Chilhowee
Mountain can be had from the ridgetops dividing the creeks. Only one of the
four potential campsites on the route is heavily used.

Start your adventure at Abrams Creek, with its intimate 16 site, warm season,
auto-accessible campground, good for a late arrival. You start in the lowest auto-

Trekking along Abrams Creek.

accessible area of the Smokies. Leave the parking area, following the gravel road beside Abrams Creek, gurgling and rushing and pooling in slow spots. I think it the most beautiful stream in the world. Reach small, hemlock shaded Abrams Creek Campground at 0.4 mile. You'll be able to analyze the 16 sites before reaching the official start of the Cooper Road Trail. Here, follow the doubletrack path, tracing an old road built connecting Cades Cove to points west. The wide track makes the hiking easy as you travel in tall woods, rising on a bluff above Abrams Creek. Dip to cross small Kingfisher Creek twice in succession.

Keep up the easy valley of Kingfisher Creek, reaching a trail intersection at 1.3 miles. Here, the Little Bottoms Trail, your return route, leaves right. You keep straight on the Cooper Road Trail, immediately reaching Cooper Road backcountry campsite #1, the park's lowest elevation camp at 1,200 feet. This pine and hemlock rich site is set along Kingfisher Creek and makes for a great one-night family backpack, a short way in with no big hills, an ideal testing ground for novice backpackers.

Next, the backpack traces Cooper Road under sweetgum, pines and mountain laurel, crossing now-small Kingfisher Creek at 1.6 miles. Climb away from the stream in fire-managed pine-oak-hickory forest, stepping over a tributary of

Buck Shank Branch at 2.7 miles. Top out at Gold Mine Gap at 3.0 miles. Keep straight, descending wide Cooper Road Trail. The walking is easy and you reach Cane Gap at 3.6 miles. Here, head left on the little used Cane Creek Trail. This doubletrack dips northeast into the once settled Cane Creek Valley, where you can still find the Buchanan Cemetery in a locale that once even housed a school in addition to multiple subsistence farms. Rock hop Cane Creek then reach Cane Creek backcountry campsite #2, elevation 1,320 feet, at 4.2 miles. I've camped here at least 15 nights and never had to share the small camp, set under a few preserved hemlocks of a now wooded flat that was once a field. Look for piled rocks as the fields were clear of stones. The old Buchanan Cemetery is less than a mile distant down trail, if you desire a side trip. A keen eye will also spot a crumbled chimney en route to the internment site.

From campsite #2, backtrack 0.6 mile on the Cane Creek Trail, returning to Cane Gap. Head left here on the wide Cooper Road Trail, noting the 0.4 mile unsigned spur to the small Lail Cemetery, also leaving from Cane Gap. The Cooper Road Trail runs the divide between Cane Creek and Abrams Creek, among sourwood, maple and oaks, along with ever present pines. The hiking is easy and you are soon at another intersection at 6.5 miles. Here, head left on the lightly trod Beard Cane Trail, cruising the southeast slope of Hatcher Mountain, slicing through a gap at 6.8 miles then entering the narrow, straight vale of Beard Cane Creek, hemmed in by Hatcher Mountain and Beard Cane Mountain. Descend in brushy woods to begin upwards of three dozen crossings of Beard Cane Creek, most easy at lower flows. A few crossings could be troublesome in winter. The area is still regenerating from a 2011 tornado that took down an incredible number of trees and obliterated Beard Cane backcountry campsite #11, now permanently closed. Rhododendron and doghobble rise in thickets as you hone your stream crossing skills. Beard Cane Creek increases it flow as you proceed downstream. At 7.8 miles, the path travels directly down the creek. Sycamore, musclewood and sweetgum trees increase in dense woods.

By 9.8 miles, the valley widens and you come along Hesse Creek, reaching Hesse Creek backcountry campsite #3 at 10.0 miles. One of my favorites, the needle covered flat lies beside Hesse Creek where it has reconverged after splitting around an island. A fire ring and bearproof food storage cables enhance the lightly used locale, sitting at a mere 1,360 feet.

From campsite #3, backtrack the Beard Cane Trail, again trying your hand—er foot—at the three dozen crossings of Beard Cane Creek, returning to the intersection with Cooper Road Trail where you were at 6.5 miles, but now you are at 13.5 miles. Now, head straight, southwesterly, on the nicely graded Hatcher Mountain Trail toward Abrams Creek. Begin ridge running among pines and oaks to reach the backpack's high point of 2,038 feet at 13.9 miles. Occasional views open through the trees of Chilhowee Mountain. Dip to step over Oak Flats

Branch at 14.8 miles, followed by a smaller tributary. Aim for the Abrams Creek valley and at 15.6 miles, the trail opens onto the stream gorge, where views open of the valley below and adjacent ridges.

Drop to intersect the Little Bottoms Trail at 16.1 miles. Here, head right on the Little Bottoms Trail, upstream along the slope of the Abrams Creek gorge. This section of the slender path makes an irregular undulating course among woods and rock outcrops, giving it the nickname "Goat Trail." More views open of Chilhowee Mountain in the distance and Abrams Creek below. Cross tiny tributaries of Abrams Creek before reaching Little Bottoms backcountry campsite #17, at 16.7 miles. This is deservedly the most popular campsite on this backpack. It is set on an old farm at 1,240 feet—you can find an old chimney as well as rock walls here. Pines, preserved hemlocks and sweetgums shade the large site with multiple fire rings, on a bend above gushing Abrams Creek, presenting swimming and fishing possibilities.

Continuing the backpack, the Little Bottoms Trail leads downstream alongside Abrams Creek, displaying alluring views of the watercourse that flows from the state line ridge near Spence Field down through Cades Cove, over famed Abrams Falls, then through this gorge before emptying into Chilhowee Lake. Cross Mill Branch then Buck Shank Branch at 17.7 miles. From here the trail climbs over a hill, then drops to cross Kingfisher Creek near campsite #1 before returning to the Cooper Road Trail at 18.4 miles. From here it is a 1.3 mile backtrack to the trailhead, and you complete your Smoky Mountain lowlands backpack at 19.7 miles.

Mileages

0.0	Abrams Creek parking area
0.4	Abrams Creek Campground
1.3	Little Bottoms Trail, campsite #1 just ahead
3.6	Cane Gap
4.2	Campsite #2
6.8	Left on Beard Cane Trail
10.0	Campsite #3
13.5	Join Hatcher Mountain Trail
16.1	Little Bottoms Trail
16.7	Campsite #17
18.4	Rejoin Cooper Road Trail, campsite #1
19.7	Abrams Creek Trail parking area

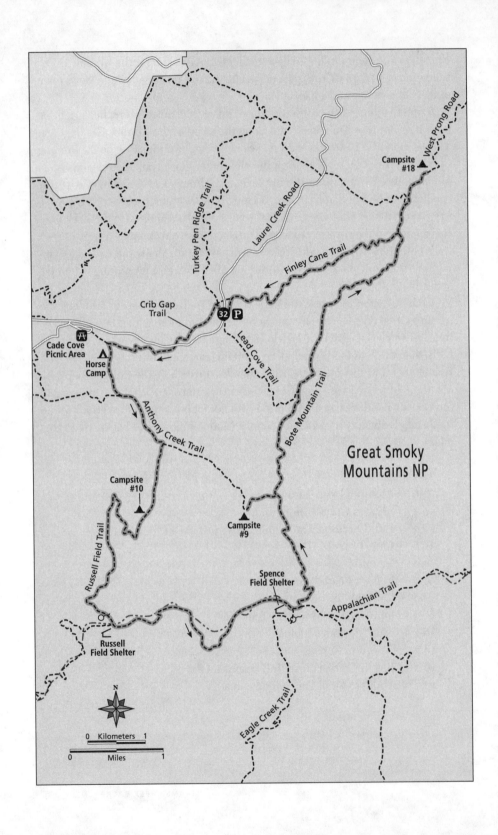

Campsite #18

West Prong Road

Laurel Creek Road

Turkey Pen Ridge Trail

Finley Cane Trail

Crib Gap Trail

32 P

Lead Cove Trail

Cade Cove Picnic Area

Horse Camp

Anthony Creek Trail

Bote Mountain Trail

Great Smoky Mountains NP

Campsite #10

Campsite #9

Russell Field Trail

Spence Field Shelter

Appalachian Trail

Russell Field Shelter

Eagle Creek Trail

N

0 Kilometers 1

0 Miles 1

32

Bote Mountain Backpack

THE BACKPACK

This circuit adventure takes place in one and only Great Smoky Mountains National Park. Start the lesser-used Crib Gap Trail to reach Anthony Creek, then ascend to the Tennessee-North Carolina state line. Join the fabled Appalachian Trail, soaking in views before descending Bote Mountain back to Anthony Creek. The final part of the trek rejoins Bote Mountain, with more vistas, then drops to West Prong Little River and creekside camping. Return via historic Finley Cane Trail. Three campsites and two trail shelters are situated along the recommended route. Note: This route can easily be shortened or altered.

Distance and Configuration: 21.4-mile loop
Difficulty: Difficult due to elevation change
Outstanding Features: Appalachian Trail, Smokies history
Elevation: 1,600 feet low point, 5,023 feet high point
Scenery: 4
Solitude: 3
Family Friendly: 1
Canine Friendly: 0 (Dogs not allowed)
Fees/permits: Fee-based permit required
Best season: Year-round
Maps: National Geographic #229 Great Smoky Mountains National Park
For more info: Great Smoky Mountains National Park, 107 Park Headquarters Road, Gatlinburg, TN 37738; (865) 436-1200; nps.gov/grsm
Finding the Trailhead: From Townsend at the intersection of US 321 and Lamar Alexander Parkway, take the parkway into Great Smoky Mountains National Park then turn right onto Laurel Creek Road and follow it for 5.6 miles to the Turkey Pen Ridge/Lead Cove trailhead, with shoulder parking on both sides of the road. GPS trailhead coordinates: 35.606650, -83.745104

Crossing one of the many signature Smokies footbridges on this backpack.

This backpacking adventure incorporates a classic Smokies loop and lesser used trails to fashion a fine overnighting circuit. I recommend 3 nights for the loop, but it can be shortened to 2 nights or extended to 4 nights. Furthermore, you can shorten the entire loop to 13 miles by starting at Cades Cove picnic area, then climbing up to Russell Field, descending at Spence Field and taking Anthony Creek Trail back to the picnic area. This aforementioned classic Smokies loop is done as both a dayhike and backpacking adventure. The recommended longer loop adds a trip to gorgeous West Prong Little River, an archetypal Smoky Mountain stream. Five designated camping areas add still more possibilities to the main route. Camp low, camp high and camp in between—your choice.

Start the adventure on the Turkeypen Ridge Trail as it leads down through woods 0.2 mile to a trail intersection in formerly settled Big Spring Cove. Look for leveled areas, indicating pre-park settlement. Head left on the lesser trod Crib Gap Trail. It follows an old road and goes nowhere near Crib Gap, rising through now-wooded upper Big Spring Cove, bisecting a few small branches then crosses Laurel Creek Road at 0.9 miles. Leave the farmland-turned-forest in a rich wildflower area. Rise to view Scott Mountain across the valley. Cut through a gap at 1.3 miles, and keep west toward Anthony Creek on an easy track.

At 1.8 miles, head left on the gravelly Anthony Creek Trail, running through Anthony Creek Horse Camp. Rise in wooded flats beside spunky Anthony Creek to bridge it at 2.2 miles. White pines tower over the thick forest that includes preserved trailside hemlocks. Bridge the stream again at 2.5 miles. The Anthony Creek valley narrows and you bridge it again at 2.8 miles. Pass alongside an old stone wall at 3.0 miles, then bridge Left Prong Anthony Creek at 3.2 miles.

Come to a trail intersection at 3.3 miles. Here, you head right on the Russell Field Trail. Cove hardwoods such as straight trunked tulip trees and Carolina silverbells dominate the forest here. The path narrows and steepens as you cross trickling tributaries. At 3.9 miles, bridge Left Prong Anthony Creek then climb to meet Ledbetter Ridge backcountry campsite #10, elevation 3,000 feet, at 4.1 miles. The small, tiered site is set on a tributary of Left Prong Anthony Creek under youngish hardwoods replacing deceased hemlocks.

The Russell Field Trail leaves the stream at 4.4 miles, angles up to Ledbetter Ridge, cloaked in galax, mountain laurel, pines and chestnut oaks. At 5.1 miles, turn abruptly south atop Ledbetter Ridge. The ascent remains gentle and almost level in places under shortish oaks and blueberry bushes. At 5.9 miles, the path

Russell Field trail shelter.

climbs while curving around McCampbell Knob. At 6.4 miles, a spur leads left to the lone remains of Russell Field, a former summer cattle grazing meadow. Dive through rhododendron tunnels to reach a signed spring at 6.7 miles. Rise to reach Russell Field shelter at 6.8 miles. Here, you will find a three sided stone refuge fronted with sheltered sitting area with inside and outside fireplaces, all at 4,360 feet atop the wooded state line ridge.

Join the well-maintained Appalachian Trail northbound from Russell Field. The path stays on the Carolina side of the state line ridge among laurel thickets and oaks, climbing to then level out at Maple Sugar Gap at 7.9 miles. Enjoy a brief level cruise before rising around the south side of Mount Squires, reaching the backpack's high point of 5,023 feet at 8.9 miles. From here, descend through woods with relic grasses from when the locale was wide open, part of the greater meadows of Spence Field. Notice the trees here are wide limbed, having risen in open terrain. The wide limbs will eventually atrophy and drop as the forest thickens.

Pass through partial clearings with winter views of Rocky Top and Thunderhead. And yes, this is *the* Rocky Top of University of Tennessee fight song fame—*"Rocky Top you'll always be/home sweet home to me/good ol' Rocky Top, Rocky Top Tennessee."* Intersect the Eagle Creek Trail at 9.7 miles. Here, turn right to access Spence Field shelter and a fine spring in 0.2 mile. The shelter is on a shoulder ridge bordered by woods and is your second chance to overnight in one of these sturdy huts.

The backpack continues through now-wooded Spence Field to intersect the Bote Mountain Trail at 10.2 miles. Here, you leave the state line ridge, switchbacking downhill past springs to run atop Bote Mountain, dividing Laurel Creek watershed from the waters of West Prong Little River. The path was the route for cattle brought up to graze Spence Field from Cades Cove, and became a deeply eroded path. Cherokee Indians built this one-time toll road from the lowlands to the Smokies crest as part of a scheme to link nearby Maryville, Tennessee with settlements on Hazel Creek in North Carolina. The natives chose the path, "voting" for this ridge, which ended up being called "Bote Mountain," since the aboriginals had a hard time with the letter "v." The next ridge east, not chosen for the toll road route, became known as Defeat Ridge.

The walking is easy and you find yourself at the intersection with Anthony Creek Trail at 11.8 miles. Here, bear left, descending from Bote Mountain through richly wooded coves with sporadic views Cades Cove's famed fields. Reach water and Anthony Creek backcountry campsite #9, elevation 3,200 feet at 12.5 miles. This larger, multi-tiered site stands along the raucous Anthony Creek.

If you want to make a shorter 1 or 2 night 13-mile loop, park at the Cades Cove camp store area, then return to Cades Cove after overnighting at campsite #9.

Trailside fungi on the AT.

Otherwise, after overnighting at campsite #9, climb .8 mile back out of Anthony Creek, returning to Bote Mountain, then heading left on the wide Bote Mountain Trail. The West Prong Little River falls away to your right as you travel astride pines, hickory, oaks and mountain laurel. Keep an eye peeled for sporadic views into West Prong and Defeat Ridge across the gulf.

At 14.5 miles, at Sandy Gap, the Lead Cove Trail drops left 1.8 miles to the starting point of this backpack. We stay on easy Bote Mountain Trail entering lower elevations where sourwood, pine and black gum trees prevail on the xeric ridge. Pass through Hickory Tree Gap at 15.2 miles. A continuous downgrade ensues and you meet the Finley Cane Trail at a mere 2,000 feet at 16.9 miles. This will be your return route but for now stay straight on Bote Mountain Trail, now a wide, road-like expanse tracking through pines and oaks, reaching a trail junction at 17.2 miles. Here, split right and descend singletrack West Prong Trail as it moderately winds its downward. Creek sounds make your pulse rise. Rhododendron thickens as you reach West Prong Little River at 17.8 miles. Here, find recommended West Prong campsite #18, at 1,600 feet. Despite the low elevation, the large camp is cool in the summer. Three main campsites are dispersed along the linear streamside flats. A sturdy log bridge spans cold, crystalline West Prong as it merrily cavorts among mossy gray boulders sheltering secretive trout.

Leave the hike's low point, backtracking 0.9 mile to once again meet the Finley Cane Trail, shaded by cove hardwoods of vine-draped tulip trees, sugar maple, and beech. Small wildflower-rich rills flowing off Bote Mountain cross the trail as it bisects gaps dividing the streamsheds. The walking is easy as you pass a horse hitching post at 19.4 miles. Curve to step over Hickory Creek at 20.7 miles. The path then drops you into almost level Big Spring Cove. Look for signs of pre-park settlers, including a now dried-up pond. At 21.3 miles, head left on a connector toward Lead Cove Trail. Step over Laurel Creek then complete the backpack at 21.4 miles.

Mileages

0.0	Turkeypen Ridge Trail/Lead Cove Trail parking area
0.2	Crib Gap Trail
1.8	Anthony Creek Trail
3.3	Russell Field Trail
4.1	Campsite #10
6.8	Russell Field shelter, join Appalachian Trail
9.7	Right 0.2 mile to Spence Field shelter, spring
10.2	Join Bote Mountain Trail
11.8	Anthony Creek Trail
12.5	Campsite #9
13.3	Rejoin Bote Mountain Trail
14.5	Lead Cove Trail leads left to parking area
16.9	Pass Finley Cane Trail
17.2	West Prong Trail
17.8	Campsite #18
18.7	Join Finley Cane Trail
21.4	Turkeypen Ridge Trail/Lead Cove Trail parking

BACKPACKING AT GREAT SMOKY MOUNTAINS NATIONAL PARK

Great Smoky Mountains National Park contains over 850 miles of trails (including 70 miles of the Appalachian Trail) threading through 522,000 acres of land, creating a host of backpacking opportunities on both the Tennessee side and the North Carolina side of the preserve. Being a national park backcountry camping is managed according to a system the park service has deemed best for the Smokies. Therefore, it pays to know the rules before you go. Peruse the park's web pages on backpacking before leaving for your trip.

When backpacking, you must stay at one of the more than 100 backcountry campsites and trail shelters. You cannot create your own site or use a non-designated campsite. You must obtain a fee-based backcountry camping permit reserving specific campsites for specific nights. These permits are most easily obtained online at www.smokiespermits.nps.gov. Permits can also be obtained in person at Sugarlands and Oconaluftee visitor centers respectively, or by phone at 865-436-1297.

Permits may be obtained at any time up to 30 days in advance of the first night of your trip. Maximum party size is 8, unless a specific site or shelter has lower limits. You cannot stay consecutive nights at a trail shelter or more than 3 nights at a single backcountry campsite. Properly dispose of human waste—most sites do not have a latrine. Carry all trash out of the backcountry and properly dispose of it. Pets are not allowed on trails in the Smokies. The above list will help better prepare for your Smokies backpacking adventure.

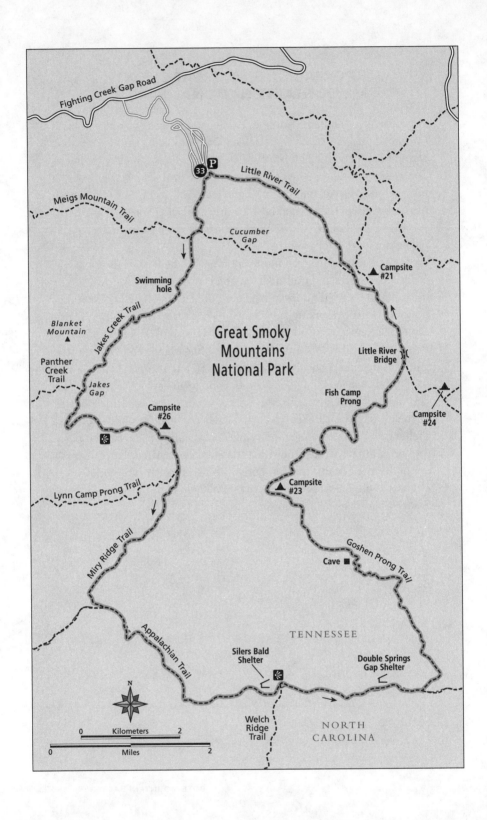

Fighting Creek Gap Road

Meigs Mountain Trail

33 P

Little River Trail

Cucumber Gap

Campsite #21

Swimming hole

Blanket Mountain

Jakes Creek Trail

Great Smoky Mountains National Park

Little River Bridge

Panther Creek Trail

Jakes Gap

Fish Camp Prong

Campsite #24

Campsite #26

Lynn Camp Prong Trail

Campsite #23

Miry Ridge Trail

Cave

Goshen Prong Trail

Appalachian Trail

TENNESSEE

N

Silers Bald Shelter

Double Springs Gap Shelter

0 Kilometers 2

0 Miles 2

Welch Ridge Trail

NORTH CAROLINA

33

Silers Bald Backpack

THE BACKPACK

This Great Smoky Mountains backpacking adventure leads you from historic Elkmont up to the Appalachian Trail and spruce-fir highlands near Silers Bald before dropping into the wild upper Little River drainage. A recommended 3 night trip, several designated campsites and a pair of trail shelters allow for varied daily distances and overall trip length of up to 5 days. The loop backpack does entail 3,600 feet of climbing, but the views, stream scenes and overall national park level beauty make it worthwhile, especially when you consider the above average trail conditions in the Smokies.

Distance and Configuration: 25.6-mile loop
Difficulty: Difficult due to overall mileage and elevation change
Outstanding Features: Views from high country, cascades along Fish Camp Prong
Elevation: 2,170 feet low point, 5,770 feet high point
Scenery: 5
Solitude: 1 on AT, 3 on other trails
Family Friendly: 1
Canine Friendly: 0 (Dogs not allowed)
Fees/permits: Fee-based permit required
Best season: April-December, late summer is ideal
Maps: National Geographic #229 Great Smoky Mountains National Park
For more info: Great Smoky Mountains National Park, 107 Park Headquarters Road, Gatlinburg, TN 37738; (865) 436-1200; nps.gov/grsm
Finding the Trailhead: From Gatlinburg take US 441 south to enter Great Smoky Mountains National Park and shortly reach Sugarland Visitor Center. From here, turn right onto Little River Road and follow it 4.9 miles then turn left into Elkmont. Follow the paved road 1.3 miles to Elkmont Campground, then turn left just before

the campground check-in station and follow this road a short distance to cross the Little River and shortly reach a parking area. From here, angle right toward "Additional Parking, Jakes Creek Trail" and in 0.1 mile reach a second parking area at the Jakes Creek trailhead. GPS trailhead coordinates: 35.652369, -83.581643

This backpack visually displays why the Great Smoky Mountains have been preserved as a national park—from crystal-clear streams tumbling between mossy gray boulders framed in towering forest, to vistas where waves of mountains stretch as far as the sky will allow to the varied woodland ecosystems that replicate traveling up the spine of the Appalachians from Georgia to Maine—the scenery will sate the wearied soul.

It will also challenge the body, but with campsites and shelters aplenty you can adjust your mileage to make the circuit backpack as rigorous or leisurely as you please. Of course, you can't take out the elevation change. After all, it is the Smoky *Mountains*.

Leave the busy Little River/Jakes Creek parking area, joining the wide Jakes Creek Trail past stone chimneys, stone steps and other reminders of the Elkmont summer home community that stood here for four score before lifetime leases went unrenewed. At 0.4 mile a park gravel road dips right but you stay left on the wide trail, entering cove hardwood forest of maple and tulip trees. At 0.7 mile, the Cucumber Gap Trail splits left. Keep straight on Jakes Creek Trail, passing the Meigs Mountain Trail leaving right. The wide gravelly path continues a gentle but steady ascent into the bosom of the Great Smoky Mountains, paralleling Jakes Creek as the watercourse drops in shadowy pools and silvery shoals. At 1.5 miles, gaze down on an alluring swimming hole bordered by big boulders, at the confluence of Jakes Creek and Waterdog Branch.

Just ahead, the doubletrack trail ends and the trail morphs to a footpath. Cross Newt Prong on a footbridge and pass one of the uppermost homesites in the pre-park Jakes Creek valley. Look for the tiered trailside lands, now covered in hardwoods. Keep climbing amidst rhododendron and yellow birch. Step over now-small Jakes Creek at 2.3 miles, then make a switchback left, rising into a wide, sloped cove. Come to signed Lower Jakes Gap backcountry campsite #27, elevation 3,520 feet, at 3.1 miles. It offers several sites down the cove, along with bearproof food storage cables, as do all the campsites and shelters in the Smokies.

Beyond campsite #27, the Jakes Creek Trail continues rising through the upper reaches of Jakes Creek watershed. Look for the square brown barked Carolina silverbell tree. Often just a shrub, it reaches record dimensions here in the park, with species over 120 feet in height. It has a small, white bell shaped flower. Make Jakes Gap at 3.8 miles. Here, an old path heads right for Blanket Mountain and

Morning on the trail near Silers Bald.

the signed Panther Creek Trail descends right. We stay left, joining the Miry Ridge Trail as it angles up the slope of Dripping Spring Mountain. At 4.3 miles, the path curves east just below the crest of Dripping Spring Mountain. At 4.9 miles, open onto a heath bald, with views of the stateline ridge across Lynn Camp Prong. At 5.7 miles, a spur leads left to Dripping Spring Mountain backcountry

Trail intersections in the Smokies feature signs like this.

campsite #26. The pleasant site, elevation 4,400 feet, is set in a level area under preserved hemlocks and hardwoods. Water is accessed via a signed spur.

Beyond campsite #26, the path gains the ridgecrest then intersects the Lynn Camp Prong Trail at 6.3 miles, Keep straight on the Miry Ridge Trail, climbing toward the state line on Miry Ridge in rich woods with a grassy understory. The Little River valley forms a huge gulf below. Curve around the east side of Cold Spring Knob to meet the Appalachian Trail at 8.7 miles. Head left, northbound on the world's most famous footpath, in northern hardwoods of cherry, maple, buckeye and yellow birch. Dip to Buckeye Gap at 9.0 miles then gently climb in stairstep fashion, flirting with the 5,000 foot mark amid wind stunted beech. Partial views open into Carolina and Tennessee.

Reach Silers Bald shelter, 5,420 feet elevation, at 11.7 miles, located in a small clearing. The attractive stone shelter with inside and outside fireplace, as well as nearby spring, is popular with backpackers and AT thru-hikers. Continuing on, the AT leads upward through beech groves to reach nearly wooded Silers Bald, once an open herding pasture. Reach a rock and the high point, 5,607 feet, at 12.0 miles. Here, a spur leads left to an outcrop and view into the Little River drain-

Author admires the scenery from a bridge over the Little River.

age and mountains beyond. Descend by switchbacks, passing the signed Welch Ridge Trail at 12.2 miles. Stay with the AT and state line ridge among stunted beech trees with sporadic views from a slender ridge known as The Narrows. Roll into Double Springs Gap and a trail shelter at 13.5 miles. This stone hut is open on the front with inside and outside fireplace. It also has a privy. True to its name, two springs flow nearby, one into Tennessee and the other into Carolina, their waters merging 100 miles distant.

Climb away from Double Springs Gap, entering full blown red spruce-Fraser fir forest that cloaks only the highest mantles of the Smokies and Southern Appalachians, a very rare ecosystem forming "sky islands" of boreal woods and its attendant plants and animals, such as the northern flying squirrel. Admire the lush, mossy evergreen copses, reaching the backpack's highpoint of 5,770 feet just before heading left on the signed Goshen Prong Trail at 14.0 miles. You are just 2 miles distant from the Smokies and Tennessee high point of Clingmans Dome, 6,643 feet.

Fully reenter Tennessee. Despite the downward trajectory of the Goshen Prong Trail, Fraser fir and especially red spruce remain present in the towering forest, as the narrow rock strewn path passes across and through springs feeding Goshen Prong. Descend Goshen Prong valley on a side slope above the watercourse, briefly pulling away and walking a level stretch of Goshen Ridge before continuing the downgrade. At 16.7 miles, pass by a small cave on a trailside bluff. Just ahead, cross a tributary of Goshen Prong below a 20 foot low flow cascade. Shortly come directly alongside Goshen Prong, where heaps of rhododendron flank the waterway, crashing and dashing down, in obedience to gravity's order.

The path joins an old logging railroad grade and the walking gets easier. At 18.4 miles reach a trail sign. An abandoned trail heads left, but we stay right, coming to Camp Rock campsite #23, elevation 3,200 feet, at 18.5 miles. The recommended site is set at the confluence of several crystalline, cool mountain streams, together forming Fish Camp Prong under a mantle of yellow birch and rhododendron copses, as well as a few preserved hemlocks. Interestingly, you are only 1.5 miles distance from campsite #27—as the crow flies. From here, the trail traces ultra beautiful Fish Camp Prong, passing a slide cascade at 20.1 miles, then by a big bluff near War Branch and stairstep cascades at 20.6 miles, all draining the highest points of the Volunteer State.

Open onto a huge densely wooded flat before coming to the iron bridge spanning the Little River at 21.6 miles. Here, Fish Camp Prong and Little River merge, forming a scenic sight. Meet the Little River Trail at 21.7 miles. Here, you can head right 0.8 mile to the fine Rough Creek campsite #24, set at the confluence of Rough Creek and Little River. It offers fire rings and bearproof food storage cables. Otherwise head left on the wide, gravel Little River Trail. The walking is easy in magnificent woodlands with sizeable sycamore and other hardwoods. Meet the Huskey Gap Trail at 22.6 miles. Here, that path leads a short piece to campsite #21, set on a slight slope a little ways back from the Little River. It offers fire rings and bearproof food storage cables.

Our circuit backpack stays on the Little River Trail, crossing the waterway on a sturdy bridge to meet the other end of the Cucumber Gap Trail at 23.1 miles. Keep straight, descending past Huskey Branch Cascades at 23.3 miles. Here, the cataract drops 25 feet in stages both above and below the trail bridge crossing Huskey Branch. Note the huge pool in the Little River at the two stream's confluence. Continue on the wide, gravel Little River Trail. The walking is a breeze then you pass through another portion of the former Elkmont cabin community, reaching the Little River trailhead and alternate parking at 25.5 miles. Here, head left and walk the road 0.1 mile to the Jakes Creek trailhead parking and hike's end at 25.6 miles.

Mileages

0.0   Jakes Creek Parking Area

0.7   Pass Cucumber Gap Trail, then Meigs Mountain Trail

The Little River presents national park–level splendor.

3.1	Lower Jakes Creek Campsite #27
3.8	Jakes Gap
5.7	Dripping Spring Mountain campsite #26
6.3	Lynn Camp Prong leaves left
8.7	Left on Appalachian Trail
11.7	Silers Bald shelter
12.0	Silers Bald
13.5	Double Springs Gap shelter
14.0	Left on Goshen Prong Trail
18.5	Camp Rock campsite #23
21.7	Left on Little River Trail, campsite #24 to right
22.6	Huskey Gap Trail and campsite #21 to right
23.1	Cucumber Gap Trail leaves left
23.3	Huskey Branch Cascades
25.5	Little River Trail parking area
25.6	Jakes Creek Trail parking area

GOOD CAMPSITES CAN MAKE
OR BREAK A TRIP

I was in the midst of an extended backpacking trip in the Smokies. I'd spent much time along the Appalachian Trail, where the wind had been blowing nonstop. Furthermore, it seemed the parade of AT backpackers was as ceaseless as the wind.

I headed for lower terrain, hoping a change of elevation would also cut down on the wind. I left the AT and dropped to the Little River and a sheltered campsite, then cast a line for trout. After fishing, I returned to the lovely, quiet campsite and concluded that when backpacking an appealing camp is as important as appealing weather.

Minimally speaking, a backcountry campsite requires two things: a flat spot and accessible water. Beyond those two necessities, look for characteristics of the land that will help you deal with the situations at hand. For example, you may want an open, breezy location if the insects are troublesome. Or you may want a sheltered location if the winds are howling. You may want shade if it is hot. Or ample fallen wood for a fire if it is cold. Find surroundings that enhance your comfort in camp.

Raising the bar, begin looking for other characteristics that will make your campsite not only functionally desirable but also aesthetically appealing. Why not go for a view if you can get it? Or look over a wildflower garden? Perhaps camp within walking distance of a waterfall. Discerning backpackers will camp near such highlights, but not too close to detract from the overlook or waterfall.

Some backpacking destinations have designated campsites that require a permit such as the Smokies or some Tennessee state parks, or have specific camping rules such as Big South Fork. Other places, like national forests, are more freewheeling. Still others have designated campsites that you can stay at without a permit. Check into specific camping regulations *before* your backpacking trip.

Also consider campsite safety. Look around for widow makers—dead standing trees that may fall during a storm. This actually happened on a backpacking trip in Alaska. My friend Scott Davis and I were camped in an aspen grove, one of which fell from wind throw around dawn. Luckily the tree, while falling, hit other trees and was slowed while plunging down onto Scott's shelter. We considered ourselves very lucky.

Don't set your campsite near a stream prone to flooding. Consider an exit strategy. Will you have to ford the river to get back to civilization? If rain is forecast, hike on to another campsite where you can avoid fords.

Therefore, whether it is practicality, aesthetics or safety, a good campsite can make or break a backcountry trip.

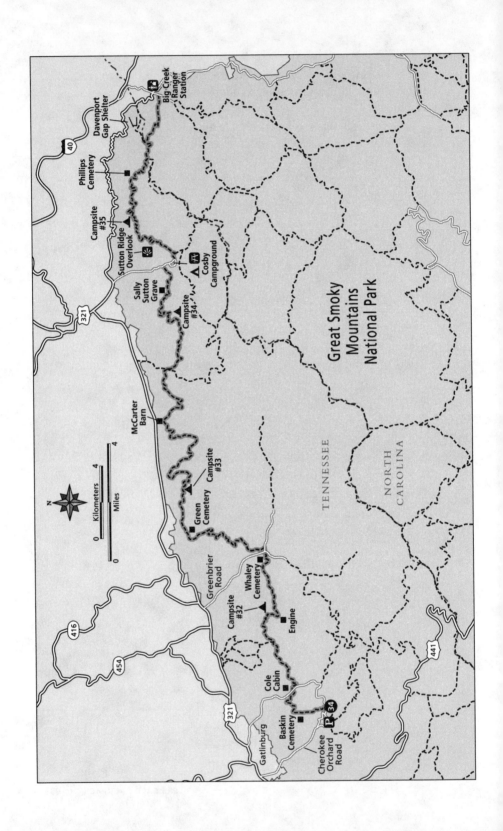

34

Old Settlers Backpack

THE BACKPACK

This backpacking adventure in the Great Smoky Mountains National Park will leave you with a sense of history and natural splendor. The backpack runs along the lower reaches of the Tennessee side of the park, winding past cemeteries, old homesites, chimneys, rock walls and other relicts of the days when hardscrabble farmers hoed the backwoods hollows. Four backcountry campsites are available for overnighting.

Distance and Configuration: 44.4 mile end-to-end
Difficulty: Difficult due to mileage
Outstanding Features: Pioneer history, streams, waterfalls, views
Elevation: 1,412 feet low point, 3,514 feet high point
Scenery: 5
Solitude: 4 (Busier in a few places)
Family Friendly: 1
Canine Friendly: 0 (Dogs not allowed)
Fees/permits: Fee-based permit required
Best season: October through April
Maps: National Geographic #229 Great Smoky Mountains National Park
For more info: Great Smoky Mountains National Park, 107 Park Headquarters Road, Gatlinburg, TN 37738; (865) 436-1200; nps. gov/grsm
Finding the Trailhead: To reach backpack's end from Exit #451 on I-40 near Hartford, exit right to bridge the Pigeon River on Waterville Road. After the bridge, turn left to follow the Pigeon River upstream. Come to an intersection with Mount Sterling Road 2.3 miles after crossing the Pigeon River. Proceed straight through the intersection and drive 0.3 mile to Big Creek Ranger Station and parking on your right. To reach the backpack's beginning from Big

Creek, backtrack 0.3 mile, then turn left on Mount Sterling Road toward Cosby, soon entering Tennessee and joining TN 32. Stay with TN 32 north for 11 miles, then turn left onto US 321 south and drive for 17.9 miles to turn left on Baskins Creek Bypass and follow it 0.7 mile to turn left on Cherokee Orchard Road. Stay with Cherokee Orchard Road for 3.6 miles to reach the second Rainbow Falls parking area. Park here, then walk up Roaring Fork Motor Nature Trail (gated in winter) and follow it 0.2 mile to the Baskins Creek Trail on your left. GPS trailhead coordinates: Big Creek Ranger Station: 35.759848, -83.105592; Rainbow Falls parking area 35.677517, -83.481665

On this backpack, you will hike amongst the greatest concentration of preserved mountain settler homesites in the Appalachians, gaining a glimpse into the lifeways of those who pioneered the lower reaches of what became Great Smoky Mountains National Park. The backpack travels easterly, roughly from Gatlinburg to the park's eastern end at Big Creek Ranger Station. The end is in North Carolina in order to provide secure parking, rather than ending at Davenport Gap, on the Tennessee-North Carolina state line.

The backpack is intended to be a four night trip, with roughly evenly spaced mileages between campsites. Although there are no long ascents or descents, the hike does undulate between streams flowing off the state line ridge looming above the route. It is along these streams you will find settler homesites. The best time to execute this backpack is when the leaves are off the trees, either late fall, winter or early spring, when you can best see the cemeteries, stone walls, chimneys, and metal remains marking sites where early Tennesseans were born, lived and died.

Start the Baskins Creek Trail, meandering through second growth woodland still recovering from the fires of 2016. Rise onto a ridge of pine, oak, and mountain laurel where views open of the Sugarlands and mountains beyond. Drop to Falls Branch, rock hopping it at 1.0 mile, then descend a tight hollow covered in rhododendron where Falls Branch falls. At 1.1 miles, a spur leads left to 0.2 mile to Baskin Cemetery. All but one grave is unmarked. At 1.3 miles, split left to Baskins Falls. It leads past a pioneer homesite, with the broken down chimney, over a ledge and down to the base of 35-foot Baskins Falls, diving in two stages over a wide rock face. Purportedly, pioneers used Baskins Falls as a natural shower.

Continue the Baskins Creek Trail, surmounting a ridge to turn up Baskins Creek. You will repeat the pattern, going over another ridge then down to the next creek, Rocky Spur Branch. Find well-tended Bales Cemetery beyond Rocky Spur Branch and just before coming to Roaring Fork Motor Nature Trail at 3.2

Baskins Falls was used as a natural shower by Smokies settlers.

Typical settler remains as seen along this backpack.

miles. From there, head left, crossing Roaring Fork then turning right onto the Grapeyard Ridge Trail. View the Alex Cole cabin and two outbuildings, moved here from the Sugarlands onto the old Jim Bales Place, where there was once a frame house.

Keep east, climbing over 500 feet, joining the north slope of Mount Winnesoka. Cut across the upper reaches of streams flowing off Mount Winnesoka

This elaborate trailside chimney continues to stand the test of time.

divided by wooded ridges. At 5.6 miles dip into formerly settled Dudley Creek, trekking alongside old stone walls marking homesites. At 5.9 miles, a trail leads left into the quasi-official network of bridle paths used by the park equestrian concessionaire. Cross Dudley Creek, then rise along Grapeyard Ridge, its tulip trees draped in a surfeit of vines. Top out then descend a wonderfully graded trail, reaching the spur to moderately used Injun Creek campsite #32 at 7.6 miles.

Here, the unusually grassy camp is set on a terraced homesite with streams on both sides of it. As with all Smokies backcountry campsites, bearproof food storage cables are provided.

Leave your first night's destination, climbing along Injun Creek on settler roads for the next few miles. Keep your eyes peeled for the famed steam engine tractor that fell in what became known as Injun Creek at 8.1 miles (An errant mapmaker misnamed the stream when told the name was Engine Creek instead dubbed it Injun Creek).

Climb over James Gap and walk a fine rhododendron lined path into aptly named Rhododendron Creek. At the height of settlement in the Smokies there were 11 homesteads in the Rhododendron Creek watershed. Today, the gurgling stream makes the only noises as you criss-cross it several times without benefit of footbridge. At 10.1 miles, leave Rhododendron Creek, turning up a side stream, then rise over a gap. Middle Prong Little Pigeon River roars below. Switchback downhill, passing a spur to the Whaley Cemetery before dumping out on Greenbrier Road at 11.0 miles. Here, turn right then bridge Porters Creek left and follow the gravel road toward Ramsay Cascades trailhead. After the third road bridge, crossing Middle Prong, look left for the Old Settlers Trail (OST) at 11.1 miles.

The Old Settlers Trail is an agglomeration of former wagon roads, woods paths, farm tracks and newer foot trail, wending through numerous watersheds along which pioneers lived before being bought out by the state of Tennessee in its appropriation of lands for what was to become Smoky Mountains National Park.

Leave once densely populated Greenbrier Cove. Rock walls soon are evident. The roar of Middle Prong Little Pigeon River stays with you as the trail crosses Bird Branch then ascends a bluff above the Middle Prong. Descend before reaching and turning up Little Bird Branch at 11.7 miles, shortly passing a homesite bordered by a mossy rock wall. An old "chimbley" (mountain vernacular) stands among scattered trees, taking over of the former farm. Ascend over Copeland Divide in a hickory-oak forest then cross upper Copeland Branch at 13.6 miles. Climb into pine and mountain laurel. In winter, vistas of the high country open to the north. The OST drops off the ridge to cross Snakefeeder Branch—on the top ten all time Tennessee mountain names list—at 14.7 miles. The path passes homesites while shambling down the deep and intimate valley, criss-crossing Snakefeeder Branch and its tributaries.

At 15.5 miles, a still-used former settler path leaves left across Snakefeeder Branch. The OST turns right here, easterly, entering a large flat of brambles, brush and trees. Pass a spur right to the Green Cemetery just before reaching wide and shallow Soak Ash Creek at 15.6 miles. Splash over the stream to soon cross Evans Creek and join a wagon track heading up the branch. At 16.0 miles, at a sign, the OST makes a hard right turn, leaving the wagon track for a different roadbed but continuing up Evans Creek.

At 16.8 miles, the OST climbs steeply away from the watershed, then levels off at some striking stone walls just before reaching Timothy Creek. Cross Timothy Creek then turn right, upstream, passing a chimney with an inverted "v" hearth. A crumbling wooden outbuilding is located toward the creek a bit, as you stand at this chimney. This homestead is a good place to explore. Remember to leave all relicts for other to discover.

Pass two long rock walls before stepping over Darky Branch at mile 17.2. The OST then climbs along a moist north facing slope. At 17.5 miles, a well-used trail leads left out to US 321. The OST veers right to a stony homesite with a chimney and Settlers Camp, campsite #33, your second night's destination, at 17.6 miles. It has two main sites, one by the trail and one uphill in a preserved hemlock grove.

The OST leaves the camp and quickly reaches Redwine Creek. Look for a rocked-in spring box just before the creek. The trail crosses Redwine Creek then works into more former farmland. Rock piles bear witness to a mountaineer's attempt to make his land more arable. Climb a ridge then dip to Ramsay Creek at 18.7 miles. Homesites with crumbling chimneys are stretched along this slender hollow where hardscrabble livin' was the order of the day. Multiple creek crossings are made beneath the black birch and even a few sycamores. Leaves Ramsay Creek behind after the 5th crossing and work east through prime farmland now shaded by a young forest rising above rock walls. Look for a double-hearthed chimney on trail right behind some high rock walls. Contemplate the long winter nights spent huddled by these hearths.

The OST meets Noisy Creek at 20.0 miles, and ascends along the attractive creek. Falling mini cascades slow into clear pools. Step over Noisy Creek at 20.3 miles where a mossy rock wall forms a terrace on trail right topped by a chimney. Climbing past another homesite, this one with a double chimney and numerous yucca plants, an exotic which settlers often planted. Tumbling Creek, a tributary of Noisy Creek, flows in front of this homesite. Make a quick double creek crossing of Tumbling Creek, followed by a short, steep pitch into quiet woods. By 21.0 miles, you may notice old growth trees overhead. Tulip trees, a few chestnut oaks, and even red maple round out the species list of ancient trees that escaped the logger's axe. Unfortunately, the old growth hemlocks have fallen prey to the hemlock wooly adelgid.

Descend by switchbacks into Texas Creek and settled country at 21.7 miles. Begin an 800-foot descent along the stream, where the valley opens and widens, as spur branches feed the cascading creek. Homesites are abundant, as evidenced by one on trail right with a double chimney. At 22.7 miles, an old roadbed continues down Texas Creek, but the OST bears right, winding among low hills and small creeks, passing a very high rock wall. Reach Webb Creek and a homesite at 23.6 miles. The signed OST crosses Webb Creek, then immediately turns upstream. A spur trail to the McCarter Barn goes straight 300 feet. The McCarter Barn, circa 1876, is a log structure with wooden shingle roofing.

Rise up Webb Creek, passing through a break in a rock wall then surmount Snag Mountain, where the quiet woods contrast with noisy creeks that the trail has followed. Just after the trail tops out it offers wintertime views of the evergreen slopes of Maddron Bald and the Smokies crest. Turn down Snag Branch at 25.1 miles, where homesites in the hollow reveal more glimpses into the lives of Tennessee mountaineers. Turn away from Snag Branch to meet its mother stream, Dunn Creek at 26.0 miles. This can be a tough crossing. Work east in flats to reach Indian Camp Creek, where there has been a footbridge in the past and may be in the future, at 26.3 miles. The OST shambles uphill through young woods to reach a trail junction in a preserved hemlock grove at 26.8 miles.

Our hike joins the Gabes Mountain Trail toward Cosby, leaving settled terrain and rising into old growth woods, where northern red oaks, buckeyes and preserved hemlocks tower overhead. Rise up above 3,000 feet then reach Greenbrier Cove campsite #34, your third night's destination, at 28.6 miles. It offers several sites strung along Greenbrier Creek, amid the boulders and old growth trees.

Next day, make the sometimes-challenging crossing of Greenbrier Creek, then rise to wind in and out of small coves where more old growth trees thrive. At 30.4 miles, split a gap on Gabes Mountain then descend by switchbacks to Lower Falling Branch. Pass the quarter-mile spur trail to the base of 45-foot Hen Wallow Falls at 31.3 miles. It is worth a detour to see the cataract flow slender of a rock face then widen to crash into a boulder jumble. The track continues east on steeply sloped lower Snake Den Mountain. Look for wooden guardrail posts, relics from the days when early Smoky Mountain tourists would drive almost to Hen Wallow Falls. Bisect interestingly named Bearneck Gap at 31.7 miles. Pass the spur to the grave of Sally Sutton at 32.1 miles then descend into formerly settled country in the Crying Creek valley.

Span streams on log bridges, passing the spur right to Cosby Campground at 33.1 miles (another camping option), then trace an old pioneer road to emerge at the Cosby Picnic Area and parking at 33.4 miles. From here, head right past the picnic shelter then uphill along the parking lot to join the signed Low Gap Trail at 33.6 miles. The wide path passes nature trail spurs and the Cosby campground road before turning left on an old pioneer road then bridging Cosby Creek to reach another trail intersection at 34.1. Here, the Low Gap Trail goes right, the Cosby Horse Trail goes left and we keep straight, joining the Lower Mount Cammerer Trail.

You've successfully navigated the Cosby maze. Lower Mount Cammerer Trail keeps its easterly direction, passing through former pioneer farms, long since forested with hardwoods, especially tulip trees. They like to reclaim former fields. At 34.4 miles, on trail right, is an old rocked-in spring. Bridge Toms Creek, rich with native brook trout, at 35.0 miles. Brook trout are the only native Smokies trout and normally are relegated to higher elevation streams, due to heavy stocking in the past of rainbow and brown trout. But Toms Creek, at 2,500 feet, still sports brookies.

After spanning Toms Creek on a footbridge, begin the short ascent to Sutton Ridge, reached at 35.3 miles. A spur trail leads right to the overlook where to your left and dead ahead is the upper Cosby Valley. You can see in the grand scheme of things how level the land in Cosby is compared to the rest of the Smokies, explaining why it was so heavily settled. Gabes Mountain stands prominently to your left.

Leave Sutton Ridge, dipping into the hollow of Riding Fork, where a long, tapered cascade drops from Rich Butt Mountain. Continue the creek/ridge pattern, working east in shady lush creek vales and over dry and piney ridges. Gilliland Creek campsite #35 appears in the flat below at 37.2 miles. This campsite, your fourth night's destination, is misnamed, as the waterway's official name is Gilliland Fork. Three campsites are tiered along the brook, while two others are on the piney hillside above the stream.

The trail leaves the campsite and resumes the creek/ridge pattern. At 39.5 miles, reach the nose of Groundhog Ridge and the Groundhog Ridge Manway, a rough unmaintained narrow track leading 1,500 feet directly up Groundhog Ridge in about a mile to Mount Cammerer.

From Groundhog Ridge, Lower Mount Cammerer Trail continues east. At 40.0 miles, a short spur heads left to the Phillips Cemetery, the highest internment on the Tennessee side of the park at 3,480 feet. Families of upper Tobes Creek were buried in this now remote spot. Continue along the slopes of lower Mount Cammerer to meet the Appalachian Trail and the Tennessee-North Carolina at 41.4 miles.

It's downhill all the way from here. Head left, southbound on America's most famous footpath, winding through the mountain laurel and galax lined path to meet the Chestnut Branch Trail in a gap at 42.4 miles (You could extend your trip by continuing the AT for another mile to reach the Davenport Gap trail shelter, then backtrack next day). The Chestnut Branch Trail dives into North Carolina, tracing a tributary before coming along bigger, beautiful and crashing Chestnut Branch at 43.4 miles.

Chestnut Branch was named for the American chestnut tree, the once dominant giant of the Southern Appalachians. Some of the largest trees in the park measured 30 feet in circumference. Chestnut acorns were the staple food for everything from bears to birds. Settlers ate them, too. Remember the words from the Christmas carol, "chestnuts roasting on an open fire." In the early 1900s, Asian chestnut trees were imported to the United States, bringing a fungus that killed the chestnuts. However, to this day chestnut trees sprout from the roots of the ancients, growing up but always succumbing to the blight. Hopefully, these chestnuts are building a resistance to the blight.

Ahead, open onto settled terrain for your last enjoyment of pre-park settler homesites, including rusted relics and huge old trailside oak tree that shaded a home, one among 10 homesites on this stream. Reach backpack's end at 44.3 miles. Here, the Big Creek Ranger Station and parking area are a short ways left.

Mileages

0.0	Baskins Creek Trail
1.3	Spur to Baskins Falls
3.2	Join Grapeyard Ridge Trail
7.6	Campsite #32
11.0	Greenbrier Road
11.1	Join Old Settler Trail
14.7	Snakefeeder Branch
17.6	Campsite #33
21.0	Old growth forest
23.6	Webb Creek, spur to McCarter Barn
26.8	Join Gabes Mountain Trail
28.6	Campsite #34
31.3	Spur to Hen Wallow Falls
33.4	Cosby Picnic Area/Campground
33.6	Join Low Gap Trail
34.1	Lower Mount Cammerer Trail
35.3	Sutton Ridge Overlook
37.2	Campsite #35
40.0	Spur to Phillips Cemetery
41.3	Join Appalachian Trail
42.3	Right on Chestnut Branch Trail
44.4	Big Creek Ranger Station

35

Snake Den Backpack

THE BACKPACK

This is a classic two night Great Smoky Mountains National Park adventure, almost a rite of passage for Tennessee backpackers. The loop is chock full of highlights, including old growth forests, waterfalls and views. Two reservable backcountry campsites comprise your itinerary. Start in Cosby, traveling through hilly terrain to visit Henwallow Falls before walking big forests to reach Sugar Cove campsite. Next, climb to the high country via the old growth trees of Albright Grove. Rise to a stellar vista then camp on cool Otter Creek. Finally, pass the vistas of Maddron Bald before making the long descent on the Snake Den Ridge Trail.

Distance and Configuration: 18.2-mile loop
Difficulty: Difficult due to elevation change
Outstanding Features: Old growth forests, views, waterfall, homesites
Elevation: 2,175 feet low point, 5,400 feet high point
Scenery: 5
Solitude: 3
Family Friendly: 1
Canine Friendly: 0 (Dogs not allowed)
Fees/permits: Fee-based permit required
Best season: Year-round; spring for wildflowers
Maps: National Geographic #229 Great Smoky Mountains National Park
For more info: Great Smoky Mountains National Park, 107 Park
   Headquarters Road, Gatlinburg, TN 37738; (865) 436-1200;
   nps.gov/grsm
Finding the Trailhead: From exit 534 on I-40 at Newport, take TN
   32 south for 5.5 miles, then stay left with TN 32 south at a stop
   sign and follow it for 8.1 more miles to turn right into the signed
   Cosby section of the park. After 1.9 miles up Cosby Road, watch
   for a road splitting left to the Cosby Picnic Area. Turn left here and
   immediately park. The Gabes Mountain Trail starts a short distance

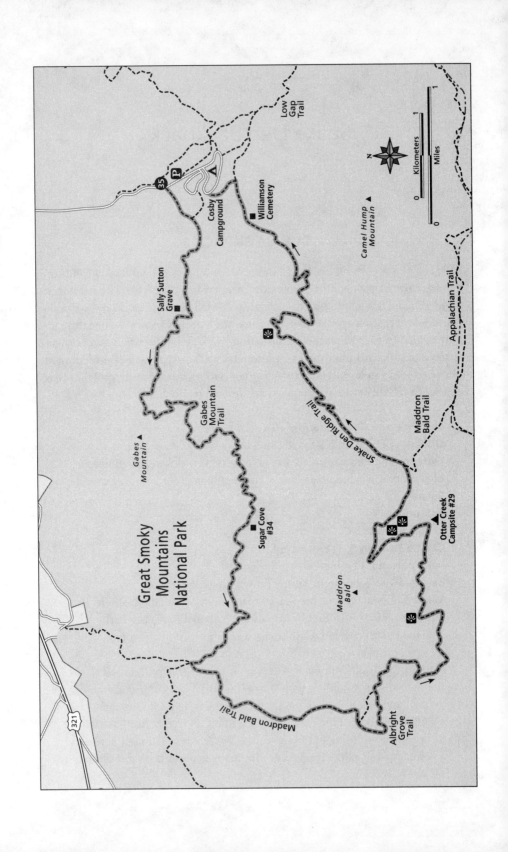

Using the food storage cables at Otter Creek campsite.

downhill, back toward the entrance to Cosby, on the west side of Cosby Road. GPS trailhead coordinates: 35.757712, -83.209637

I've executed this backpack in all seasons and it never fails to please the eye. You likely can't find a loop backpack in Tennessee with more old growth trees on the route. You can even camp among them at your first night's destination at Sugar Cove. In addition to the big trees the trailside scenery is first rate, including clear-as-air creeks, and views from the heath balds of the high country. The reservable designated campsites are average, not destinations in and of themselves. Be apprised the backpack does have an aggregate elevation gain/loss of nearly 5,200 feet. This allows you to enjoy multiple environments, from formerly settled lands to cove hardwood forests to heath balds to red spruce forests.

Leave Cosby Picnic Area on the Gabes Mountain Trail under oak and hickory forests flanked by mountain laurel and rhododendron. The coves of Cosby were among the most heavily settled areas of the pre-park Smokies. Reach a trail junction at 0.3 mile. Here, a path heads left to Cosby Campground. Stay right here to bridge Rock Creek on one of the signature Smokies log bridges with a handrail. Curve northwest for Bearneck Cove. More substantial tributaries have

Hen Wallow Falls.

small bridges. Bridge Crying Creek before coming to an old auto turnaround at 1.1 miles, in Bearneck Cove—one of the top ten all-time Tennessee mountain appellations. Ascend past rock piles, where a local mountaineer tried to make this stony land easier to plant.

The Gabes Mountain Trail, long ago known as the Messer Trail, works up Crying Creek then climbs to reach a small gap where you can find the spur leading right to the lonesome grave of Sally Sutton, marked with native rocks and a newer marble rectangle. The path dips to a tributary of Crying Creek then slices through Bearneck Gap at 1.7 miles. From here, traverse steeper terrain on the slopes of Gabes Mountain among rock outcrops and vine-draped tulip trees.

At 2.3 miles, a signed spur descends 0.1 mile to Hen Wallow Falls. Here, Lower Falling Branch skims down a wide sheet over a layer of naked for 60 feet before bespattering a heap of boulders. Here, you will leave most dayhikers behind. The path crosses Lower Falling Branch, then switchbacks up its vale, crossing it a couple more times before rising to bisect a gap on Gabes Mountain at

3.7 miles. Ahead, curve around the upper reaches of greater Sugar Cove, drained by Greenbrier Creek. Old-growth tulip trees, buckeyes and Carolina silver-bells rise in the cathedralesque coves. Unfortunately the big old hemlocks are gone, decimated by the hemlock wooly adelgid. But the fallen trees have created light gaps where future giants will take their place.

The trail leads you across crystalline Greenbrier Creek to Sugar Cove campsite #34, at 5.3 miles. Several camps, shaded by several old growth trees, including some preserved hemlocks, are strung out in tiers along the crashing waterway. Metal fire rings and bearproof food hanging cables enhance the locale.

Continuing on, the Gabes Mountain Trail rises to Buckeye Lead, slicing through another gap. More old growth trees are found within sight of the trail. Hop over Buckeye Creek. Descend to cross Cole Creek at 6.3 miles, then wander down its valley. The mountain slope eases and you enter former fields and farms now regrown with a wide biodiversity that belies its former cleared state when East Tennessee's mountain folk farmed this rocky terrain.

Come to a trail intersection at 7.0 miles. Head left on the wide Maddron Bald Trail, rising on a gravel doubletrack through lightly sloped woods, aiming for gorgeous Indian Camp Branch. Curve to its valley where you will find rock walls from former settlements.

At 8.0 miles, reach an old auto turnaround. The trail becomes more primitive as it rises forth, leaving previously inhabited terrain, and returning to old-growth woods of northern red oak, maple, tulip trees and basswood. A host of other plants and trees round out the picture. Cross Indian Camp Creek on a long footbridge at 8.5 miles. Climb away, reaching a trail junction at 8.7 miles. Keep right with the Albright Grove Trail as it loops through an old growth forest, altered by the falling of so many giant hemlocks.

Return to the Maddron Bald Trail at 9.4 miles. Turn right and soon come to a bridgeless, potentially challenging crossing of Indian Camp Creek, just upstream of its confluence Otter Creek. Make more crossings of Indian Camp Creek at 10.5 miles then at 10.8 miles, just below a stairstep cascade slaloming among gray boulders. The terrain steepens. Make an easier crossing of Copperhead Branch. Climb from here, looking for red spruce trees—harbinger of the high country—that will accompany you for the next several miles.

The Maddron Bald Trail reaches the point of a ridge and a heath bald at 11.1 miles. A heath bald is a low brushy cluster of shrubs, found along ridges, primarily of rhododendron, mountain laurel, sand myrtle and blueberry. Take the spur leading left to an overlook at a rocky point, elevation 4,215 feet. The vista opens north into East Tennessee through the Indian Camp Creek valley through which you just hiked. The evergreens of Maddron Bald rise to your right, while Snag Mountain and Pinnacle Lead form a wall to your left. What a view.

Beyond the view, turn into steeply sloped Otter Creek valley amidst an ever-green world of spruce, moss and ferns. Reach Otter Creek backcountry campsite #29, elevation 4,525 feet, at 11.9 miles. The small, often chilly campsite has a few tiered flats alongside noisy Otter Creek with slopes rising sharply from the waterway. The camp also features two metal fire rings and bearproof food storage cables.

From Otter Creek, climb to reach the ridgeline of Maddron Bald at 12.6 miles. Make a hard right turn and continue climbing among tunnels of laurel above which rise wind-flagged spruce trees. At 12.9 miles, come the first of a few intermittent lookouts from trailside rock outcrops, flanked by low growing sand myrtle and other windswept plants. Look out. The peaks of Old Black and Pinnacle Lead give way to lower terrain sloping toward the lowlands. Scan the horizon for heath-covered lesser ridges. Enjoy some level hiking before making a final climb in spruce in spruce to meet the Snake Den Ridge Trail at 13.5 miles. You are at the backpack's high point of 5,400 feet.

Head left on the Snake Den Ridge Trail, running along official USGS-named Snake Den Mountain, declining a stony, often wet path under a mantle of yellow birch and red spruce with the land falling away sharply from the trail. Cruise downhill, often using switchbacks. Partial vistas open where the trail passes through heath balds. Views open east of the Smokies crest, including low slung Mount Cammerer lookout tower. A short spur leads left to a view of the cove of Cosby at 15.6 miles. From here, drop to rock hop Inadu Creek at 16.1 miles. Inadu is Cherokee for snake. This must've been once "snakey" place when names were being handed out. The rest of the hike can be a wildflower rich area as the mountain slopes lessen.

Bridge Rock Creek at 17.1 miles, returning to formerly settled lands. Come to an auto turnaround used by park personnel at 17.2 miles. Stay left here on the gravel track, passing the Williamson Cemetery at 17.4 miles. Notably Ella Costner, 1894-1982, is buried here. The Tennessee State Legislature once bestowed upon the World War II prisoner-of-war the title "Poet Laureate of the Smokies."

At 17.7 miles, a horse trail keeps straight to intersect the Low Gap Trail. The Snake Den Ridge Trail stays left on the gravel road, reaching Cosby Campground near campsite #B51, at 18.0 miles. From here, work your way through the campground downhill to the picnic/hiker parking area, completing the classic backpack at 18.2 miles.

Mileages

0.0	Cosby Picnic Area
2.3	Spur to Hen Wallow Falls
5.3	Sugar Cove Campsite #34
7.0	Left on Maddron Bald Trail

8.7	Right on Albright Grove Loop
11.1	View
11.9	Otter Creek Campsite #29
12.9	Views from Maddron Bald
13.5	Left on Snake Den Ridge Trail
16.1	Cross Inadu Creek
17.2	Left on gravel doubletrack
17.7	Stay left toward Cosby Campground
18.0	Reach Cosby Campground
18.2	Cosby Picnic Area

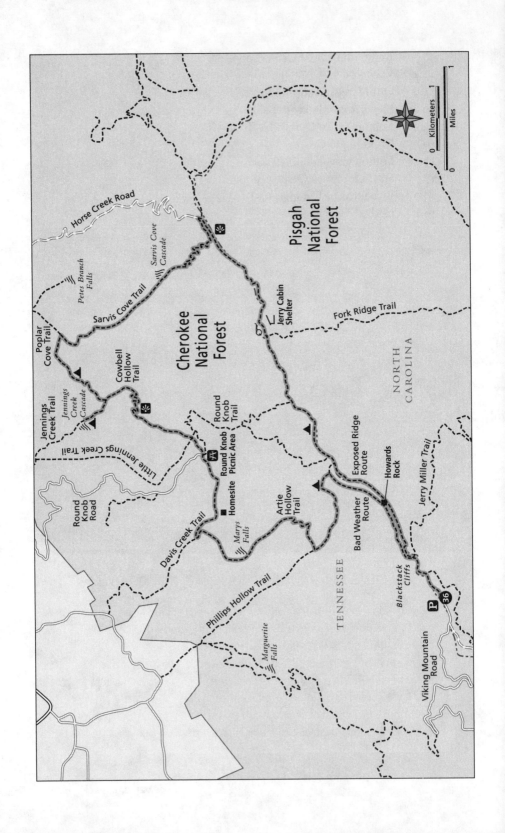

36

Bald Mountains Backpack

THE BACKPACK

This loop backpack combines incredible Appalachian Trail views with lesser used side trails of the Cherokee National Forest's Bald Mountains Scenic Area in Greene County. See waterfalls, homesites, remote creeks—and very few people off the AT. Start the circuit with fast and far reaching views from Big Firescald Knob. Pass Jerry Cabin Shelter then the fields of Coldspring Mountain before leaving the AT for remote Sarvis Cove. Next cross over to pretty Jennings Creek, then rise to Round Knob before roller coasting down to Davis Creek. The next three miles are arguably the hardest in this guide—up primitive Artie Hollow Trail, and then up ultra-steep ascent Phillips Hollow, returning to the AT. From there the trip's end back to the trailhead will seem a breeze.

Distance and Configuration: 17.0-mile loop

Difficulty: Difficult due to 3 mile stretch of Artie Hollow/Phillips Hollow Trails

Outstanding Features: Blackstack Cliffs, Big Firescald Ridge, waterfalls, remoteness

Elevation: 2,068 feet low point, 4,565 feet high point

Scenery: 5

Solitude: 2 on AT, 5 on other trails

Family Friendly: 1

Canine Friendly: 2

Fees/permits: No fees or permits required

Best season: Early fall through late spring

Maps: National Geographic #782 French Broad and Nolichucky River, Cherokee and Pisgah National Forests

For more info: Cherokee National Forest, Unaka Ranger District, 4900 Asheville Highway, Greeneville TN 37743, (423) 638-4109, www.fs.usda.gov/cherokee

Traversing the field of Coldspring Knob on a chill winter morn.

Finding the Trailhead: From the intersection of US 321 and TN 107
in Greeneville, take Asheville Highway/TN 107W/TN 70S for
14.8 miles to turn left on Viking Mountain Road (If you reach
North Carolina and Allen Gap you've gone too far). Follow Viking
Mountain Road for 7.9 miles to reach Camp Creek Bald. Here, the
road splits—head left for 0.3 mile to a circular turnaround. The
parking area is on the right just before you reach the turnaround.
GPS trailhead coordinates: 36°01'52.4"N, 82°42'19.3"W

The Bald Mountains Scenic Area is deserving of the moniker. Along with adjacent
Shelton Laurel Backcountry in North Carolina's Pisgah National Forest, this
section of the Cherokee National Forest delivers beauty and ruggedness high
and low. This specific backpack presents two distinct segments. The first part
is on the well-trod and maintained Appalachian Trail. After leaving the AT, be
prepared for rugged, primitive, lightly marked and maintained paths that collectively create a challenging roller coaster ride between steep sided stream hollows and the ridges that divide them. The trails are truly challenging and equally
rewarding with waterfalls, wildflowers, some views and an everywhere-you-look
beauty that must be earned. Campsites can be easily found on the Appalachian

On the AT atop Big Firescald Knob.

Trail, including Jerry Cabin shelter. Camps are more limited on the lesser used trails, though savvy backpackers can find small flats suitable for overnighting. I recommend this as a two night trip, even though the mileages suggest a 1 night trip is viable. Artie Hollow and Phillips Hollow are truly rugged tracks that will test your mettle. I have tramped them many, many times and find the area quite rewarding. Do not do this loop in summer! All trails but the AT will be overgrown.

Leave Camp Creek Bald parking area by walking just a few feet west on the entrance road then cut back east on a blue-blazed doubletrack. Trace it for 0.3 mile then split right on a blue-blazed foot trail that quickly meets the AT. Here, head left on the rocky AT, northbound among rhododendron and yellow birch. A short distance ahead, a well-used spur climbs left to the Blackstack Cliffs and a stellar view into East Tennessee. Don't pass this by. Resume the AT and meet the Jerry Miller Trail at 0.6 mile. It leaves right for Carolina but we keep on the AT and quickly the Appalachian Trail splits. Take the right fork, the "Exposed Ridge Route," climbing to the stony crest of Big Firescald Knob. The "Bad Weather Route" is part of our return.

The rugged trail rises in rock and stunted vegetation. By 1.3 miles, multiple vistas open east to waves of Carolina mountains and west into the hills of East Tennessee. Reach signed Howards Rock at 1.4 miles. What panoramas in all directions! Make sure and look back at the towers of Camp Creek Bald. The views diminish and the Exposed Ridge Route and Bad Weather Route reunite at 2.2 miles. The walking becomes easier as you continue northbound on the united AT. Descend to reach Licklog Gap and a level but dry wooded campsite at 2.6 miles. Climb to reach Round Knob Trail at 3.0 miles. That trail leads left to a gated road and onward for a total of 2 miles to Round Knob Picnic Area. This is a viable loop shortcut.

The AT then traces a former roadbed, making an easy track through an area with an incredible display of painted trilliums in April. At 3.7 miles, pass the Fork Ridge Trail descending right, then descend to find Jerry Cabin Shelter at 3.8 miles. The three-sided stone refuge also has a nearby spring. Fine, level campsites are a short distance downtrail at Chestnutlog Gap.

From there, the AT climbs Coldspring Mountain, opening onto mown fields at 4.8 miles, a slender mix of grass, brush and trees. Look back toward the towers of Camp Creek Bald before leaving the meadows at 5.1 miles. Just ahead, join the signed Sarvis Cove Trail as it cuts left, back across the narrow meadow to soon reach the end of four-wheel-drive-only Horse Creek Road. Here, head left from the turnaround on a brushy, narrow, faint, primitive track that quickly descends a very steep slope using innumerable switchbacks. At 6.2 miles, come along the stream of Sarvis Cove. The descent moderates while passing Sarvis Cove Cascade, a 10-foot ledge drop, at 6.5 miles. Just ahead, cross the tumbling stream twice in succession. Descend the right bank on a wider trail flanked with rhododendron, rock-hopping the stream again at 7.5.

Meet Poplar Cove Trail at 7.9 miles. Here, turn acutely left and climb to a gap and dry campsite at 8.4 miles, the only level place around. Descend in oaks, pines and laurel toward Jennings Creek. At 8.9 miles reach Jennings Creek. For a recommended campsite, leave right, crossing Jennings Creek twice to reach a small campsite and Jennings Creek Cascade, a waterfall with an outsized pool, at 9.2 miles. From there, backtrack up Jennings Creek, and continue up the stream, joining the Cowbell Hollow Trail. Pass rock piles and an old homesite to cross Jennings Creek. Climb, switchbacking among xeric pines, Catawba rhododendron, and greenbrier. Views open south to the stateline ridge. Cut through a gap, easing the climb, then meet the Little Jennings Creek Trail at 10.7 miles. Keep straight here, reaching Round Knob Picnic Area, with a historic picnic shelter and a spring, at 10.8 miles.

From here, join the Davis Creek Trail, leaving near the picnic area restroom. Wind through evergreens then descend toward Davis Creek. Step over a tributary of Davis Creek at 11.6 miles, bisecting a widening cove and former homesite. Come along Davis Creek, tracing it downstream to cross the tributary once more. At 11.9 miles, an unofficial bootleg equestrian trail rises right. Here, stay left on a rocky eroded path to meet Davis Creek. Cross the stream then reach Artie

Hollow Trail at 12.0 miles. Head left on the Artie Hollow Trail. Get your mojo on. Begin ascending the right side of Davis Creek then cross the rocky stream of Artie Hollow. Storms and lesser use leave a rough track. Expect to criss-cross the stream, push through brush and work around blowdowns in a temperate jungle. The hollow is steep-sided, almost wall-like. At 12.9 miles, come to Marys Falls on your right. The 35-foot spiller dances down a rock ledge. The lack of a beaten down trail to Marys Falls testifies to infrequent visitation.

Continue battling up Artie Hollow, criss-crossing the stream as it stair-steps over layered rock. Rhododendron grows thick here. At 13.4 miles, cross over to the right hand bank, then here the trail goes right up a heavily overgrown tributary. At 13.5 miles, the trail switchbacks right up and away from the water. Bisect the ridge dividing Artie and Phillips Hollows, then dive a steep slope, at times tracing an old fire line. Cross a small stream then gratefully meet the Phillips Hollow Trail at 14.1 miles. Don't sweat that this trail isn't on the National Geographic map—the path is there and is easier but steeper than Artie Hollow. Head up Phillips Hollow, crossing the stream of the hollow, now on the right hand bank. Hike up a clear trail grade that becomes very steep, cleaving a boulder garden ahead. Small streamlets spill over the path. The trail becomes fainter as you level off at Fox Cabin Gap at 15.0 miles. Congratulations, you just climbed 1,100 feet in 0.9 mile! Campsites can be found at Fox Cabin Gap. From here the brier bordered track curves right, east, to meet the Bad Weather Route of the AT at 15.1 miles.

You'll never be so glad to see a well maintained trail. Here, head right, southbound on a more level than not track. This was the main AT before the Exposed Ridge Route was built over Big Firescald Knob. Meet the Exposed Ridge Route, then Jerry Miller Trail at 16.4 miles. From here it is 0.6 mile back to the trailhead.

Mileages

0.0	Camp Creek Bald Parking Area
0.3	Northbound on AT
0.6	Pass the Jerry Miller Trail then right with Exposed Ridge Route
1.4	Howards Rock
2.2	Exposed Ridge Route/Bad Weather Route converge
2.6	Licklog Gap, campsite
3.0	Round Knob Trail leaves left
3.7	Pass Fork Ridge Trail
3.8	Jerry Cabin Shelter, spring, Chestnutlog Gap
4.8	Fields of Coldspring Mountain
5.1	Left on Sarvis Hollow Trail
6.5	Sarvis Hollow Cascade
7.9	Left on Poplar Cove Trail

8.4	Dry ridgetop campsite
8.9	Right on Jennings Creek Trail
9.2	Campsite, Jennings Creek Cascade, backtrack
9.5	Intersection, straight on Cowbell Hollow Trail
10.7	Pass Little Jennings Creek Trail
10.8	Round Knob Picnic Area, join Davis Creek Trail
12.0	Left on Artie Hollow Trail just after crossing Davis Creek
12.9	Marys Falls
13.4	Trail splits up right hand hollow
14.1	Left up Phillips Hollow
15.0	Fox Cabin Gap, very lightly used campsites
15.1	Meet Bad Weather Route of AT
16.4	Bed Weather Route, Exposed Weather Route meet
17.0.	Camp Creek Bald, complete backpack

37

Roan Highlands Backpack

THE BACKPACK

Trace an unmatched section of the Appalachian Trail on this end-to-end backpack, starting near the town of Unicoi and making your way up to 6,285 foot Roan High Knob. From there cross world famous balds with world class panoramas of the Southern Appalachians, including Round Bald, Jane Bald, Hump Mountain and more. Campsites and shelters abound, including the highest elevation shelter on the entire Appalachian Trail.

Distance and Configuration: 30.0-mile end-to-end
Difficulty: Difficult due to distance; can be shortened
Outstanding Features: Grassy balds, spruce-fir highlands,
    views extraordinaire
Elevation: 6,285 high point, 2,865 low point
Scenery: 5
Solitude: 2
Family Friendly: 1
Canine Friendly: 1
Fees/permits: No fees or permits required
Best season: March-November
Maps: National Geographic #783 Cherokee and Pisgah National
    Forests—South Holston and Watauga Lakes
For more info: Cherokee National Forest, Watauga Ranger District,
    4400 Unicoi Drive, Unicoi TN 37692, (423) 735-1500,
    www.fs.usda.gov /cherokee
Finding the Trailhead: To reach the end point on US 19E from the
    intersection of US 321 and US 19E in Elizabethton, take US 19E
    south for 20.9 miles to the Appalachian Trail road crossing, just
    beyond Bear Branch Road. To reach the starting point from the
    US 19E endpoint, take US 19E north for 11.5 miles, then turn

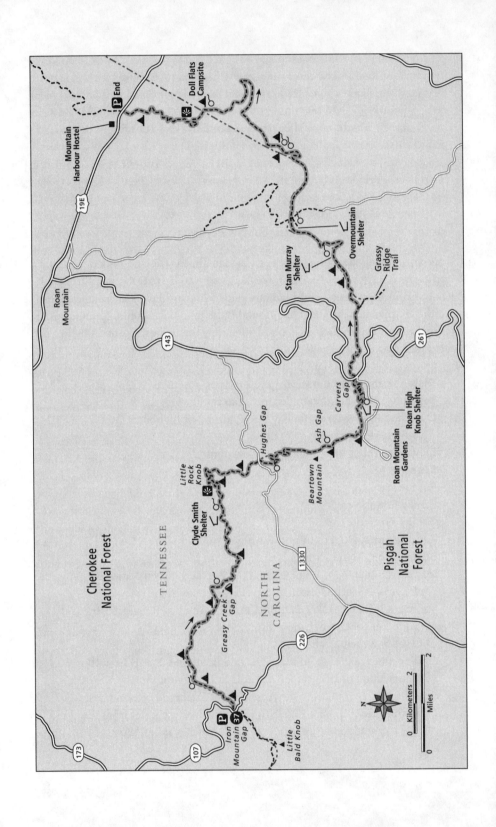

left on TN 173 west and follow it for 6.5 miles to turn left on TN 107 east and follow it for 4.6 miles and Iron Mountain Gap at the Tennessee-North Carolina state line. GPS trailhead coordinates: US 19E 36.177265, -82.011766; Iron Mountain Gap 36.142693, -82.233147

Ask any Appalachian Trail thru-hiker to name five highlights of their hike and the Roan Highlands are sure to make the list –deservedly so. The miles of open mountaintop meadows revealing continual stunning highland panoramas fashion a memorable sight. This backpack takes you not only through the meadows but also amidst the rare Southern Appalachian spruce-fir forest cloaking Roan High Knob.

Water and campsites are abundant along the route, enabling you to adjust your daily mileages on the fly. I recommend this as a 3 night trip but it can run, 2, 3, or 4 nights. A word of warning, the Roan Highlands can be bitterly cold in winter and navigating your way across the balds in fog, snow or rain can be challenging. A portion of the backpack stays above 4,500 feet for 17 straight miles. Try to tackle the open lands when the skies are clear.

Since this is an end-to-end hike, you will either need two cars or a shuttle. A reliable hostel/shuttle is located near the backpack's endpoint, Mountain Harbour, www.mountainharbour.info, in business since 2003. They offer safe, fee parking as well.

Start the backpack at Iron Mountain Gap. Cross TN 107 on a curve, northbound on the Appalachian Trail. Quickly rise in maple, buckeye and oak. At 0.3 mile, find a dry campsite in a gap to your right. Come along an old fence line with locust posts still standing, with a few remaining clearings, like the one at 0.9 mile presenting a view of Unaka Mountain. Just ahead, find level dry campsite on a knob then descend to a clear site of an old highland farm, perched at 4,000 feet, at 1.3 miles. Note the gnarled apple trees. Here, a signed spur trail leads left to a spring.

Continue roughly tracing the state line delineating Tennessee and North Carolina atop Iron Mountain. Pass through still-weedy Weedy Gap at 1.5 miles. Climb and regain the ridgecrest, reaching a small, dry campsite at 2.0 miles. Ascend among hardwoods, now staying above 4,000 feet, passing a dry hilltop campsite at 3.5 miles. Descend to reach Greasy Creek Gap at 4.2 miles and a recommended camping area. Water can be had on the signed old road into Tennessee.

Work your way out of Greasy Creek Gap, regaining the crest in a maple grove, passing a dry campsite on trail left at 5.0 miles. Continue ridge running among hardwoods with occasional rhododendron and hemlock adding an evergreen touch. At 6.1 miles, a signed spur leads left to the Clyde Smith shelter, a three

Backpackers loading their hammocks on Roan Mountain.

sided wooden affair sleeping 6 or so. Flat tent sites are located behind the refuge and a spring serves the site standing at 4,400 feet.

Continuing onward at 6.5 miles in a gap, a spur leads left to a spring. Work your way up stony Little Rock Knob to reach a small cliff and fine view into Tennessee all the way to Johnson City and beyond at 7.2 miles. Trailside, look for the first red spruce trees that will accompany you much of the ensuing journey. At 7.3 miles, pass a dry mountaintop campsite, then wind downward on a well graded, well routed trail, reaching a gap and level campsite at 8.8 miles. Circle around a knob and descend past young chestnuts to reach Hughes Gap at 9.4 miles. Here, Cove Creek Road leads right toward the town of Roan Mountain. Begin a prolonged ascent to Beartown Mountain, passing a short spur to a spring at 9.8 miles. The AT climbs into maple, buckeye and birch, with scads of stinging nettle in summertime. Red spruce increase in number as you switchback upwards atop narrow, rocky ridge. Top out then cruise mixed woods with hardwoods and

Impatient backpacker waiting for his water to boil.

tall regal spruce with an understory of grasses, rolling into Ash Gap at 12.2 miles, elevation 5,330 feet, with a large scenic camping area and a spur trail to a spring.

From here, backpackers work up a shoulder ridge of Roan Mountain. Numerous switchbacks ease the climb as you enter full blown red spruce-Fraser fir forest, with its moss and fern understory lending a fairyland look. Level out and at 13.5 miles come to a dry campsite near a clearing, the former site of the

Verdant meadows grace the spine of Hump Mountain.

old Cloudland Hotel. It operated from 1885-1910, eventually sold and hauled off board by board. From there, the AT descends past an old standing chimney, joining the former wagon track leading to the Cloudland Hotel. At 14.2 miles, come to the spur rising right to the top of Roan High Knob and the highest shelter on the entire Appalachian Trail at 6,250 feet. Once a ranger cabin with nearby fire observation tower, the repurposed four-sided shelter with a wooden door also avails tent sites and a spring near at hand.

From the cabin spur, the AT traces the old hotel access, once known as the Hack Line Road, down Roan High Knob in gorgeous evergreen woodlands. Spring branches run down the track. Traverse numerous switchbacks, crossing spring branches on footbridges then pop out at busy Carvers Gap with its large parking area at 15.4 miles. Cross TN 143 and begin the glorious rise onto the famed balds of Roan Mountain. Cut through a patch of woods then pass a pair of poor, waterless campsites amid a few scraggly evergreens at 16.0 miles.

Top out on Round Bald at 16.2 miles. Look back at the massif of Roan Mountain before rolling along this very popular trail segment. Trek amid stone, brush and grasses with extensive views. Rock outcrops beckon a stop. Gaze around at the wonderment of mountains around you, including the dark wooded Roan High Knob. At 17.4 miles, stay left with the Appalachian Trail as the Grassy Ridge Trail rises right. Most day hikers are left behind. The AT enters brushy woods occupied with mountain ash, yellow birch and spruce with spring seeps spilling over the path. Descend by switchbacks, finding a small overhang that would be a passable rain shelter at 18.0 miles. Continue the downgrade, reaching a dry campsite at 18.4 miles.

Continue in wind gnarled hardwoods, passing a level dry campsite under maples at 18.9 miles. Drop to make Low Gap and the Stan Murray trail shelter, elevation 5,050 feet, at 19.1 miles. The three sided wooden refuge sleeps 6, has a spring nearby, fire ring, a picnic table and adjacent tent sites. From there, work around Elk Hollow Ridge then pass through buckeye-laden Buckeye Gap at 20.3 miles. Continue straddling the state line to reach historic Yellow Mountain Gap at 21.0 miles. Back in 1780, the Overmountain Men from what became Tennessee marched through this pass en route to defeat the British at South Carolina's Battle of Kings Mountain, turning the tide in the Revolutionary War. Campsites and water are near the gap, and the Overmountain shelter, an old barn, is 0.3 mile distant, as is a spring. The Overmountain Victory Trail extends into Tennessee and North Carolina. Climb away from the gap onto Yellow Mountain, running the margin of woods and field. Extensive panoramas open into North Carolina, across Roaring Creek and beyond. Look for the red Overmountain shelter in the meadows below.

Reach the meadows of Little Hump Mountain at 22.3 miles, after passing an old woods road leaving right. Top out at 22.7 miles, near an inviting outcrop.

Views open up in all directions, including east to Grandfather Mountain. Wind in and out of pockets of beech. At 23.1 miles, a spring branch crosses the trail and at 23.2 miles come to recommended wooded campsites in a gap on Little Hump Mountain. Another spring is passed at 23.4 miles, then a second wooded campsite. Descend then open onto the magnificent balds of Hump Mountain, bisecting grassy Bradley Gap at 23.8 miles. You can see your goal ahead—the grassy crown of Hump Mountain. The AT runs up the spine of the ridge, revealing views all about.

Reach the apex of Hump Mountain, elevation 5,587 feet, at 24.5 miles. Eye-popping vistas extend in all cardinal directions. A clear sky reveals a host of mountains. The rest of the backpack is almost all downhill from here as you circle Hump Mountain in grassy splendor, reentering woods at 25.4 miles. Parts of the path ahead are extremely rocky. Spring seeps cross the trail. The track eases as you near Doll Flats. Bisect a meadow then reach woods, the Tennessee state line and the Doll Flats camping area at 27.1 miles. Here, level, wooded campsites and a spur trail to water leave this a well-liked camping area, elevation 4,560 feet.

Beyond Doll Flats, the Appalachian Trail resumes a steady descent in rocky woods, coming alongside some impressive clifflines. Pass a partial view then make a switchback near Morgan Branch. Wind in and out of coves rich with straight trunked tulip trees. Turn into Wilder Mine Hollow at 29.3 miles. Reach a designated camping area at the old Wilder ore mine at 29.4 miles. A flat spot and water are available. Pass a couple more campsites before bridging Buck Creek then rise a bit to make US 19E, completing the backpacking adventure at 30.0 miles.

Mileages

0.0	Iron Mountain Gap trailhead
0.3	Late arrival campsite
1.0	Campsite
1.3	Spring
2.0	Campsite
3.5	Campsite
4.2	Greasy Creek Gap, campsites, spring
5.0	Campsite
6.1	Clyde Smith shelter, spring, campsites
6.5	Spur to spring
7.2	View, campsite ahead
8.8	Campsite
9.4	Hughes Gap
9.8	Spur to spring
12.2	Ash Gap, campsite, spring

13.5	Campsite near old Cloudland Hotel
14.2	Spur to Roan High Knob shelter, spring
15.4	Carvers Gap, TN 143
16.0	Non recommended campsites in a few trees
17.4	Grassy Ridge Trail leaves right
18.4	Campsite
18.8	Campsite
19.1	Stan Murray shelter, spring, tent sites
21.0	Yellow Mountain Gap, campsites, spring, Overmountain shelter
22.7	Top of Little Hump Mountain
23.1	Spring crosses trail, campsite 0.1 mile ahead
23.4	Spring to right of trail, campsite 0.1 mile ahead
24.5	Top of Hump Mountain
27.1	Doll Flat campsites, spring
29.4	Wilder Mine Hollow campsites, stream
30.0	US 19E, backpack's end

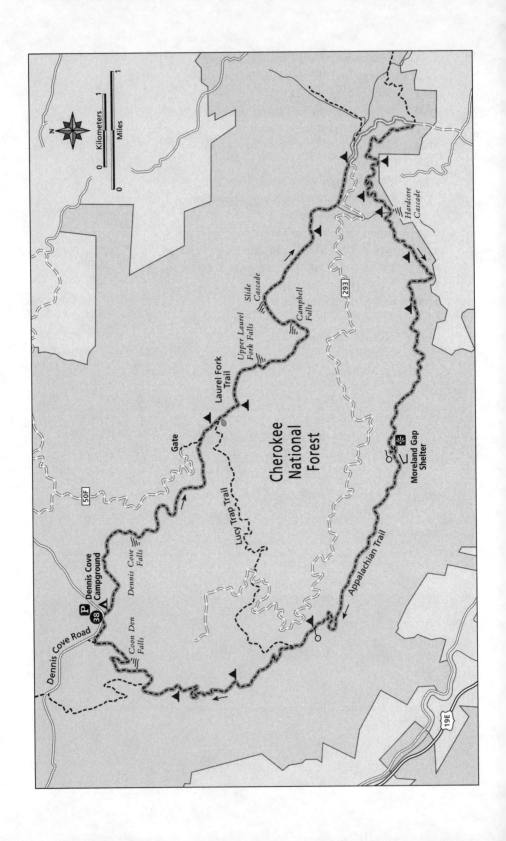

Dennis Cove Road

P 38 Dennis Cove Campground

Coon Den Falls

Dennis Cove Falls

50F

Gate

Lucy Trap Trail

Laurel Fork Trail

Upper Laurel Fork Falls

Slide Cascade

Campbell Falls

293

Cherokee National Forest

Moreland Gap Shelter

Appalachian Trail

Hardcore Cascade

19E

N

Kilometers

Miles

0   1

0   1

38

Laurel Fork Backpack

THE BACKPACK

This scenically diverse loop explores the waterfall-rich valley of upper Laurel Fork, repeatedly fording Laurel Fork and its tributaries before joining the Appalachian Trail, ridge running its way back to the trailhead, passing views and yet more waterfalls en route.

Distance and Configuration: 18.5-mile loop
Difficulty: Difficult due to fords
Outstanding Features: Mountain stream, waterfalls, views
Elevation: 4,210 high point, 2,580 low point
Scenery: 4
Solitude: 3
Family Friendly: 1
Canine Friendly: 1
Fees/permits: No fees or permits required
Best season: April through October
Maps: National Geographic #783 Cherokee and Pisgah National Forests—South Holston and Watauga Lakes
For more info: Cherokee National Forest, Watauga Ranger District, 4400 Unicoi Drive, Unicoi TN 37692, (423) 735-1500, www.fs.usda.gov /cherokee
Finding the Trailhead: From the intersection of US 19E and TN 67 in Hampton, take TN 67 east and follow it 0.8 mile to join Dennis Cove Road, leaving right at an angle. Drive Dennis Cove Road for 4.9 miles to reach the bridge over Laurel Fork, just before reaching Dennis Cove Campground. Park in the gravel area on the left just before reaching the bridge over Laurel Fork. GPS trailhead coordinates: 36.256968, -82.111612

Backpacker fording Laurel Fork on a sunny summer day.

Trekking poles aid your fords of Laurel Fork.

Looking out from White Rocks Mountain on the AT.

This is a deceptively challenging backpack, yet very rewarding as it reveals the wild beauty of upper Laurel Fork, deep in the recesses of the Cherokee National Forest. Trips can last from 1-3 nights, as campsites are well spaced out, availing a chance to lay up on Laurel Fork, then spend a night on the Appalachian Trail, or pound your way up Laurel Fork then camp about halfway along the circuit. A total of 18 stream fords make this a warm season only proposition. Start on the Laurel Fork Trail, where you will earn your waterfall sightings with the continual stream fords on lightly maintained trail. Laurel Fork avails an opportunity to fish this stream where brown, rainbow and brook trout secret in the shadows. After the 18 fords of Laurel Fork (not counting crossing tributaries), a short spur takes you to Forest Road 293. Walk this quiet gravel road to pick up the fabled Appalachian Trail, cruising the slopes of White Rocks Mountain. Up here, you wind through alluring mixed forests with plenty of campsites from which to choose, including an AT trail shelter. The trail here has neither extensive rocky sections nor prolonged climbs or descents. It's relatively easy for the AT in Tennessee. After leaving the AT, you join the Coon Den Falls Trail, and a chance to visit tall Coon Den Falls before completing the backpack.

From Dennis Cove Road, join the Laurel Fork Trail up the right hand bank of Laurel Fork. Dennis Cove campground and picnic area stands across the creek. At 0.5 mile come to the first ford where an overhead sign displays trout creel limits. This is also one of a few remaining steel cables that once stretched across many of the creek fords. The second ford is not far ahead. Here, the trail follows an old blasted railroad grade that bisected a stream bend. At 0.6 mile, come to ford #3, with deep spots and irregular boulders. If you can make these first three fords then you can do the rest.

Continue up the valley on and off the old railroad grade and at 1.0 miles, a spur trail leads right to Laurel Fork and a 10-foot cascade with a huge pool. Soon leave the railroad grade, traversing rugged slopes before rejoining the railroad grade at 1.1 miles just above 25- foot Dennis Cove Falls, with its two-tier drop and large plunge pool. Continue upstream, fording Laurel Fork at 1.4, 1.7 and 2.0 miles, between trail segments thick with rhododendron. Cross the stream again at 2.1 miles and open onto a meadow. Here, walk toward the left hand side of the clearing, toward a gnarled old apple tree.

Make ford #8. You are on the right hand bank. Pass through a smaller clearing then make ford #9 at 2.6 miles. Here, a doubletrack trail leads left .3 mile to a parking area at the end of Forest Road 50F. The Laurel Fork Trail keeps straight, entering Frog Level and its mown fields. Make ford #10 while traversing truly level Frog Level. Campsites can be found in the woods directly along Laurel Fork. At 2.8 miles, reach a dug pond and the Lacy Trap Trail. That faint trail bisects our loop. Keep straight on the Laurel Fork Trail to immediately make ford #11. At 3.2 miles, come to a campsite under holly trees. At 3.3 miles, make ford #12, then climb above Laurel Fork on the right hand bank. At 3.5 miles, a short spur trail drops to Upper Laurel Fork Falls, a narrow, 20-foot cataract diving into a narrow stone cleft. Cautiously descend the short spur into a misty rock defile.

Ahead, step over Moreland Branch, entering on your right. Here, you enter a cathedral of tall yellow birch towering over doghobble and rhododendron thickets. Ford at 3.8 miles, and pass a seldom used campsite before fording back over to the right hand bank. At 4.5 miles, a short spur drops to 18-foot Campbell Falls. It spills over a wide rock ledge. The path travels close to its brink. Cross Laurel Fork again at 4.7 miles, then climb along a slide cascade where Laurel Fork spreads wide over a sloped rock slab. By 5.0 miles, Laurel Fork has ceased its cataracts. Continue on the old grade, stepping over Bunton Branch, entering on your left at 5.3 miles. Ford the stream again at 5.5 and 5.7 miles to enter a small meadow. You are on the left hand bank. At the end of this small meadow, at 5.8 miles, look across the creek for a campsite set in white pines. The trail continues up the left hand bank in a notoriously muddy section, then fords over to the right hand bank at 6.0 miles.

Two more fords and you are at the Bitter End at 6.6 miles. Here, the Laurel Fork Trail keeps straight for Cherry Flats but you split right on a doubletrack trail that climbs to reach gravel Forest Road 293 at 6.7 miles. Head left on the road, rising to meet the Appalachian Trail at 7.6 miles. You are 3,400 feet in elevation. Head right, southbound on America's most famous footpath. The well maintained and cleared AT will seem like a superhighway after cloistered, overgrown, and ragged Laurel Fork Trail. Wind over knobs then drift into a rhododendron-choked tributary of Laurel Fork, where you will find a very small campsite after crossing the tributary at 8.4 miles. Rise a bit and find a level but dry campsite at 8.9 miles. The Appalachian Trail dips into another tributary of Laurel Fork, reaching Hardcore Cascades, a two-tiered 14-foot fall followed by lesser drops, and a sloped campsite just after the creek crossing, at 9.3 miles.

The AT keeps a westerly direction on the north slope of White Rocks Mountain, winding in rhododendron thickets as well as more open oak forests. Pass a level, dry campsite on trail right at 9.8 miles. Begin hiking in and out of little branches, reaching a good level campsite at 10.5 miles, located near one of these tiny creeks. Beyond this campsite the AT rises to make the crest of White Rocks Mountain at 11.0 miles, where oaks, pine and mountain laurel are more prevalent. Descend by switchbacks to a view at 12.2 miles. Here, the Roan Mountain massif rises across the Doe River Valley below you. Continue descending to reach Moreland Gap and a trail shelter at 12.4 miles. Here, a three-sided concrete block refuge stands and a spur trail drops north from the gap to a spring. Tent sites are nearby the shelter.

The AT rises from Moreland Gap, running the ridgecrest. Partial views open among the rocks and trees. Top out a little over 4,200 feet. At 14.1 miles descend by switchbacks passing a pair of small springs before opening to a gap and wildlife clearing with a recommended trailside campsite under a big maple tree at 14.6 miles. A blue blazed spur drops south from the campsite to a spring. From here, rise on the AT, crossing a gated forest road at 14.8 miles, where the Lacy Trap Trail meets the AT. Hike under a powerline ahead, then pass southward views of Unaka Mountain. Come to lesser-used dry campsite at 15.7 miles.

The AT descends, using several switchbacks, entering cove hardwood forests of buckeye and tulip trees. Pass a small, level but dry campsite in a gap shaded by tulip trees at 16.6 miles. Continue the descent, meeting the Coon Den Falls Trail at 17.0 miles, while the AT keeps straight. The Coon Den Falls Trail used to be the old AT, before it was rerouted. Come along Coon Den Branch then steeply drop along a sharp, irregular slope. At 17.6 miles, switchback right, returning to Coon Den Branch at 17.8 miles. Here a spur trail climbs the creek a short distance to the 80-foot narrow cataract dashing over a rock ledge. The spiller is boldest in winter and spring. From there, the trail descends through a narrow rock cleft, passing a lesser fall, and continues down in a sea of rhododendron. At 18.2 miles, the Coon Den Falls reroute splits right. Take it, while the old route keeps straight. Curve to run parallel to Laurel Fork and Dennis Cove Road, emerging at the trailhead parking area at 18.5 miles, completing the adventurous backpack.

Mileages

0.0	Dennis Cove trailhead
0.5	First ford
1.1	Dennis Cove Falls
2.6	Spur to FR 50F, Frog Level, campsites in wood along creek
2.8	Lacy Trap Trail leaves right
3.2	Campsite
3.5	Upper Laurel Fork Falls
3.8	Seldom used campsite after ford to left bank
4.5	Campbell Falls
5.8	Campsite across creek
6.6	Right at Bitter End, join FR 293
7.6	Right on AT
8.4	Small campsite along creek
8.9	Dry campsite
9.3	Hardcore Cascades, campsite
9.8	Dry campsite
10.5	Level campsite
12.2	View
12.4	Moreland Gap shelter, campsites, spring
14.6	Campsite, spring near wildlife clearing
14.8	Cross gated forest road, Lacy Trap Trail
15.7	Dry campsite
16.6	Dry campsite
17.0	Right on Coon Den Falls Trail
17.8	Coon Den Falls
18.5	Dennis Cove trailhead

STRATEGIES FOR STREAM CROSSINGS

I was taking a newbie backpacking in the Cherokee National Forest along the Laurel Fork Trail. It was summertime, a great time to be along the mountain stream, fishing, swimming and camping. Problem was the trek entailed over 18 fords of Laurel Fork. It didn't take the newcomer long to figure out that fording streams with a backpack has its challenges.

When backpacking along streams and rivers you may be faced with having to cross a body of water without benefit a bridge. Have a strategy for successfully crossing the waterway. For starters, every ford is different. The crossing may be deep, shallow or some combination of the two. The stream may be flowing fast or slow, or somewhere in between. It may be rocky or have irregular boulders. Water temperature is another variable. In winter, your feet and legs can go numb before you're back on dry land. Finally, consider water volume. Is the stream flooding? If so, turn back. No backpacking adventure is worth endangering your life.

So what are the best techniques for crossing creeks big and small? First, decide whether you can rock hop the creek or it will necessitate a ford. Whether rock hopping or fording, trekking poles help you maintain balance. Use a stout stick if you are pole-less. When rock hopping assume every rock may be slick. Factor in the weight of your pack when balancing atop a rock. Logs are especially prone to being slick. Be doubly careful when using a log to cross a stream. Logs with bark give better traction than those stripped of bark.

Whether rock/log hopping or fording, plan out a route all the way across the stream. Remember—the widest parts of the streams are usually the shallowest and still waters run deep. Therefore, go for the wider moving waters rather than narrower deep pools.

Before entering the water, loosen your waist belt and shoulder straps of your pack. This way you can ditch your pack if knocked over by the stream. Backpackers have drowned in water less than 4 feet deep after being knocked over and swept downstream then held down by a weighty, wet pack.

While fording, face upstream to brace against the current, keeping at least two points on the stream bottom at all times—one foot and one trekking pole, both feet, etc. When walking in the water, don't try to walk atop submerged rocks—you'll slip off into deeper water. You are already wet so there's no real advantage to walking atop submerged rocks. Try to pick the route with the least depth change. Go for gravelly or small rock stream bottoms rather than open slippery stone slabs or singular big boulders.

I often cross sans shoes. Sometimes I use a pair of sandals/camp shoes for stream crossings, but usually go barefooted if I want to keep my shoes dry, especially if I have but one or two total crossings for the whole trip.

Ties your shoe laces together and hang your shoes around your neck before crossing. On the other hand, if I have numerous crossings such as the above-mentioned trip on Laurel Fork I wear hiking shoes I don't mind getting wet and staying wet the entire trip, crossing in shoes and socks every crossing.

So when you have to cross a stream without a bridge while backpacking, have a strategy for successful crossings.

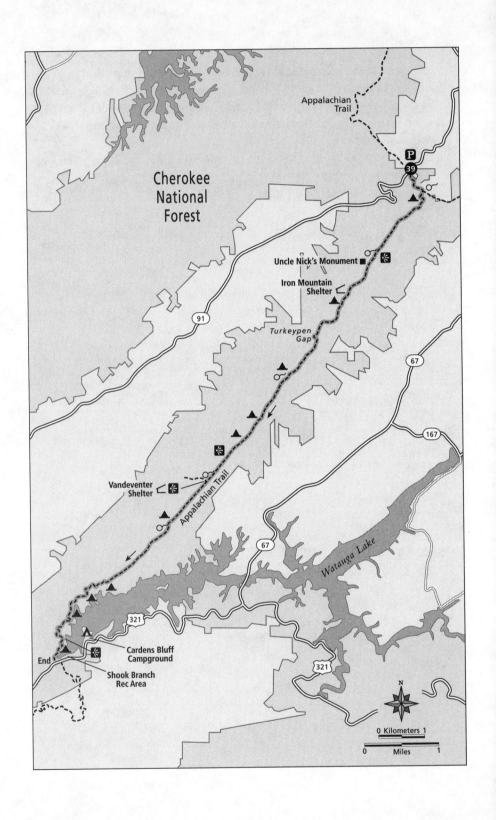

Appalachian
Trail

Cherokee
National
Forest

P
39

Uncle Nick's Monument ■

Iron Mountain
Shelter

91

Turkeypen
Gap

67

167

Vandeventer
Shelter

Appalachian Trail

67

Watauga Lake

321

Cardens Bluff
Campground

End

Shook Branch
Rec Area

321

N

0 Kilometers 1

0 Miles 1

39

Big Laurel Branch Wilderness

THE BACKPACK

This end-to-end overnight adventure uses the venerable Appalachian Trail to traverse the spine of Iron Mountain through the Big Laurel Branch Wilderness. Start high atop Cross Mountain, then head south on the AT, rolling the ridge past a hermit's home, views, and two trail shelters before dropping to gorgeous Watauga Lake. Roll along its shores before ending the adventure near the community of Hampton.

Distance and Configuration: 20.7-mile end-to-end
Difficulty: Moderate-difficult
Outstanding Features: Views, wilderness, Watauga Lake
Elevation: 4,177 high point, 1,959 low point
Scenery: 5
Solitude: 3
Family Friendly: 2
Canine Friendly: 3
Fees/permits: No fees or permits required
Best season: Year-round
Maps: National Geographic #783 Cherokee and Pisgah National
     Forests—South Holston and Watauga Lakes
For more info: Cherokee National Forest, Watauga Ranger District,
     4400 Unicoi Drive, Unicoi TN 37692, (423) 735-1500,
     www.fs.usda.gov /cherokee
Finding the Trailhead: To reach the hike's endpoint from the
     intersection of US 19E and US 321/TN 67 in Hampton, take US
     321 South for 3.0 miles to a parking area on the left side of the road
     near the Cherokee National Forest sign, just before Shook Branch
     Recreation Area. From there, continue on US 321 South/TN 67 for
     6.6 miles, then veer left, staying with TN 67, as US 321 leaves right.
     Remain on TN 67 for 12 more miles to turn left on Spear Branch

The view from behind Vandeventer shelter.

Road and follow it for 1.8 miles to turn left onto Cross Mountain Road. Stay with Cross Mountain Road for 3.6 miles to reach the trailhead at the intersection with TN 91. GPS trailhead coordinates: Watauga Lake: N36°18'06.6", W82°07'43.7"; Cross Mountain N36° 28.882', W81° 57.629'

This Appalachian Trail trek presents panoramas, varied camping opportunities from trail shelters to lakeside camps as well as a final advantage—you end up 1,500 feet lower than where you started, availing more downhill than uphill, though you still undertake 3,140 feet of ascent, compared to 4,686 feet of descent. Not only do your views come from high but also along Watauga Lake. You'll pass through designated Big Laurel Branch Wilderness, too, for around 10 miles of the trek.

Water is limited the first 17 miles of the hike, get it where and when you can. You may have company at the trail shelters but other than that expect to camp in solitude. Along the lake you will hear and see both motorboats on the water in season, as well as vehicles along US 321 across the water. Don't let it bother you, the scenery outshines such disturbances. AT thru-hikers can crowd this section in April. Other than that any time of year is fine for backpacking.

Leave the Cross Mountain trailhead southbound on the AT in mostly level woods, roughly paralleling Cross Mountain Road in hardwoods. At 0.8 mile, pass a marked spring while bridging branches flowing off Cross Mountain. At 0.9 mile, find a late arrival campsite on trail right. By 1.4 miles, the AT has turned south on the crest of Iron Mountain and will keep a south-southwest tack until reaching Watauga Lake. The path runs under hardwoods with scattered pines, mountain laurel and rhododendron. The ridge features protruding outcrops—often with views and sharp drops along its eastern flank while the west facing slopes are generally less declivitous.

Break the 4,000 foot barrier and at 3.1 miles a view opens left of the Doe Creek valley below, backed by Stone Mountain. Just beyond this vista a blue-blazed trail drops right 50 yards to a spring, likely the upwelling used by the famed hermit Nick Grindstaff, whose trailside memorial you see at 3.4 miles. He resided alone atop Iron Mountain hereabouts for over four decades, dying at the age of 71, back in 1923. Ironically, his monument receives far more visitation than he ever got a century back.

Roll along the ridge and reach concrete block Iron Mountain trail shelter at 4.6 miles. A few campsites can be had near the shelter. Water is found at 4.8 miles, as a stream crosses the AT. A recommended campsite is located on a rise just beyond the stream. Keeping south, bisect a powerline cut near the high point of the hike, at 5.4 miles. Vistas open north all the way to the Old Dominion. From there, descend to brushy Turkeypen Gap at 6.4 miles. The trailbed remains mostly foot friendly as you roll on the ridge, entering the Big Laurel Branch Wilderness.

Drop to a gap and recommended campsite at 7.7 miles. The spring is down a short piece to the east while the favorable campsite is to the west of the trail. From there, top out at 8.5 miles, then its downhill more than not. Pass a dry campsite at 9.2 miles. The AT enters craggy, rocky terrain mixed with mountain laurel, pines and stunted hardwoods. The footbed remains challenging all the way to Watauga Lake, though you are mostly going downhill.

Reach Vandeventer trail shelter at 11.5 miles. An outcrop behind the shelter presents a highlight reel panorama of Watauga Lake and mountains beyond. Water can be had from a spur trail that leaves the AT about 100 yards to the south then drops to a campable gap about 0.3 mile down the mountain. Back on the AT, pass a campsite on trail right at 13.1 miles, then descend from the ridgecrest to reach a spring in a hollow at 13.3 miles. Rise back to the crest then continue more down than not on a slim, stony ridgeline, occasionally using switchbacks. At 15.8, pass a small dry campsite in pines.

Pond Mountain rises across Watauga Lake from the AT crossing at Watauga Dam.

Come to a campsite and Watauga Dam Road at 16.4 miles. You are now under 2,300 feet. Cross the road and regain the ridgeline before dropping to a dry campsite and TVA dam access road at 17.3 miles. Head right on the paved access road to reach and cross Watauga Dam at 17.7 miles, with first rate vistas of the impoundment behind which rises Pond Mountain. Leave the road and the AT nears a sloped lakefront campsite at 18.0 miles. Continue working along the lake. Turn into and cross a small stream at 18.9 miles, where a short spur goes to the sloped Watauga Lake shelter site, its concrete foundation still standing. Cross a ridge then step over Griffith Branch at 19.3 miles. Come along the lake again, enjoying aquatic vistas. At 19.9 miles, come to a large campsite overlooking the impoundment. Ahead, the AT squeezes between the water and Oliver Road. At 20.0 miles a blue-blazed spur goes right to Oliver Road. Curve around small branches feeding the lake then reach US 321 and the trailhead parking area up steps to your right, just before bridging Shook Branch at 20.6 miles. There

This backpack leads you alongside Watauga Lake.

is no overnight parking at Shook Branch Recreation Area, therefore you must either park on US 321 or pay a small fee to park at nearby Boots Off Hostel and Campground. They also provide fee shuttles.

Mileages

0.0	TN 91 trailhead atop Cross Mountain
0.8	Spring just to left of trail
0.9	Campsite
3.1	View to east, trail to spring on right just ahead
3.4	Uncle Nick Grindstaff Monument
4.6	Iron Mountain shelter
4.8	Stream, campsite shortly beyond stream
5.4	Bisect power cut
6.4	Turkeypen Gap

7.7	Campsite, spring in gap
8.5	High point of backpack
9.2	Dry campsite
11.5	Vandeventer shelter/view, spring in vicinity
13.1	Campsite to right of trail
13.3	Spring in hollow
15.8	Small dry campsite in pines
16.4	Campsite, Watauga Dam Road
17.3	Campsite, right on TVA dam access road
17.7	Cross Watauga Dam, views
18.0	Sloped lakefront campsite
18.9	Cross stream, old Watauga Lake shelter site
19.3	Cross Griffith Branch
19.9	Large lakeside campsite to left of trail
20.0	Spur right to Oliver Road
20.6	Steps to parking on US 321, backpack's end

BEING A TRAIL ANGEL REALLY CAN WORK LIKE MAGIC

Fresh fruit, cookies, candy bars. They were just what were needed for an afternoon of magic on the Appalachian Trail. I decided on a one-night backpack trip on the AT. To add to the adventure, I wanted to help out by providing fresh food and snacks to any Appalachian Trail thru hikers encountered.

For anyone who is a bona fide backpacker, the term "Trail Magic" is familiar and may bring back happy memories. Unexpected tasty treats are the most common trail magic, and are a welcome sight for those dedicated thru-hikers, trudging mile after mile on minimal rations.

To thru-hikers, we are known as "Trail Angels." All that is required to be a trail angel is to position yourself somewhere on the Appalachian Trail, usually near a trail junction, road crossing, campground, or parking area, with a smorgasbord of edible goodies for the hikers. The good eats can be extravagant, such as grilled hot dogs, hamburgers with all the fixings, ice cream or some perishable dessert, or a simple set up of fresh fruit (too heavy for the hikers to carry as part of their daily meals) and soft drinks.

Cookies and candy bars are always on the menu. Hikers seem to crave sweets and can't get enough. And when they do have them, the treats don't last long enough.

For my afternoon of Trail Magic, I chose the AT road crossing at Iron Mountain Gap, near Watauga Dam. I was excited and energized to be sharing fresh fruit and sweet snacks with my fellow outdoorsmen.

It wasn't long before the first hiker came by. Super Dave (his "trail name") was a young man in his early 30's, trim build with shoulder length hair, scruffy beard and a smile on his face. As Super Dave unloaded his pack we chatted about his hometown (Portland, Maine), his profession (works on oil rigs all over the world) and his purpose for hiking the full 2,100 miles of the Appalachian Trail (adventure).

Super Dave wasn't your typical thru hiker—usually a graduate fresh out of college or a mature retired executive. He was in that "middle zone," occupied by few. I asked Super Dave all the questions he probably expected (Have you seen a bear? What has been the most gorgeous scenery on the trail? What do you think about our neck of the woods?) I was living his adventure with him—just two compadres sharing their passion for backpacking.

I highly recommend becoming a Trail Angel. The thru-hikers wander through Tennessee's segment of the Appalachian Trail from late March through April. It is an opportunity to show Southern hospitality—Tennessee-style. I promise any small act of kindness will be so graciously received that it will have a far greater impact on the giver.

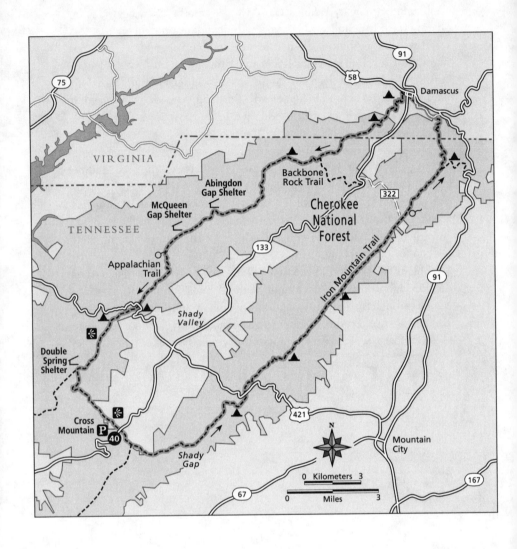

75

91

58

Damascus

VIRGINIA

Abingdon
Gap Shelter

McQueen
Gap Shelter

Backbone
Rock Trail

Cherokee
National
Forest

322

TENNESSEE

133

91

Appalachian
Trail

Iron Mountain Trail

Shady
Valley

Double
Spring
Shelter

Cross
Mountain

P
40

Shady
Gap

421

N

Mountain
City

67

Kilometers

Miles

167

40

Shady Valley Backpack

THE BACKPACK

The long, exciting 3-4 night loop circles Johnson County's bucolic Shady Valley. Start on the lesser used Iron Mountain Trail, cruising a high ridgeline, making your way through Damascus, Virginia to join the fabled Appalachian Trail, returning to Tennessee atop Holston Mountain. Stay high, passing trail shelters en route to the trailhead. The backpack offers ample views, campsites, shortcuts and bailouts, as well as a chance to resupply in Damascus.

Distance and Configuration: 41.9-mile loop
Difficulty: Difficult due to distance
Outstanding Features: Long loop, views, resupply opportunity
Elevation: 4,170 high point, 1,930 low point
Scenery: 5
Solitude: 3 (5 on Iron Mountain Trail, 1 on Appalachian Trail)
Family Friendly: 1
Canine Friendly: 2
Fees/permits: No fees or permits required
Best season: Early fall through early spring, early summer
Maps: National Geographic #783 Cherokee and Pisgah National
     Forests—South Holston and Watauga Lakes
For more info: Cherokee National Forest, Watauga Ranger District,
     4400 Unicoi Drive, Unicoi TN 37692, (423) 735-1500,
     www.fs.usda.gov /cherokee
Finding the Trailhead: From exit 24 on I-26 near Johnson City, follow
     the signs for Elizabethton, joining US 321 north/TN 67 east. Travel
     for 8.6 miles to reach US 19E and a traffic light. Turn left here, now
     joining US 19E north just a short distance to cross the Watauga
     River. Next, turn right on TN 91, Stony Creek Road. Follow TN
     91 for 18.4 miles to reach a gap with Cross Mountain Road to your
     right. The parking area is on the right just beyond Cross Mountain

Road. Alternate directions: From Bristol, take US 421 south for 20 miles to Shady Valley and a four-way stop. Turn right here on TN 91 south and follow it 4 miles to the Cross Mountain trailhead, on your left. GPS trailhead coordinates: 36.481367, -81.960483

The 3-4 night Shady Valley Loop is a backpacking adventure to which Tennessee trail treaders aspire. The unusual combination of the ridgetop Iron Mountain Trail, sporting solitude and views, with a trip through the trail town of Damascus, Virginia, then finishing the circuit on America's favorite pathway—the Appalachian Trail—adds up to a winning combination, especially when you factor in no shuttle needed for a 40-plus mile circuit.

And the scenery is fine. During the leafless season, backpackers will be treated to continual views of adjacent valleys as well as ridges beyond. The drop off into Doe Valley from Iron Mountain is nearly sheer in places. The patchwork fields and woods of Shady Valley please the eye. In Damascus you will see small town

Rainy afternoon at Abingdon Gap shelter.

America and some big streams while striding the famed Virginia Creeper Trail. Then you climb from the citified clamor up Holston Mountain, where vistas of South Holston Lake, the Holston River Valley and Shady Valley all vie for your attention. Near hike's end you travel through the old Osborne Farm, where meadows open to first rate panoramas of the peaks and vales of East Tennessee.

For a 40-plus mile hike it isn't too difficult. Iron Mountain Trail is more rugged and rocky, and has more ups and downs over knobs and swales. The big descent and climb comes when entering and exiting Damascus. Remember, Damascus offers a chance to resupply your larder, from groceries to sandwiches to coffee and even backpacking necessities at one of the outdoor stores in town. Once atop Holston Mountain, the AT is fine, in great shape, with fewer ups and downs. That being said, the entirety of the adventure features over 7,000 feet of vertical variation, but spread over 40 miles that ain't bad.

Campsites with water are limited, especially on Iron Mountain where established campsites are very few in number. Campsites aren't going to jump out at you on Iron Mountain —look for them. Get water when and where you can. Campgrounds and hostels are available in Damascus for those inclined. The Appalachian Trail segment has several established campsites—most without water—and two trail shelters, three-sided concrete block structures, with springs nearby. Remember, the Appalachian Trail can be quite busy during the thru-hiker spring season as well as anytime during the warm season.

This loop is best executed from early fall through early spring, then from mid-May through mid-June. In late summer Iron Mountain Trail can be brushy, and you want to avoid the rush of AT thru hikers from April through mid-May. In autumn, water sources can be limited. The "Mileages" section below is comprehensive and details step-by-step turns for this adventure.

Mileages

0.0   TN 91 trailhead atop Cross Mountain, join paved Cross Mountain Road southeast

1.2   Left on signed Iron Mountain Trail at power line, beyond high point on road

1.9   Top out near flats suitable for camping, no water

2.1   View from outcrop into Doe Valley, campsite, no water

2.9   Shady Gap, water to right. Rise with blazed singletrack Iron Mountain Trail, beware other roads and trails spoking away from the gap

3.2   Regain ridgecrest, northeast-bound on narrow ridge

4.7   Gap, curve around headwater of Sidney Branch

5.5   Battleham Gap, water to south, campsite, views ahead of Grindstone Knob

This part of the AT follows an old road through former farmland and pasture.

6.1   Sandy Gap, US 421, climb

6.9   Grassy clearing, campsite, water to left, keep northeast

7.8   Curve easterly, descending into watersheds divided by small gaps

8.0   Small stream, climb to gap

8.3   Pass second small stream

8.5   Good established campsite to left of trail

9.1   Regain ridgecrest, keep northeast amid upthrust rocks, winter views

11.3   Gap, campsite, spring down to left, ahead keep on ridge with upthrust rocks

14.2   Pass under powerline

14.3   Cross Forest Road 322, potential loop shortcut left on FR 322 to Backbone Rock then up Backbone Rock Trail; Iron Mountain Trail climbs

14.8   Reach trailside spring after climbing over knob, campsites in nearby pines

16.9   Camp Ahistadi Trail leaves right, begin prolonged descent for Damascus

18.2	Enter Virginia, continue descending by switchbacks
19.6	Reach paved Orchard Hill Road, end of Iron Mtn. Trail, head left on road
20.3	Bridge Whitetop Laurel Creek in Damascus; food and camping supplies immediately nearby, left on Virginia Creeper Trail, bridge Whitetop Laurel Creek again
20.9	Bridge Beaverdam Creek, enter Damascus City Park near red caboose, left on Appalachian Trail through the park
21.2	Leave park, right on Water Street, AT leads uphill between 2 houses
21.6	Dry campsite on old roadbed overlooking Damascus, climb
23.0	Campsite, blue blazed spur to water; roll over knobs
24.6	Reenter Tennessee, marked with a sign
25.9	Backbone Rock Trail drops left 2.8 miles to TN 91 and Backbone Rock
27.1	Attractive dry campsite in gap under large trees, other dry campsites ahead
31.2	Abingdon Gap shelter, trail left to spring, campsites nearby
32.3	Cross FR 69 in McQueen Gap, climb wide old roadbed
32.6	Pass 1934-built, small McQueen Gap shelter, sleeps 2, no water; climb over old fire tower site then descend
33.7	Pass rock wall and spring just to left of trail in gap, campsites nearby
34.0	Double Springs Gap, good campsite, no easy water
34.6	Pass alongside stone fence
35.9	Low Gap, US 421, spring and picnic table by road, campsites .1 mile ahead, climb
37.5	Reached cleared view into Shady Valley and Virginia beyond
38.5	Surmount Locust Knob, paralleling old fence posts from grazing days
38.9	Holston Mountain Trail leaves right at gap, Double Springs Shelter just below, campsites, water. AT curves southeast onto Cross Mountain
39.8	Cross small creek, campsite to left
40.8	Step over stile, entering fields of old Osborne Farm, trace Appalachian Trail through rolling grasses marked with big stones, Iron Mountain rises in the distance
41.4	Come to bench and view into Shady Valley, join all access trail segment
41.9	Return to trailhead and TN 91, completing the loop